THE COLORADO TRAIL
The Official Guidebook

On the way to Rolling Mountain (13,693'), San Juan National Forest

Text by Randy Jacobs
Photography by John Fielder

A portion of the proceeds from the sale
of this book benefits the Colorado Trail Foundation.

Fourth Edition

Westcliffe Publishers, Inc., Englewood, Colorado

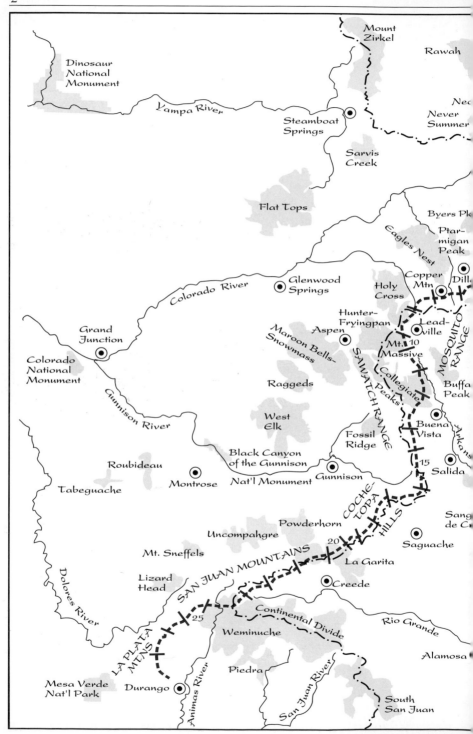

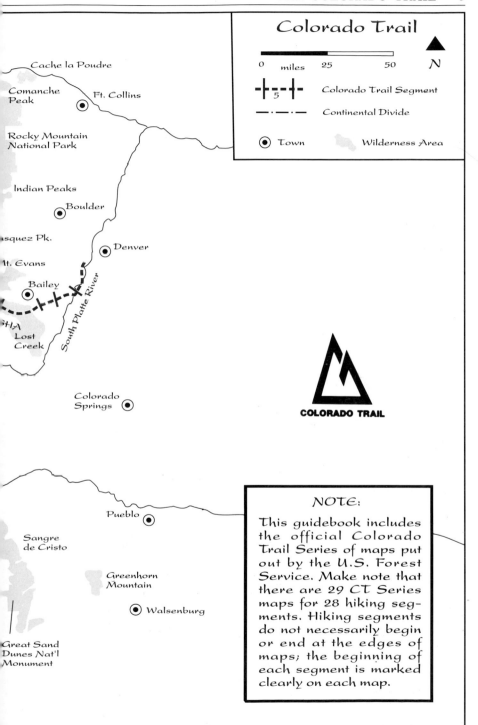

Colorado Trail

0	miles	25	50	N

⊣⊦--⊦ Colorado Trail Segment
5

—·—·— Continental Divide

⊙ Town   Wilderness Area

Cache la Poudre

Comanche
Peak   Ft. Collins

Rocky Mountain
National Park

Indian Peaks

Boulder

squez Pk.

Mt. Evans

Bailey

HA
Lost
Creek

South Platte River

Denver

Colorado
Springs

Pueblo

Sangre
de Cristo

Greenhorn
Mountain

Walsenburg

Great Sand
Dunes Nat'l
Monument

COLORADO TRAIL

NOTE:

This guidebook includes the official *Colorado Trail Series* of maps put out by the U.S. Forest Service. Make note that there are 29 CT Series maps for 28 hiking segments. Hiking segments do not necessarily begin or end at the edges of maps; the beginning of each segment is marked clearly on each map.

TABLE OF CONTENTS

Foreword, by Gudy Gaskill 9

Introduction 11
    History of the Colorado Trail 12
    Colorado Trail Heritage 15

Hiking the Colorado Trail 23
    Using This Guide 23
    Planning Your Hike 24
    Supplying Your Hike 26
    Trail Markers 26
    Regulations & Backcountry Ethics 27
    Backcountry Precautions 31
    Mountain Biking the Colorado Trail 33

Natural History of the Colorado Trail 35
    Geology Along the Trail 35
    Colorado Ecosystems 39

Segment 1 46
    CT Map 1:   50-51
Segment 2 52
    CT Map 2:   56-57
Segment 3 58
    CT Map 3:   62-63
Segment 4 64
Segment 5 68
    CT Map 4:   72-73
Segment 6 74
    CT Map 5:   80-81
Segment 7 82
    CT Map 6:   86-87
Segment 8 88
    CT Map 7:   96-97
Segment 9 98
    CT Map 8:   104-105
Segment 10 106
    CT Map 9:   110-111
Segment 11 112
    CT Map 10: 118-119   CT Map 11: 120-121
Segment 12 122
    CT Map 12: 126-127

Segment 13...128
   CT Map 13: 134-135
Segment 14...136
   CT Map 14: 142-143
Segment 15...144
   CT Map 15: 148-149   CT Map 16: 150-151
Segment 16...152
   CT Map 17: 156-157
Segment 17...158
   CT Map 18: 162-163
Segment 18...164
   CT Map 19: 168-169
Segment 19...170
   CT Map 20: 174-175
Segment 20...176
Segment 21...180
   CT Map 21: 186-187
Segment 22...188
   CT Map 22: 194-195
Segment 23...196
   CT Map 23: 200-201
Segment 24...202
   CT Map 24: 208-209
Segment 25...210
   CT Map 25: 216-217
Segment 26...218
   CT Map 26: 222-223
Segment 27...224
   CT Map 27: 230-231   CT Map 28: 232-233
Segment 28...234
   CT Map 29: 238-239

Mountain Bike Detours 241
Gudy Gaskill's Highlights & Pitfalls....................................256
Chart: Mileages Between Hiking Segments 258

Appendix A: Forest Service Addresses.......................................260
Appendix B: Equipment Checklist 261
Appendix C: Colorado Conservation Groups.........................262
Appendix D: Map Sources...262
Appendix E: Recommended Reading.......................................263
Index 264

International Standard Book Number: 1-56579-084-7
Library of Congress Catalog Number: 94-60963
Text copyright Randy Jacobs, 1994. All rights reserved.
Photographs copyright John Fielder, 1994. All rights reserved.

Published by Westcliffe Publishers
2650 South Zuni Street
Englewood, Colorado 80110

Publisher: John Fielder
Editor: Suzanne Venino
Designer: Leslie Gerarden
Graphics Production: Mark Pearson
Proofreader: Bonnie Beach and Caryl Reidel
Printed in Hong Kong

Writer Mark Pearson contributed to the sections on minimum impact camping and wilderness precautions.

The topographic maps published in this guidebook were reproduced from maps prepared by the U.S. Department of Agriculture, Forest Service.

WARNING: While every effort has been made to make the trail descriptions in this book as accurate as possible, some discrepancies may exist between the text and the actual lay of the trail. Some routes may have changed and others will change; previous hazards may have expanded and new ones may have formed since publication of this edition. This book is not intended to be instructional in nature but rather a guide for those who already have the requisite backcountry training, experience, and knowledge. Proper clothing and equipment are essential. Failure to be fully prepared for backcountry travel may subject hikers to extreme physical danger, injury, or even death. Westcliffe Publishers and the author assume no responsibility for the safety of users of this guide. Individuals are liable for all costs incurred if a rescue is necessary. The State of Colorado pays the cost of rescuing anyone in possession of valid Colorado fishing or hunting license.

The Colorado Trail Foundation awards certificates to hikers who have completed the entire trail. For further information, contact the Colorado Trail Foundation, P.O. Box 260876, Lakewood, CO 80226; phone: 303-526-0809.

Front Cover: Hiking the Colorado Trail in the Rico Mountains, San Juan National Forest

ACKNOWLEDGMENTS

Any interpretive guide would be an utter failure if it did not attempt to weave various anecdotal comments of interest into its descriptive narrative. The Colorado Trail guide is no exception to this practice. However, this guide has attempted to go further because of the uniqueness of the topic. The Colorado Trail is more than a wilderness trail that threads its way through spectacular mountain scenery. It has been a labor of love to a diverse assortment of individuals, mostly volunteers, who have insured its existence for us all.

In the process of compiling and revising this work through four editions, it has been impossible for me to separate the Colorado Trail hiking experience from the tremendous effort that brought the trail into existence; my association as part of the endeavor has simply been too long and too deep. This warm association has been my continuing inspiration for the guide.

There have been many people over the years, too many to list, who have helped me in my role as hiker, trail builder, surveyor, and interpreter. These people have helped me discover the incredibly multi-dimensional aspects of the Colorado Trail experience. In so doing, they have, sometimes unwittingly, played a part in the development of this guide. Some have been long, heart-felt acquaintances; others were unknown fellow hikers who briefly entered my life at trailside and shared their innermost thoughts on their trek.

However, in this parade of significant people, a few stand out for special mention. Gudy Gaskill inspired me in the early 1980s with her impulsive enthusiasm for building the Colorado Trail. This association resulted in years of back-breaking trail building for me as well as countless and repetitious miles recording the state of the trail for the purpose of this guide. I thank Dave Gaskill, Gudy's patient husband, whose humorous cynicism eventually snapped me back into reality from an overly altruistic illusion of volunteerism, and who, as a professional geologist, contributed to the geologic chapter of this guide. I will always be grateful to Peter D. Rowland, who helped immensely by providing trail survey information from Molas Pass southward, by shuttling me to and from trailheads, and by housing me on my many trips to Durango. I remember with great fondness the hours spent with Hugo Ferchau, a long-time contributor in various aspects to the trail, a board member of the Colorado Trail Foundation, a Western State College professor of biology, and the contributor of the natural history section of the guide. The hours we spent conversing and philosophizing changed and deepened my understanding of the Colorado Trail as an environmental experience and literally redirected my life. Finally, over the years it has been my great pleasure to work with various individuals of the U.S. Forest Service. These dedicated people are no doubt the ones most responsible for the reality of the Colorado Trail today. All worked side by side with volunteers to accomplish the goal, giving of themselves far beyond their official duties and responsibilities.

The Colorado Trail volunteers, including our friends in the Forest Service, constitute a family of sorts. As in all families, there has been a certain amount of dissension and conflict, but through it all there radiates much love and devotion. It is my hope that in your travels on this very special trail, a portion of this love and dedication will shine through to you. Happy Trails!

— R.J.

FOREWORD

Colorado! The name rolls off the tongue and brings to mind visual images of red rock walls, cascading waterfalls, lofty Rocky Mountain peaks, alpine meadows bedecked with wildflowers, and a unique outdoor lifestyle. This lifestyle has created a state of vigorous, healthy, and robust young men and women, who flock to the mountains to practice their climbing and mountain biking skills in the summer and a multitude of snow sports in the winter. They live sincerely, work longer, and play harder. It is truly a magnificent state.

I have traveled all over the world, climbed and hiked in many different climates and environments, but each time as the plane brings me safely down to terra firma, my mind always comes back to the same question. Why did I ever leave Colorado? Colorado is home, a big friendly state with such a variety of scenery! Who could ever forget the azure blue sky, the color deepening as the day draws to an end, the spectacular cumulus clouds that billow up before the afternoon showers, and the show of golds, oranges, and crimsons in the sky on a late summer evening? Who could forget the tunnel of golden aspen, with a treasure of gold coins covering the fragrant earth on a crisp autumn day? Or the brilliance of ice crystals, shimmering a million colors in the early morning sun? This is heaven underfoot!

The Colorado Trail, a wilderness path designed to traverse some of the most scenic areas of the Rockies and the Continental Divide, is a unique experience for both the body and the soul. In this revised guidebook to the trail, author Randy Jacobs has managed to describe all the wonders and beauty that you will see along the Colorado Trail. He chronicles the trees, flora, and fauna that you will encounter along the way. He stirs the imagination with his geological observations, creating a desire to know more of the area's ancient history and the powers of nature that formed this landscape. The Colorado Trail has also become a living history lesson, as Randy relates the tales of its earliest inhabitants, from Indians to turn-of-the-century miners and railroad barons. His guidebook makes the trail an educational reality.

We have received many wonderful letters from trail users from all over the world. The peace, solitude, and beauty has given us all a new look at our place on the earth. The Colorado Trail has changed many lives. Our daughter, Polly, who just recently came off the trail, wrote these words in one of her journal entries: "I walk the spine of rocks around the curve of the mountains. Awareness vibrates — color, textures of plants radiates from the earth with vibrancy and life. Rock gardens of immense beauty gift my eyes. Tufts of shimmering bird feathers alight on rough bark. Rusted lichen paint the granite, life's green light dances on the ground. The smell of nature's perfume rises from the earth. The sound and touch of changing wind breathe against every hair on my body. Aliveness. Gratitude."

That is the affect the trail has on body and soul. That is the Colorado Trail!

— Gudy Gaskill

Sunrise, Snow Mesa, Rio Grande National Forest

INTRODUCTION

The Colorado Trail is a continuous, non-motorized recreational trail that traverses Colorado for 471 miles from Denver to Durango. It passes through seven national forests and six wilderness areas, crosses five major river systems and penetrates eight of the state's mountain ranges. What makes the trail even more impressive is that it was created through a massive volunteer effort involving literally thousands of dedicated people.

The Colorado Trail is administered through an unusual public/private joint venture between the U.S. Forest Service and the Colorado Trail Foundation. Because of this special relationship, the trail has been built and maintained largely through donated funds for just a small fraction of the cost that would otherwise have come out of taxpayers' pockets.

The Colorado Trail truly reflects the richness of the long-term partnerships created among the Colorado Trail Foundation, the U.S. Forest Service, and the numerous volunteers who made the dream of the trail a reality. Indeed, the real heroes in the building and the maintenance of the Colorado Trail are the volunteers. People from every state and many foreign countries provided the painstaking manual labor needed to hack this trail from the mountainsides. The stories behind these volunteers are numerous, but the commonality among them seems to be the satisfaction derived from having contributed to a tangible natural resource that will be a legacy for generations.

The Colorado Trail Foundation is a charitable and educational nonprofit Colorado corporation organized and operated solely by volunteers. The mission of the foundation is: to preserve the sense of community associated with the unique, high-altitude experience achieved by participating in trail activities; to support environmental education; to be a place for healing and self-renewal, and facilitate an appreciation for the value of natural systems; to support multiple use, non-motorized family recreation in a wide variety of unpopulated ecosystems; and to maintain a cooperative effort that involves volunteers and promotes a sense of public ownership.

There are no salaries paid to the officers or the trustees of the Colorado Trail Foundation. All money raised by the foundation is used to supply and equip base camps, purchase food for trail crews, and provide transportation. A portion of the profits from the sale of this book will support future work on the Colorado Trail.

While the Colorado Trail is now linked from Denver to Durango, much work still needs to be done to reroute certain sections, to build loops, and to fully realize the goals of the trail planners. Everyone who uses the Colorado Trail, or anyone interested in the trail, its maintenance and preservation, is encouraged to become a "Friend of the Colorado Trail" by making an annual tax-deductible donation so that funds will be available to continue the necessary maintenance and improvements to the trail. Please mail donations to The Colorado Trail Foundation, P.O. Box 260876, Lakewood, CO 80226.

As a Friend of the Colorado Trail you will receive a quarterly newsletter reporting on recent developments along the trail and listing upcoming ones. You will also receive information about all Colorado Trail Foundation meetings,

Wildflowers, Weminuche Wilderness

functions, and accredited educational courses, and you will be invited to participate in fully supported treks and special occasion hikes on the trail.

In addition to making a charitable donation and becoming a Friend of the Colorado Trail, you can further help by volunteering to serve on a trail crew or you can even "adopt" a section of the trail to maintain as your own.

HISTORY OF THE COLORADO TRAIL

The concept of a Colorado Trail was fresh and exciting back in 1973. There was talk of creating a recreational corridor across the state by linking existing trails, and in the July issue of *Colorado Magazine*, editor Merrill Hastings proposed a trail between Denver and Durango. But if anyone is to be given credit for the idea of today's Colorado Trail, it would have to be Bill Lucas.

As head of the U.S. Forest Service's Rocky Mountain region, Lucas was aware of the growing demands that recreation put on national forests. The increase in visitation was alarming, and he hoped to reduce the pressure on existing trails. He organized a public meeting of interested groups to discuss the possibility of a recreational corridor complete with side trails, access points, and eventually even a hut system. Additional considerations were the reality of shrinking budgets.

The November 1973 meeting raised more questions than it answered, but it did result in the establishment of the Colorado Mountain Trails Foundation (CMTF), a nonprofit organization created to work with the Forest Service to make the Colorado Trail a reality by using primarily volunteer labor. Initially funded with a $100,000 grant from the Gates Foundation, as well as numerous smaller grants, the CMTF planned to make the trail a Colorado Centennial-United States Bicentennial project. Gates promised additional funding, assuming progress on the trail continued, and completion was tentatively set for 1978.

In its first years, the CMTF worked with the Forest Service in organizing volunteers to inventory existing trails to be considered for the main route as well as for the side trail system. Dr. Hugo Ferchau, a biology professor at Western State College in Gunnison, spent his summers leading groups of students from Lake Pass to Molas Pass to document existing trails. In the meantime, Gudy Gaskill had been named executive trail director by the CMTF to recruit volunteers for inventories elsewhere on the proposed route and to begin trail construction.

When an environmental assessment was undertaken by the Forest Service, it was estimated that three-quarters of the route followed existing trails. Based on this report, an official decision was made on the route of the Colorado Trail, with various alternate routes proposed.

At the same time, questions were being raised about the ability of the CMTF to continue coordinating the trail effort. The organization had exhausted nearly all of its original seed money on overhead costs and, although not officially disbanded, had become polarized and seemed to be unable to establish a unified course of action for the project.

Here the story of the Colorado Trail might have come to a end were it not for Gudy Gaskill. Gaskill had been recruiting volunteers for the CMTF from its infancy and also chaired the Colorado Mountain Club's (CMC) Trail and Hut Committee, which was established to organize volunteer crews to preserve the

A trail crew constructing new tread (Photo by M. John Fayhee)

state's network of hiking trails. When the CMTF foundered, Gaskill continued to organize volunteers through the CMC. Slowly, year by year, mile by mile, headway continued on the Colorado Trail.

The first section of the trail to be completed by Gaskill and her volunteers was in the South Platte district, the section closest to Denver. Next the crews moved to the Leadville and Salida districts, where, in 1984, they were visited by journalist Ed Quillen. The resulting "Trail to Nowhere" cover story in the *Denver Empire* (December 9, 1984) was decidedly pessimistic in describing the jubilant beginnings and unfortunate downfall of the CMTF, and it raised serious doubts about whether the trail would ever be finished. The article did, however, attract the attention of one influential Coloradan — Governor Richard Lamm.

With the support of the governor's office behind the project, an ambitious schedule was devised for finishing the original links and thus finally joining Denver to Durango via a hiking trail. The resulting two-year plan, which was coordinated by the Forest Service, called for completing nearly 60 miles of trails through six forest districts during the 1986 and 1987 seasons, using primarily volunteer labor. Almost half of the total mileage would be constructed in the Animas District of the San Juan National Forest, where the Hermosa Highline detour would reroute trekkers around the originally proposed route, thus avoiding a heavily used trail along Vallecito Creek in the Weminuche Wilderness. Other areas needing attention were a 20-mile stretch between Copper Mountain and Tennessee Pass and neglected sections around Twin Lakes Reservoir and Mount Princeton.

Concurrent with this renewed focus on the Colorado Trail, a new Colorado Trail Foundation (CTF) was formed to organize volunteers, provide leaders, supply trail crew base camps, and coordinate trail construction with the Forest Service. The new board of directors consisted of individuals determined to complete the Colorado Trail and was headed by the energetic Gaskill.

The effort put forth during those years by the volunteers was unprecedented. In 1986, some 400 volunteers labored in 20 trail crews building new tread. The following year, nearly a thousand volunteers happily took up their tools in 46 trail crews. The complicated logistics taxed the CTF's volunteer organizers, many of whom used their own vehicles to help the Forest Service supply and relocate base camps. Also challenged were the dedicated Forest Service liaisons who worked tirelessly alongside the volunteers.

The volunteers and Forest Service personnel enjoyed a tremendous feeling of accomplishment when, on September 4, 1987, "golden spike" ceremonies were held simultaneously at Molas Pass, Camp Hale, and Mount Princeton to commemorate the linking of the Colorado Trail from Denver to Durango. The ceremony, however, did not mark the completion of work on the trail; since then, CTF volunteers and the Forest Service have been busy each summer maintaining the existing trail and building new tread to improve substandard sections. In addition, work has progressed on connector and loop trails extending from the main corridor. Eventually, shelters along the trail may eliminate the need for long-distance trekkers to shoulder the extra weight of tents.

Please join us for a walk on a unique hiking trail built by the people and for the people. We encourage you also to explore the many side, loop, and connector trails. And, as you travel the Colorado Trail, you will be a part of the continuing effort to preserve a unique aspect of Colorado's colorful heritage.

COLORADO TRAIL HERITAGE

The heritage of the Colorado Trail is in many ways a reflection of the unique history of the mountain West, and its story goes back much further than the mid-1970s when the first trail crews took to the hills. It was the intention of the founders to create a hiking trail that would not only emphasize the incredible natural beauty of the state, but one that would also incorporate significant historical and cultural features. Today the Colorado Trail includes long-forgotten Indian trails, abandoned mining roads, and narrow-gauge railroad grades. It also reflects the consequences of more contemporary developments, such as logging and water projects.

The Indians

For generations the Ute Indians hunted in the mountains and parks of present-day Colorado. As settlers began moving into the area, skirmishes erupted between the Indians and newcomers. These battles eventually forced the Utes into exile in a small corner of the southwestern part of the state.

Prior to an 1863 treaty made with the Utah Tabeguache band, the Utes had laid claim to most of the mountainous areas of Colorado. The 1863 treaty, however, limited them to a reservation with boundaries that followed the Continental Divide on the east and south, the Colorado and Roaring Fork rivers on the north, and the Uncompahgre River on the west. Five years later, they were restricted even further, as pressure from the ever-increasing flood of migrating Easterners and mining entrepreneurs persuaded the government to move the Indians farther west to a reservation in western Colorado bounded by the 107th meridian. Two agencies were set up to distribute goods and food to the Indians, one to the north on the White River and the other to the east on Los Piños Creek at the foot of the Utes' ancestral Continental Divide passage over Cochetopa Pass.

The promise of profitable mining in the San Juan Mountains resulted in a council at the Los Piños agency in 1872, when the government attempted to persuade the Utes to turn over even more of their land. They were not successful this time. Chief Ouray, official representative of all the Ute bands, "with rare eloquence, demolished every detail of their carefully arranged program," as one observer put it, adding that the great chief put "them to shame by exposing the violation of their pledges, the injustice and wrong of their attempt to nullify a contract which had been agreed to and ratified by the Senate of the United States." The commissioners remained persistent, however, and the following year Felix Brunot, with the help of Otto Mears, persuaded the Utes to turn over nearly four million acres in what was to become the high-producing San Juan mining district around present-day Silverton. This infamous agreement came to be known as the Brunot Treaty.

By 1879, tensions were high because of continuing relocations and attempts to convert the nomadic Indians into farmers. When White River agent Nathanial Meeker plowed up the Utes' horse track for planting, the Indians responded by killing Meeker and nine other agency employees and by attacking a cavalry unit sent to subdue them. The White River Utes, who were responsible for the killings, were driven out of Colorado along with the Uncompahgre Utes to a reservation in Utah. The Southern Ute bands were removed to two small reservations in southern Colorado bordering New Mexico.

Chief Ouray, who had attempted to save his Indian nation by cooperating with the government, witnessed the tragic decline of the Ute people, whose culture and important contributions are unknown to most people today. Several towering mountain peaks in the southern Sawatch Range immortalize some of the names of these mountain people.

Early Explorers and Expeditions

For centuries, the Spanish had been entrenched in regions south of present-day Colorado, but they had little if any knowledge of the region that would eventually be traversed by the Colorado Trail until Fathers Escalante and Dominguez traveled through the western San Juan country. During a 1776 expedition seeking a less-perilous southern route to California, the friars' explorations took them on a roundabout tour of western Colorado and eastern Utah. In their journal they described the La Plata and San Miguel mountains northwest of Durango, as well as the sites of many future settlements. Escalante and Dominguez never made it to California, but their discoveries helped New Mexico Governor Juan Bautista de Anza when he traveled the eastern San Juan Mountains, the Cochetopa Hills, and the San Luis Valley three years later.

De Anza led an army north from Santa Fe in pursuit of a Comanche band that was terrorizing Spanish colonists. Along the way de Anza noticed that the Rio Grande had its beginnings on the eastern flank of the San Juans, not farther to the north as previously had been assumed. He was the first white man to lay eyes on the ancient Continental Divide crossing known to the Utes as Cochetopa, or "Pass of the Buffalo." He correctly deduced that farther west, beyond the ridges seen from the San Luis Valley, flowed the headwaters of the western San Juan rivers described by Father Escalante. De Anza continued north to Poncha Pass, descended into the Arkansas Valley near today's Salida, and viewed the skyscraping Sawatch Range before disposing of Comanche Chief Greenhorn's war party near the Wet Mountains.

In the adventurous half century between 1813 and 1863, expeditions in the American West were sponsored by the War Department's newly formed Corps of Topographical Engineers. Major Steven Long's 1820 expedition, which skirted the east slope of the Rampart Range, was organized under the auspices of the Corps. Long's group was timid about penetrating the Rockies, but they did struggle a few miles up Platte Canyon, which would later become the eastern trailhead of the Colorado Trail. The group then headed south, where the party's botanist, Edwin James, ascended Pikes Peak and discovered the blue columbine, Colorado's state flower.

Later expeditions, led by Captain John Charles Fremont, probed the La Garita Mountains, South Park, and the upper Arkansas River Valley. Fremont, the son-in-law of influential Senator Thomas Hart Benton, conducted several expeditions into the Rockies for the Corps. He is probably best known in Colorado for the disaster that struck his expedition during the winter of 1848-49 in the rugged La Garita Mountains. His party was stranded in a fatal blizzard, and there were rumors that the survivors had resorted to cannibalism.

In 1853, Congress authorized the Corps to conduct preliminary transcontinental railroad surveys through the Rockies. Captain John W. Gunnison explored what seemed to be the only logical route through Sangre de Cristo

Eroded volcanic ash formations below Snow Mesa

Pass, across the San Luis Valley, and over Cochetopa Pass. Unfortunately, the river drainage west of Cochetopa Pass cut down into the impregnable gorge of the Black Canyon. Even more unfortunately, Gunnison and seven others in the party were killed later that summer in Utah by a band of Piutes out to avenge the murder of their chief's father by a group of uprooted settlers. The railroad was eventually built through Wyoming, and as a further reminder of the tragic end of the Gunnison expedition, Cochetopa Pass has remained a rather minor Continental Divide passage.

The Great Surveys

After the Civil War, the most significant of the Colorado surveys were led by Ferdinand Hayden and by Lieutenant George Wheeler. The Plains Indians were used to seeing Hayden digging in worthless soil and, thinking him a harmless eccentric, gave him a name that roughly translated as "man-who-picks-up-stones-running." By 1869, Hayden had lobbied Congress to fund his civilian United States Geological Surveys of the Territories. During the three summers between 1873 and 1875, the Hayden Survey covered most of Colorado's high country, climbing and naming many of its summits, which were used as triangulation points. Hayden skillfully staffed his teams with competent topographers, geologists, and experts in fields ranging from anthropology to paleontology. After a decade of exploring and preparing invaluable maps and reports, the Hayden Survey came to an end in 1879 with the creation of the United States Geological Survey.

The Wheeler Survey, unlike Hayden's civilian expedition, was sponsored by the War Department and concentrated mainly on topographic features. Its premature demise in 1878, before the completion of its work, was at least partly due to the intense competition among the surveys. As a result, Wheeler never gained the prominence that Hayden did. Both of these great surveyors, however, provided maps and valuable information that guided railroad builders and prospectors and led to further taming of the West.

Early Entrepreneurs

The Colorado Trail meanders through a wide band of territory known as the Mineral Belt, which begins west of Boulder and trends southwesterly to Silverton. The riches of this region supported some of Colorado's most rip-roaring boom towns of old. These towns were eventually connected by a web of stage roads, trails, and railroads, some of which remain as part of the Colorado Trail today.

An early route for prospectors was pointed out by explorer John Fremont in 1844. A group of Southerners used the route, later called Georgia Pass, and panned their way to prosperity in the 1850s at Parkville, near the headwaters of the Swan River. At the same time the miners were digging their first placers in Parkville, prospectors were filtering into California Gulch near the headwaters of the Arkansas River. A rich placer boom in the 1860s was responsible for the brief appearances of the towns of Oro, Granite, and Dayton. But the real boom came in 1878 when miners uncovered silver deposits concealed in lead carbonate, which gave the rejuvenated camp its new name of Leadville. For a short time, the satellite communities of Kokomo and Robinson in the Tenmile Mining District competed with Leadville for prominence.

It was in the Leadville area that an eccentric entrepreneur, Horace Austin Warner Tabor, made his fortune as a prospector and merchant. He and his wife, August, the first white woman in the valley, would become legendary Colorado figures whose lives were changed drastically by the boom and bust cycles of mining.

Lieutenant Charles Baker, who tired of the Yankee company in California Gulch, followed the Continental Divide south into the San Juans, where his party panned unsuccessfully for gold around Bakers Park. Even though it meant trespassing on the Ute reservation, Baker pushed south to test the soil at a new location on the Animas River just north of present-day Durango, which he christened Animas City. Being a Confederate, he took a brief leave from prospecting to fight in the Civil War, but was killed by Indians when he returned to southwestern Colorado after the war. The area was still technically closed to white men but other prospectors uncovered rich mineral deposits and, when the Brunot Treaty removed the Utes in 1873, the area boomed with the production of silver, gaining its new name — Silverton.

Toll Roads and Railroads

Entrepreneur Otto Mears built roads out of the San Luis Valley along routes that had been pioneered by earlier explorers. Mears' objective, in which he was quite successful, was to maintain toll booths and freighting companies to supply the boom towns with goods he produced in the valley. His first enterprise was to build a road north over Poncha Pass to the placer mines on the upper Arkansas River. Mears next teamed up with Enos Hotchkiss to build the Saguache-San Juan toll road via Cochetopa Pass in 1874. Originally intended to go up the Lake Fork, over Cinnamon Pass, and then down into Silverton, the stretch of road was delayed when Hotchkiss discovered the Golden Fleece Mine while building a road near Lake City.

Mears did more than build toll roads. As the San Juans produced more minerals, he developed an interconnecting network of railroads to serve them. The most prominent was the Rio Grande Southern, whose twisting 168 miles of narrow-gauge track between Durango and Ridgway passed through some of the Rocky Mountains' most stunning scenery.

In 1870, General William Jackson Palmer incorporated the Denver & Rio Grande and planned to build his railroad from Denver to Mexico City. But plans changed and Palmer's railroad, using narrow-gauge track and equipment that could climb steeper grades and turn tighter corners, became Colorado's premier railroad. The small cars and locomotives were soon puffing over passes and into mining communities to the cheers of the citizenry.

Spurring the D&RG on were competing mountain railroads, such as Governor John Evans' Denver, South Park & Pacific and the Colorado Midland. The DSP&P was constructed in the 1870s from Denver up Platte Canyon to Kenosha Pass. From there, one branch continued across South Park to Leadville and Gunnison via the legendary Alpine Tunnel. The other branch ascended the Continental Divide at Boreas Pass to serve Breckenridge and the Tenmile Mining District. The entire line survived until the 1930s.

The more ambitious standard-gauge Colorado Midland was built by a feisty Easterner named John J. Hagerman, who came to Colorado to die of tuberculosis and instead lived to build a railroad. The Midland was a well-respected but short-lived railroad that linked the silver mines at Aspen to the Eastern Slope via Leadville and the breathtaking 11,528-foot Hagerman Tunnel on the craggy north shoulder of Mount Massive.

The prosperity of the late 1800s in Colorado was based largely on the mining of silver, and by 1893 the value of silver production exceeded that of gold by nearly four to one. Thus the silver camps of the San Juans, Leadville, and the Tenmile District were in a precarious state when the Sherman Silver Purchase Act was repealed that same year and the nation moved toward a monetary system based on the gold standard. The battle over the monetary standard caused turmoil nationwide and was at least partly to blame for the Panic of 1893. Silver mining districts across Colorado went into a collapse from which they never fully recovered. Horace Tabor, the silver king of Leadville, lost everything and died a pauper. Many other fortunes were wiped out as well.

About this same time, a drunken cowboy by the name of Bob Womack stumbled across a peculiar-looking rock outcrop while herding cattle and laid first claim to the gold field on the banks of Cripple Creek. Displaced miners from the silver camps poured into the gold district in the shadow of Pikes Peak with restored hope, but life would never be quite the same with the passing of Colorado's silver era.

Modern Development

A perplexing ore penetrating the slopes of 13,555-foot Bartlett Mountain at the head of Tenmile Creek on the Continental Divide baffled early day prospectors. Specialists at the Colorado School of Mines finally identified the mineral as molybdenum. The mining claim, named Climax because of the loftiness of its location, was not developed until 1911, when molybdenum's value in the production of steel was realized. The mine has been a mainstay of the upper Arkansas Valley economy ever since. The Climax Molybdenum Mine is widely known as the state's most notorious strip mine, and it is no longer possible to see the summit of Bartlett Mountain because it has been shaved away over the years. Today the mountain's remains clog the headwaters of Tenmile Creek, under the ignominious tailing ponds that have completely buried the historic sites of Robinson and Kokomo.

Other Colorado valleys have also disappeared, not buried under mine tailings but drowned under thousands of acre-feet of water. Denver began damming waterways as early as 1890, building the Castlewood Dam on Cherry Creek in that year and Cheeseman Dam on the South Platte River in 1905. In addition, Eastern Slope water districts cast longing eyes west of the Continental Divide. They laid ambitious plans to siphon off significant flows from the Colorado River watershed and transport the runoff to thirsty cities using an intricate system of diversion points, tunnels, and reservoirs.

The most prominent water project along the Colorado Trail today is the Fryingpan-Arkansas diversion system, known locally as the Pan-Ark. This complex system diverts 69,200 acre-feet of water per year from the Western Slope's Fryingpan River, a tributary of the Colorado, to the Arkansas River using a network of six reservoirs, 16 diversion structures, and ten tunnels. The Pan-Ark project was begun in the 1960s to supply Eastern Slope municipalities and agricultural water users. Summit County's Dillon Reservoir, named for the little community it flooded, and 23-mile-long Roberts Tunnel comprise a system that funnels excess flow from the Blue River eastward into the headwaters of the North Fork of the South Platte River, eventually to flow from faucets throughout the Denver area.

Besides supplying water for Denver, Dillon Reservoir is also a center for summer water sports in one of the state's most highly developed, year-round recreation areas. Once an active mining region, Summit County typifies the metamorphosis that has taken place in Colorado's mountain communities. The county's economy now revolves around its appeal as a vacation destination focusing on the ski resorts in the surrounding area.

Many of these ski resorts had their beginnings in the army installation at Camp Hale from 1942 to 1945. The winter ski training that the troops received at the Rocky Mountain outpost was not lost upon the men of the 10th Mountain Division, and some of the veterans returned to Colorado after the war to build ski resorts, thus helping the state develop its reputation as the nation's premier winter recreation area. A landmark along the route of the Colorado Trail, Camp Hale is one of the state's most recent and unusual ghost towns.

The latest development proposed along the Colorado Trail is the Two Forks Dam and Reservoir, which would inundate scenic Platte Canyon 25 miles southwest of Denver. If built, Two Forks Reservoir would be larger than Dillon Reservoir and would drown several miles of the trail in the craggy canyon. The question of Two Forks, which set off battles between development and environmental interests for nearly a decade, was at least temporarily resolved in 1990 when EPA chief William Reilly vetoed the project as then proposed.

Balancing the demands of a growing state with an unparalleled natural setting and a dynamic tourism industry is no small task. And if the past is indeed prologue to the future, then development is destined to continue. However, this trend is not without a price — a price that includes visual deterioration, loss of wildlife habitat, and the construction of highways that disrupt peaceful mountain settings. Still, despite all the development, many isolated niches remain seemingly untouched. The 471 miles of the Colorado Trail highlight the continuing history of a remarkable state, forming a thread that weaves together Colorado's past and present and creating a rich legacy for its future.

HIKING THE COLORADO TRAIL

The Colorado Trail assumes varying characteristics as it meanders through eight mountain ranges with dissimilar topographic and geologic features. For its entire 471 miles, the trail imposes diverse demands on its users, and their ability to adjust to those changing demands determines how much they will enjoy their trek. There is always something along the way to challenge some and intimidate others.

As with other trails in the state, the Colorado Trail is not developed to the point that it can be followed blindly. Nor should it be, especially in the many wilderness areas through which it passes. This guide assumes that all users of the Colorado Trail are familiar with basic backcountry techniques, precautions, and orienteering skills. For those who are not, organizations such as the Colorado Mountain Club hold regular sessions to acquaint neophytes with these practices before they venture out on the trail. This guide includes sections on safety and backcountry etiquette as well as an equipment checklist.

USING THIS GUIDE

The 28 trail segments described in this guide begin and end at points accessible by vehicle. Many have additional access points within the segment. The average length of a segment is 17 miles, although actual distances vary from 9 to 29 miles. Most segments could conceivably be completed by day hikers with light loads, although some segments would make for a very long day. Backpackers with heavy packs could take many days to cover some of the longer segments. Through-hikers going from end to end should figure on two months to complete the entire trail, assuming they hike about 9 miles per day, with a day off per week for side trips or relaxation.

The trail descriptions are laid out progressing from Denver to Durango. Each description indicates the distance of recognizable landmarks from the beginning of the trail segment. Accompanying the mileage is the elevation of that landmark. As accurate as humanly possible, the official mileages included in this guide were obtained by the Colorado Trail Foundation using a "rolotape" along the entire length of the trail. Also included are altitude profiles that give a graphic summary of the elevation gain and loss for each segment.

As a special feature, this guidebook includes the official Colorado Trail Series of maps put out by the U.S. Forest Service. Make note that there are 29 CT Series maps for 28 hiking segments. Hiking segments do not necessarily begin or end at the edges of maps; the beginning of each segment is marked clearly on each map.

In addition to the official CT Series topographic maps, U.S. Forest Service (USFS) and U.S. Geological Survey (USGS) maps are also referenced for each segment. The USFS maps for individual national forests provide information on towns, campgrounds, backroads, and highways. USFS maps and the CT Series contain all the information you need for hiking the Colorado Trail.

Instructions for reaching trailheads and trail access points are given at the beginning of each segment. Generally, "trailhead" refers to an official access point with a parking area, which is sometimes primitive and skimpy. "Trail

Sunrise reflections, Notch Lake, Mount Massive Wilderness

access" refers to a point where the trail crosses or approaches a vehicular artery but where no official parking is provided. One of the priorities in the next few years is to increase and improve the number of trailheads on the Colorado Trail. In the meantime, be careful where you park your car.

The abbreviation "FS" refers to Forest Service roads. FS-543, for example, means Forest Service Road 543. These roads can generally be traveled by conventional automobiles; if not, a "4WD" designation identifies the road as suitable for four-wheel-drive vehicles only. Keep in mind that some backcountry roads open to conventional automobiles can be rendered impassable during inclement weather, even to 4WD vehicles.

The Colorado Trail is generally a footpath, but in places it follows roads of varying quality, and trail descriptions refer to several types of roads. A "jeep track" is the lowest quality of road and typically appears as a parallel double track or trail separated by a hump of grass. Jeep tracks usually run through meadows or tundra and may either be closed to vehicular traffic or still actively used. A "jeep road" or "log road" may likewise be opened or closed to vehicles. These are often rough, narrow, and sometimes steep. The guide also refers to "old roads," which are usually long-abandoned supply routes that now more closely resemble rough, widened trails.

"Route" is a term sometimes used to describe the Colorado Trail in general. However, for stretches where the trail is so obscure that no tread is visible, "route" is used to indicate the lack of an obvious trail. A "posted route" or "cairned route" has been marked with either wooden posts or rock cairns.

PLANNING YOUR HIKE

Only a few of the total number of those hiking the Colorado Trail do so straight through from one end to the other. A more realistic and certainly less taxing plan is to travel segment by segment and take advantage of the various side trips available off the main trail. This guide serves both through-hikers as well as segment hikers on a single-day hike or a multi-day backpack.

One of the main considerations in planning a hike for early summer is lingering snow. The portions of the trail below 9,500 feet are generally snow-free from May to November, depending on weather extremes and the orientation of the trail. Above 9,500 feet, the hiking season can be dramatically shorter. If you intend to sample different segments of the trail, choose areas where conditions are optimal. Long-distance trekkers, however, cannot be choosy about avoiding a snowed-in segment if it happens to lie in their path. Many high crests and ridges are likely to be laden with snow until early July, especially on their north sides. Crossing any snow field is risky and should be done only with adequate mountaineering equipment and experience.

Those planning a terminus-to-terminus through-hike should consider that from Denver it is some 70 miles before reaching timberline on Georgia Pass; from Durango, however, timberline is less than 20 miles away at Kennebec Pass. Thus, a trek starting from Denver could begin earlier in the season. In any event, setting out from Denver before the third week of June, or from Durango before the first week of July, is generally impractical because of the hazards of lingering snow.

The logistics of returning from your trek takes some planning. For those doing a through-hike, Denver and Durango are connected by regular air service.

For segment hikers, several towns along the way are served by regular bus routes, although this service has been drastically reduced in recent years. Those wishing to take advantage of railroad passenger service may do so by planning a hike in the Durango and Silverton area, where a narrow-gauge railroad runs between the two towns daily during the summer. For information on fares and schedules, write to the Durango and Silverton Railroad, 479 Main Avenue, Durango, CO 81301, or call (303) 247-2733.

Day hikers have more and less complicated options. They can hike as far as they wish and then return the same way to their starting point; they can arrange a car shuttle between trail access points; they can have friends hike from the other direction and swap car keys with them on the trail; or they can take advantage of the many side trails that cross the Colorado Trail and loop back to the starting point.

Whether you are day hiking or backpacking, the isolation from civilization south of US-50 can be overwhelming. Therefore, it is worthwhile to prepare one's psyche for this portion and have a compatible companion along. This part of the Colorado Trail is less visited than other sections and in places is more of a challenge to follow. In addition, the high route through the San Juans, which parallels the crest of the Continental Divide, may very likely be blanketed with snow until mid-July. This compounds the area's isolation and heightens the need for hikers to keep a steady head and possess good mountaineering and orienteering skills.

Boots and feet take a beating on the trail. Even though there are some sections where lightweight boots or athletic shoes may seem appropriate, only heavier footgear will get you through high-altitude hikes across the snow fields and talus slopes on the Continental Divide. If your boots are broken in but not yet nearing the end of their life, they will likely see you through the entire trek.

Clothing, the traveler's first line of defense against the elements, deserves careful consideration. The Colorado Trail experiences extremes of mountain weather conditions, with the warmth of the lower elevations in the Rampart Range and Arkansas Valley contrasting sharply with the exposed alpine ridges of the San Juan Mountains. A variety of clothing layers (inner layers of moisture-wicking materials, such as silk or polypro, and outer layers of insulating wool or fleece), plus waterproof rain gear, is essential. It is conceivable that some items, especially socks, will wear out in 471 miles, so pack extra or plan to resupply.

The Ten Essentials

Many outdoor education organizations teach the idea of the ten essentials. Here is a list of items considered necessary for surviving most unexpected events while in the wilderness.

- matches, striker, or lighter
- knife
- emergency shelter, such as a poncho or ground cloth
- food and water
- first aid kit
- signaling devices, such as a mirror or whistle
- map and compass

• sunglasses and sunscreen
• extra clothes
• flashlight with extra batteries and bulb

These items should be carried in your pack at all times, even on the most innocuous seeming hikes, since you never know when you could run into unexpected conditions or get the urge to go just a little farther than planned.

SUPPLYING YOUR HIKE

With the exception of Copper Mountain, most groceries and sporting goods stores are located in towns well off the trail. A highlighted box within each segment describes the various services available in towns along the way and also indicates the town's distance from the trail.

If you are planning an extended trek, it would be impractical to carry all your food. One way of handling this is to pack your nonperishable meals into boxes before leaving and mail them to yourself in care of "General Delivery" to post offices in towns along your route. Another alternative is to rely on friends or relatives to meet you with fresh supplies at access points along the trail.

Drinking water is readily available on the Colorado Trail, although there are a few sections where adequate supplies are as far as 20 miles apart. These require some planning and foresight if you do not want to be caught at a dry camp. Unfortunately, cattle grazing is common along most of the route, and all water, with the exception of tested potable supplies at campgrounds, should be treated or filtered.

TRAIL MARKERS

The Colorado Trail is well marked and maintained, however, it is surprising how quickly the extreme environment of the Rockies can alter a trail's appearance. Overgrown vegetation, downed trees, and avalanches can render the trail difficult to follow regardless of how well it was originally marked. Even the cumulative effects of hundreds of human and equine feet on the trail can have a significant impact. Portions of the trail have been altered by these forces, not to mention ongoing construction, rerouting, and maintenance.

Over the years, official Colorado Trail markers have varied considerably. Their one common, eye-catching characteristic has been the incorporation of the trail's logo. Trail markers are usually triangular or diamond shaped and made of wood, metal, or plastic. Reflective metal markers were once used extensively on the trail, but have been discontinued because of their expense and appeal to souvenir hunters. Less expensive, triangular plastic markers have been used most recently. This guide generally does not refer to trail markers and signs because they are often vandalized or stolen.

In more remote stretches and wilderness areas, the Colorado Trail is marked by wooden posts, rock cairns, and blazes on tree trunks. Some older blazes are almost completely healed over and difficult to see. A number of Forest Service districts use carsonite posts to identify the route. These are tall slats, dark brown in color, and made of a material resembling fiberglass. They tend to nod conspicuously back and forth in anything but the lightest breeze. You might also encounter routes marked with blue diamonds that identify cross-country ski routes. South of US-50, where the trail follows along or near the

Setting up camp along the Colorado Trail

© M. John Fayhee

crest of the Continental Divide, it coincides with the Continental Divide Trail for long distances. In these sections, you may see occasional CDT trail markers along your route.

REGULATIONS AND BACKCOUNTRY ETHICS

The Colorado Trail lies almost entirely on national forest lands. In some areas, the route uses right-of-ways and easements across or adjacent to private property and patented mining claims. Negotiations for certain easements are still underway. Keep in mind that right-of-ways can be withdrawn by owners if problems associated with their use arise; please respect private property and all no-trespassing postings. Remember also that federal law protects cultural and historic sites on public lands, such as old cabins, mines, and Indian sites. These cultural assets are important to us all as a society and are not meant to be scavenged for personal gain or enjoyment.

Preserving wild lands for future generations requires some foresight and common sense by recreational visitors. Proper preparation will ensure your visit is safe and enjoyable, and attention to a few basic techniques will make the impact of your visit invisible to those who follow.

Most hikers by now have heard of "low impact camping" or, as the Forest Service says, "leave no trace." The general idea is to tread lightly upon the land, leaving no lasting mark of your visit. Leaving no trace requires a number of things: proper equipment, education about techniques, appropriate group size, and length of stay, as well as consideration of season of use and weather conditions. An ill-prepared, large group camped out in a fragile meadow during a several-day downpour will have much more impact than a small, well-equipped party camped on rocky soil.

Group Size

Wilderness areas, national forests, and state recreation areas set their own regulations for group size, dogs on leashes, and other issues. Limits on group size range from six to 25 people, but good wilderness practice suggests groups no larger than eight to 10. Pack animals should not exceed the number of people in a group.

Campsites

When camping in well-traveled areas, it is best to select sites where the ground is already compacted and vegetation is trampled. Research shows that most impacts to a pristine site occur within just a few days of camping, so once a noticeable campsite has been created, impacts will increase only moderately with continued use.

However, when traveling where few obvious sites exist, hikers should select a new site rather than one where impacts are just barely beginning to be noticeable. When selecting a campsite in a pristine area, try to choose a resistant area like sandy terrain or the forest floor instead of more delicate sites, such as alpine tundra. Camp at least 200 feet from water sources, trails, and scenic locations to avoid water and visual pollution.

Fires and Stoves

The crush of recreational visitors has exacted a heavy toll on many wild areas because of one particular activity: campfires. Wilderness etiquette today demands the use of stoves in all situations to avoid the ugly and ecologically destructive sight of blackened earth, multiple fire rings, and denuded vegetation that blemishes far too many backcountry campsites. Build fires only if you must, and in these instances use existing fire rings if possible. Choose small diameter sticks from the forest floor for firewood and never break the lower branches from trees. Do not put whole logs in the fire, for they usually don't burn completely and leave unsightly charred remains.

If you need to build a fire where none previously existed, either build it on top of a thin layer of dirt scattered over flat rock, or dig a pit, saving the topsoil and sod to replace when the ashes are cool the next morning. In both cases, this helps to prevent the fire's heat from sterilizing the top layer of soil.

Human Waste

Many of us have at one time or another encountered human feces and toilet paper strewn near a trail or campsite. Nothing dampens expectations of a back-country experience as quickly. Fortunately, proper disposal of human feces is both clean and easy. Experienced backpackers use the "cat hole" method, whereby you dig a hole six to eight inches deep with a lightweight aluminum or plastic trowel. This places the feces into a biologically active layer of soil where decomposition occurs fairly quickly. Toilet paper decomposes slowly, so many experts recommend carrying a cigarette lighter to burn your toilet paper before filling in the hole. Of course, be extremely careful of fire conditions.

Tampons and sanitary napkins must be thoroughly burned in a very hot fire because animals will dig them up if buried. Since Colorado is not grizzly country, this refuse can also be bagged and carried out of the wilderness without fear of attracting bears.

Pack Animals

Pack stock can do a great deal of damage to wilderness campsites if not properly tended. Never hitch horses to trees or picket them with a metal pin in one place since the animals quickly trample all semblance of vegetation. Instead, hobble pack stock, erect temporary corrals using electric fence, or tether stock to lines strung between trees that allow for relatively unconfined movement by the animals.

Horse packers should make use of readily available lightweight camping and cooking equipment to reduce the number of pack stock required and the weight of each animal's load. This will save wear and tear both on trails and campsites. Take care in selecting watering holes for horses: pick gravely stream banks over lakeshores and soft meadows. Also, an increasing problem in wild areas is invasion by exotic plant species that are typically found in hay; horse packers should use only weed-free feed such as pellets or certified hay.

More and more backcountry visitors are employing less traditional pack stock, such as llamas and goats. The lighter weight and grazing preferences of these animals can lessen the impacts caused by larger, heavier horses.

Noise Pollution

Silence is one of the great joys of wilderness. Many who tread here yearn to escape the horns, clangs, shouts, squeals, and clamor of civilization. Please realize that sounds carry great distances in the virgin silence of an alpine valley. Courtesy dictates that you leave radios at home and refrain from shouting or otherwise raising a ruckus.

Peak Bagging Ethics

Many hikers are drawn to Colorado's backcountry by "fourteeners" — peaks over 14,000 feet in elevation. There are nine fourteeners that can be accessed from the Colorado Trail, and a popular pastime is climbing, or "bagging," these high peaks. Alpine environments are extremely fragile, however, and unable to withstand the impact of hundreds of feet. Damage can be minimized by following a few basic ethics.

On rocky approaches to high peaks, alpine plants are few and far between, so avoid trampling the hardy survivors. Most climbing routes follow ridgelines to the summit, but many mountaineering guidebooks describe descents down scree slopes and suggest "skiing" these scree chutes in a controlled rockslide. This practice creates scars visible for great distances, increases erosion, and obliterates any chance plants might have at establishing a foothold. Use common sense and refrain from sliding down scree slopes.

BACKCOUNTRY PRECAUTIONS

A few simple precautions can make your hike along the Colorado Trail safe and memorable. Without taking the time in advance to prepare properly for backcountry travel, you may still have a memorable trip, but they might not be the kind of memories you anticipated.

Water

Drinking untreated water should be avoided due to a waterborne parasite called *Giardia lamblia*, which can cause severe intestinal distress if ingested. *Giardia lamblia* is transferred via fecal matter from infected animals. Minute cysts that survive for weeks or even months in frigid waters can enter a new host and cause a disease called giardiasis. The severe flu-like symptoms of giardiasis may not show up for weeks after exposure and can last up to six weeks or more. Though medicines exist, the *Giardia* cysts are difficult to destroy and the illness may return intermittently. Mammals such as elk and beaver, which are prevalent in the backcountry, commonly carry the *Giardia* cysts and hikers should assume all major water sources to be contaminated.

To guard against giardiasis, any water source of uncertain origin should be treated by boiling, filtering, or the addition of chemicals. Some experts say boiling water at any altitude kills *Giardia* cysts; others claim a roiling boil for three to five minutes is required. Most commonly available water purification filters also remove the cysts but be sure to check the manufacturer's instructions. Iodine is the only chemical widely recommended for water purification because water temperature and siltation influence the effectiveness of chlorine. Iodine, however, leaves an aftertaste and may need to be camouflaged by flavored drinks.

Hypothermia

Hypothermia is the lowering of the core body temperature to less than 95°F. This condition can be either chronic or acute. Chronic hypothermia is the gradual lowering of body temperature over many hours, or even days, and is frequently the result of continued exposure to damp and windy conditions. It can be extremely serious because once symptoms appear, a hiker's sources of internal energy have been severely depleted. Two symptoms characterize chronic hypothermia: exhaustion and lack of coordination. A person experiencing chronic hypothermia will be unable to walk 30 feet in a straight line heel-to-toe. Intense shivering and mild confusion may also occur.

Chronic hypothermia should be treated by preventing further heat loss, primarily by replacing wet clothes with dry ones, getting out of the wind, and wrapping the victim with numerous layers of insulating clothing. Victims of chronic hypothermia are extremely dehydrated and should be given warm fluids to drink. They should be warmed with hot packs (such as hot water in plastic water bottles) applied to their palms and the soles of their feet, or by the time-honored method of cuddling with one or two other hikers in a sleeping bag. Hypothermia victims need to rest in order to recover their energy, but if their symptoms appear to be worsening, they should be evacuated immediately since they can slip into a semicomatose state.

Cascade Creek, San Juan National Forest

Acute hypothermia results from immersion in cold water and occurs within two hours. A good rule of thumb is that anyone who has been immersed in 50°F. water for more than 20 minutes is suffering from severe loss of body heat. A serious concern with acute hypothermia victims is a phenomenon known as "afterdrop," whereby the victim's core temperature continues to drop even as he or she is being warmed. Because the skin temperature is so low, substantial amounts of additional heat can be lost simply as blood circulates from the body core to the skin surface. Preferred treatment is immersion in hot water (105°F.), but a more practical field treatment is a blazing campfire. Huddling in a sleeping bag with one or two bare-skinned rescuers is another means of adding substantial heat to the victim.

Of course, the best cure is prevention. Proper attire, including layering and protection from wind and rain, is a must. Hikers should be in good physical condition, eat food of high nutritional value, and drink plenty of liquids at regular intervals, as much as 16 ounces per hour. Plan your itinerary in a reasonable fashion to prevent exhaustion.

Altitude Sickness

Experts suggest acclimatizing yourself before venturing above 9,000 feet in elevation. Since most of the Colorado Trail is above 9,000 feet, this applies to the majority of hikes. Many people experience mild symptoms of altitude sickness in the form of headaches, nausea, and lack of appetite. More severe symptoms include coughing and a staggering gait. If these symptoms occur, be sure to rest, breathe deeply, and consume quick-energy foods such as dried fruit or candy. Aspirin will relieve headache symptoms, but the only sure-fire cure for altitude sickness is to retreat to lower elevations. Altitude sickness is a serious ailment and occasionally kills climbers in the Himalayas and other high mountain ranges. Hikers should be watchful for symptoms and administer treatment immediately since altitude sickness can quickly cause serious complications or even prove fatal.

Lightning

Much of the Colorado Trail is above timberline, an area susceptible to lightning strikes. Most long-time hikers have experienced the eerie sensation of hair rising when they were caught on an exposed ridge as an electrical storm approached. It is not a sensation one easily forgets.

With lightning, as with most things, prevention is the best medicine. The months of July and August are the height of the summer thunderstorm season in Colorado's high country, but lightning can and does strike most months of the year. Plan to be off mountain summits by 1:00 P.M. in the summer. If you find yourself above timberline during a storm, take the following precautions: avoid standing on mountaintops or ridges, in open areas, under a lone tree, in shallow caves (ground currents can be fatal), or at the base or edge of cliffs. Your best bet is to crouch in a boulder field or, in a worst case scenario, sit on a small rock with folded clothing or other insulating material beneath you. If you can get to lower elevations, huddling in a forest is significantly safer than being caught above timberline.

Other Precautions

The thin atmosphere of high elevations not only makes breathing more difficult, but also magnifies the power of the sun. Exposed skin will tan and burn far more quickly at altitude, so apply liberal amounts of high-strength sunscreen frequently. Be prepared for extended exposure to intense solar radiation by wearing a long-sleeved shirt, long pants, a hat, and sunglasses.

At the opposite extreme, beware of frostbite on winter ski excursions and during those surprise fall snowstorms. Frostbite is the localized freezing of soft tissue, often affecting body parts such as noses, earlobes, fingers, and toes that are exposed to chilling winds.

Winter exploration of the Colorado Trail can be an exhilarating outdoor adventure, but it also brings with it the danger of avalanches. Every year, more and more backcountry explorers lose their lives in snowslides. Before venturing into the high country, consider snowpack and weather conditions and assess the likelihood of avalanches along your route. Most avalanches occur on north- and east-facing slopes with vertical angles between 25 and 55 degrees. Slides are most prevalent after rapid changes in weather conditions, including wind, temperature variations, and snowfall. If abundant snow has fallen after an extended warm period, avalanche conditions will most likely be extreme. Be prepared by carrying beepers and shovels; avoid avalanche slopes by skiing in the forest or along ridges; if you must cross suspected avalanche routes, do so one at a time. If caught in a slide, shed your gear and try to "swim" to the surface. When the slide has stopped, create an air pocket in front of your mouth to breathe. Information about avalanche conditions can be obtained from the Colorado Avalanche Information Center at (303) 371-1080.

MOUNTAIN BIKING THE COLORADO TRAIL

Mountain bikes, sometimes called fat-tire bikes, are becoming more popular and will be encountered increasingly on the Colorado Trail. They are not, however, allowed in wilderness areas. A section in the back of this guide describes detours for mountain bikes around the six wilderness areas through which the official route passes. These detours generally use county roads, Forest Service roads, and highways. Mountain bikers can also custom-design their own detours using Forest Service maps and a state highway map.

For more information about hiking the Colorado Trail, write to:
The Colorado Trail Foundation
548 Pine Song Trail
Golden, CO 80401

NATURAL HISTORY OF THE COLORADO TRAIL

GEOLOGY ALONG THE COLORADO TRAIL

To venture along the Colorado Trail is to catch a glimpse of Colorado's history, a great deal of which is linked to the extraction of mineral wealth. For more than a hundred years Colorado towns have prospered and declined according to the fortunes of the mining industry. A far earlier history, however, is that of the land through which the trail passes. Much of the natural beauty of Colorado can be attributed to the geologic forces that have shaped the varied landscapes of this Rocky Mountain state.

In eastern Colorado lies the westernmost edge of the Great Plains, a rolling landscape that abruptly gives way to mountains at an altitude of about 5,000 feet. Underlying the plains are interlayered beds of a variety of rocks: shale, sandstone, conglomerate, limestone, coal, and volcanic ash. These beds vary in age from the geologically recent to as much as 570 million years old. In the Denver Basin (see Figure 1) this 13,000-foot-thick sequence of sediments lies above a still older Precambrian basement consisting of crystalline granitic and metamorphic rocks. Geologists learn much about the earth by "reading" the rocks, and they postulate a history here that dates back 1.8 billion years.

Some of the sedimentary rocks are visible along the Front Range, where they have been bent, broken, and brought to the surface by the forces that pushed the mountains upward. Most notable are the Fountain Sandstone flatirons, which make up the Red Rocks amphitheater and other points of interest, and the hogbacks of the Dakota and Morrison formations seen from Interstate 70. This dramatic meeting of plains and mountains provides a fine setting for the Colorado Trail as it begins its winding course through the ranges and valleys of western Colorado.

At the start, the trail moves westward across the Front Range, the core of which is made of basement rocks that have been uplifted again and again during the past 330 million years. In many places the older rocks — schists, gneisses, quartzites, marbles, and metamorphosed volcanics — have been intruded by younger granitic bodies, such as the Pikes Peak batholith.

West of the Front Range, the Colorado Trail passes to the north of South Park, a wide basin underlain by sedimentary rocks like those of the plains. These rocks were intruded by mineralized stocks of granodiorite porphyry during a mountain-building period known as the Laramide Orogeny, which occurred 40 to 70 million years ago.

The trail continues through part of the Breckenridge mining district, a region famous for its gold. The largest gold nugget ever discovered in Colorado was found here and can be seen today at Denver's Museum of Natural History. The mining of gold and silver was Colorado's principal industry in the late 1800s, when placer gold in streambeds lured eager prospectors into the mountains in search of source veins and lodes. Today we recognize far more diversity in the state's mineral wealth: limestone, sand, gravel, building stone, lead,

Volcanic outcrop below Mount Ouray, Gunnison National Forest

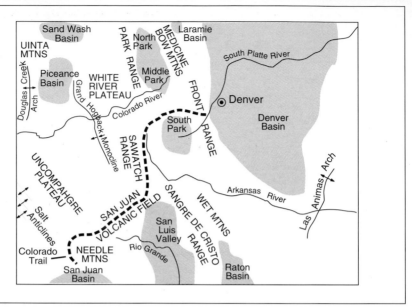

Figure 1- Geological structures underlying the Colorado Trail

molybdenum, zinc, coal, oil (including oil shale), and natural gas. One more commodity ought to be acknowledged — snow! Obviously, the winter sports industry depends on this annual accumulation in the mountains; less obvious, perhaps, but incredibly important, is the fact that each year as the snowpack melts, water is stored in forest soils, alluvium, and porous rocks, ready to supply the needs of every living thing.

The trail goes up and over the Tenmile Range, a block of uplifted, ancient metamorphic rocks. Beyond Copper Mountain it passes through an area of layered rocks that have been intruded by quartz monzonite and granodiorite porphyry dikes and sills. It crosses a 20-million-year-old rhyolite near Camp Hale and goes on to Tennessee Pass and the gold-bearing strata of the Cambrian, Devonian, Mississippian, and Pennsylvanian periods.

South of the pass, ancient gneisses and schists (1.7 billion years old) are cut by silver-producing veins of the St. Kevin-Sugar Loaf mining district. Early Indians once extracted turquoise from deposits in this area. The trail skirts Turquoise Lake on a 1.4-billion-year-old granite batholith and crosses moraines left behind by now-extinct Sawatch glaciers. At one time glaciers dammed the Arkansas River, forcing it to carve out a new channel on the east side of the valley.

The upper Arkansas Valley, part of the long, north-south Rio Grande rift, is bounded by a steplike series of parallel faults on the east and by the Sawatch fault zone on the west, along which many hot springs are located. One of these springs is at Mount Princeton, where the trail passes the Chalk Cliffs, a hydrothermally altered part of a 30-million-year-old quartz monzonite batholith. Farther south, near the summit of Mount Antero, aquamarine (beryl), topaz, garnet, and other rare minerals are found. Topaz and garnet are also found in the valley near the town of Nathrop.

Southwest of Marshall Pass is the San Juan Volcanic Field, a point of considerable geologic interest. Between 35 and 22 million years ago, this area was the scene of violent eruptions from many enormous craters. These craters, or calderas, are the present-day sites of such gold and silver mining camps as Creede, Platoro, Silverton, Lake City, and Bonanza. Layers of volcanic rock from both passive and explosive eruptions cover the area to a depth of thousands of feet. Younger volcanic rocks, about 3.5 million years old, are also present.

Along the north flank of the Needle Mountains uplift, the trail passes through spectacular Precambrian terrain in the Grenadier Range. This includes upthrust beds of quartzite, slate, and phyllite. An erosional nonconformity between 1.4-billion-year-old Precambrian rocks and an overlying layer of quartzite represents a gap in time of about 600 million years.

Beyond Molas Lake the trail works upward through successively younger sedimentary rock layers. Some of these are different from the rock units found in eastern Colorado. Others, such as the Dakota, Morrison, Entrada, and Leadville formations, are equivalent in make-up and age to rocks in other parts of the state. Still others are partially equivalent to formations found elsewhere. The Mancos Shale of western Colorado, for instance, was deposited in the same sea as the Pierre Shale of eastern Colorado, but the western rocks are older than the eastern ones. This is because the ancient sea gradually migrated eastward, altering both the time and place of deposition.

The ridge south of Grizzly Peak consists of clays and marlstones of the Morrison Formation (well known as a source of dinosaur bones) and also of the ancient beach and lagoon deposits that comprise the Dakota Sandstone. These are intruded by igneous rocks in the form of dikes, sills, and laccoliths. From this divide, the trail affords splendid views of the area's mountain ranges: the San Miguel, the San Juan, the La Plata, and the Needles.

Heading southward to the La Plata Mountains, the trail crosses red shales, siltstones, mudstones, grits, and conglomerates. The La Plata Range consists of sedimentary rocks that were domed up during the Laramide Orogeny by the intrusion of sills, laccolith, and stocks. The dome was subsequently dissected by erosional forces and is the location of a mining district that has produced gold- and silver-bearing telluride, ruby silver, copper, and lead ores since 1873.

The trail continues to wend its way southward to Junction Creek and descends by way of successively younger strata to arrive at the trail's southern terminus — Junction Creek Trailhead outside of Durango.

More extensive descriptions of the Colorado Trail's geology can be found in U.S. Geological Survey publications, including the Geological Map of Colorado. USGS publications are available by mail from the USGS Branch of Distribution, P.O. Box 25286, Denver, CO 80225; or over the counter from USGS Map Sales, Denver Federal Center, Building 810, Lakewood, CO. Free, non-technical pamphlets from these agencies include such topics as: *Mountain and Plains, Denver's Geological Setting; Landforms of the United States; Volcanoes of the United States; Earthquakes; Geologic Map, Portraits of the Earth; Geologic Time; Prospecting; Collecting Rocks;* and many others. A further source of information is the Colorado Geological Survey, 1313 Sherman Street, Room 715, Denver, CO 80203.

— David L. Gaskill and Denise R. Mutschler

COLORADO ECOSYSTEMS

This brief look at Rocky Mountain ecology is intended for those new to the Colorado Trail as well as for locals who have rarely ventured into its vastness. Veterans of these wilds could probably write an equally good account of its flora and fauna. Regardless, there is no question that the natural history of this region is the reward for the effort of hiking the trail. The opportunity to observe the Rocky Mountain ecosystem underscores the need to *walk*, not run, while on the trail. In ten years of leading groups of students through the Rockies, it has been my experience that hikers who reach camp two hours before the rest can rarely relate any interesting observations. They might as well have worked out in a gym. To get the most out of your sojourn on the Colorado Trail, take the time to look, to sit, to let nature present itself to you, and to soak up all that it has to offer. You may pass this way but once.

Observing Wildlife

For some reason, we commonly use the term "wildlife" to refer only to animals. There is less drama associated with plants because we can prepare for our encounters with them, whereas animals tend to take us by surprise — they are there all of a sudden and gone all of a sudden. As a botanist, I recognize that most people would rather talk about a bear than about bearberries.

The native fauna of the Rockies may readily be viewed from the Colorado Trail. Having been over most of its length, I cannot think of a single day's hike that did not reveal much of the Rocky Mountains' wildlife. By the same token, I have seen students hike for days without seeing a single animal. This apparent contradiction can be explained by the fact that native animals are not in a zoo. They have instincts and learned behavior to avoid threatening situations, such as encounters with people. You must meet the animals on their own terms, and several general rules may be followed.

Dawn and dusk are when animals tend to be most active. They require water regularly, so streams and lakes provide good vantage points. Many animals will learn to ignore you if you are part of the scenery, which means being relatively quiet and still. Obtain local texts and become familiar with the behavior of the animal or animals you wish to observe. You will probably have the most success with birds, but do not discount what might be considered the less dramatic animals, such as the small nocturnal rodents. A log to sit on at night and a flashlight will often allow you some captivating moments. Rising early in the morning and getting on the trail ahead of the group can also increase your chances of seeing wildlife. Early season hikers should note that fawning of deer and calving of elk occur in June; try not to be disruptive if traveling during this time of year.

Some hikers may be fearful of encountering wildlife, but there is little need for worry. I have seen mountain lion and bear at reasonable distances, and I am sure they have observed me much closer. I have seen bear droppings on the trail on a cold morning that were so fresh the steam was still rising off them. My wife woke up from a nap one afternoon, and there were fresh bear claw marks on a tree over her head. But in ten years, none of the groups we have led through the mountains have ever been attacked. Use good judgment, for an

Lupine wildflowers near Copper Mountain

animal seeks food, not your company. If you have no food in your tent, you will generally not be bothered. If you choose to keep food, even nuts or a candy bar, in your tent, you may wake up at night to find a hole cut in the floor and confront the steely eyes of a mouse or pack rat. After arriving in camp, place your food away from the sleeping area — 75 to 100 yards is a good distance. Mosquitoes are the wildlife you will most likely encounter, and they too are looking for a meal, so bring repellent. You might encounter an occasional flock

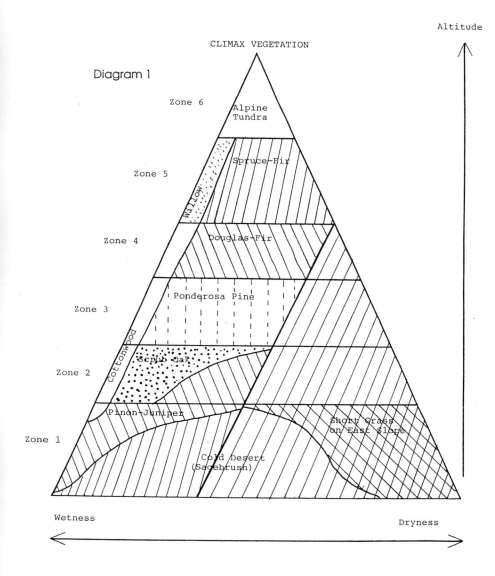

Ferchau, 1970

of domestic sheep, especially in the San Juan Mountains. If you do, remain calm and avoid eye contact, for sheep are easily spooked and you could unintentionally cause the flock to panic and run.

Some hikers feel the hiking experience is not complete without their dog. To be sure, when a backpacker is on the trail alone, companionship is pleasant. When hiking in a group, however, a dog can be a nuisance. If you are interested in being a part of the surrounding ecosystem, your dog should be left at home.

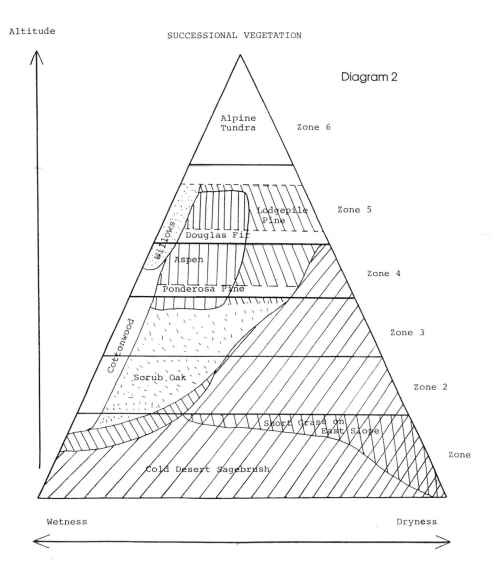

Altitude

SUCCESSIONAL VEGETATION

Diagram 2

Alpine Tundra — Zone 6

Lodgepole Pine — Zone 5

Willows

Douglas Fir

Aspen — Zone 4

Ponderosa Pine

Cottonwood — Zone 3

Scrub Oak — Zone 2

Short Grass on East Slope

Zone

Cold Desert Sagebrush

Wetness   Dryness

Ferchau 1970

Plant Communities

The highly variable topography of the central Rocky Mountains provides a kaleidoscopic variety of vegetation. The accompanying diagrams give some indication of the vegetation types encountered on the Colorado Trail, as well as their relationships to each other. Note that the zones are not defined by elevation alone, but depend also on local climatic factors. In the field, matters are generally more complicated. In areas that have been disturbed by fire or logging, for example, different types of vegetation will exist in different relationships. Diagram 1 (page 38) shows the relationships between various plant communities in a "climax" situation, that is, in an ecologically stable, undisturbed environment. When the land has been disturbed, the plants proceed through a "succession" phase before eventually evolving back into a climax state. Diagram 2 (page 39) shows the relationships between various types of vegetation during succession. Because of the severe climate and short growing season in the Rockies, successional vegetation patterns may persist for more than a hundred years. In addition, a single hillside may be covered with successional vegetation in one place and climax vegetation in another.

Riparian Vegetation

This is the vegetation found along streambanks, and it plays a variety of important roles, such as controlling erosion and providing cover and feed for wildlife. On the Western Slope, lower elevation streambanks are dominated by assorted cottonwood trees, alder, maple, and red-osier dogwood. With increasing elevation cottonwoods become less evident while the shrubs persist, eventually being dominated by willows. On the Eastern Slope cottonwoods are not as evident, but, as on the Western Slope, a mixture of shrubs prevails, becoming increasingly dominated by willows at higher elevations.

Despite what appears to be very aggressive growth by riparian species, they are among the most sensitive to human activity. Because of their proximity to water, they are typically among the most threatened and endangered.

Sagebrush Country

Sagebrush, the cold desert scrubland of the Rockies, can be found from low to surprisingly high elevations. It is interspersed with grasses and is the primary grazing land of central and western Colorado. It is also quite dry, with little water available for hikers; ranchers typically maintain water supplies in stock tanks for their cattle, but those supplies are definitely not recommended for human use. During the day, this environment can become quite hot, while at night even summertime temperatures can drop to near freezing. Watch out for ticks in June.

Scrub Oak and Piñon-Juniper Woodland

This dryland plant community is most evident along the Colorado Trail where it climbs through the foothills above Denver. It will also be seen occasionally at higher elevations on the driest and most stressed sites, until near Kenosha Pass. Junipers tend to be widely spaced with grasses interspersed in between, while the scrub oak tends to be clumped together so closely as to be almost impenetrable. This sort of vegetation makes for good game habitat, and hikers should be prepared for deer to pop up almost anywhere, particularly in early June. In late summer, the scrub oak/piñon-juniper woodland is prone to wildfires, which can move rapidly through the dry terrain. Such fires are often started by lightning strikes and occasionally by hikers — so be extremely careful with campfires.

Ponderosa Pine

This is the lowest elevation timber tree. Because of its good lumber quality and proximity to civilization, it has been the most extensively cut. Thus, you may see large, old ponderosa pine stumps among woodland vegetation, indicating a logged forest where the tall pines have not yet returned. Long-needled trees, ponderosa pines tend to grow well spaced with grasses flourishing between them. As a result, ranchers like to graze their stock among the ponderosa pine, particularly in early spring. On the Eastern Slope, ponderosa pine is found on less-stressed, south-facing hillsides. On the Western Slope, it is the tree one encounters above the open, arid countryside of the sagebrush community.

Douglas Fir

This predominant tree is not to be confused with the giant firs of the Pacific Northwest, although it is related to them. Here in the Rockies, we have the runts of the litter. The Douglas fir occupies moist, cool sites. On the Eastern Slope it is found on the hillsides opposite the ponderosa pine, and on the Western Slope it grows above the level of the ponderosa pine. In either case, as a result of the more moist environment and shorter growing season, Douglas fir trees tend to grow closer together with little ground cover underneath. These trees are found on both the Eastern and Western Slopes, but because they are likely to burn in forest fires, much of that habitat is occupied by successional vegetation. Hikers, again, should remember to be careful with fire.

Spruce-Fir Forest

This, the highest elevation forest, is composed of Engelmann spruce and subalpine fir. Because of late snowmelt, moist summertime conditions, and early snowfall, this vegetation type has been least altered by fire. Many of the spruce-fir forests in the Rockies are as much as 400 years old. These dense forests tend to contain many fallen logs, which can be a deterrent to hiking. Because the logs are typically moist, hikers walking over them may be surprised when the bark slips off and they lose their footing. Ground cover may be lacking in spruce-fir forests, and a thick humus layer may be present.

As one approaches timberline, the spruce-fir stands tend to be more open. The trees are clustered with grasses and beautiful wildflowers interspersed between them. These clusters provide refuge for elk during the night. At timberline the trees are bushlike, weather beaten, and wind shorn. They often grow in very dense clumps which provide ideal shelter for hikers if necessary. Winds of 50 mph can whistle by virtually unnoticed while you sit in a clump of timberline trees. Animals are aware of this, too, and while waiting out a storm, you may have the pleasure of observing a great deal of small mammal activity.

Lodgepole Pine and Aspen

These are ordinarily successional species which can occupy a site for up to 200 years. The lodgepole pine often succeeds disturbed Douglas fir and spruce-

fir communities and grows on the driest sites. Its seeds are opened by fire, and a wildfire will cause the deposition of thousands of seeds, and, a few years later, the appearance of many dense stands of seedlings and saplings. These pine stands are often referred to as "horsehair." There is virtually no ground cover in the deep shade beneath the saplings; competition is fierce between the closely spaced trees, and the dryness of the site encourages repeated fires.

Aspen trees occupy more moist sites. A clump of aspen among lodgepole pines suggests a potential source of water. Aspen reproduce from root suckers, and any ground disturbance, such as a fire, causes a multitude of saplings to appear. On drier sites, aspen is typically interspersed with Thurber fescue, a large bunchgrass. In moderately moist sites the ground cover will consist of a multitude of grasses, forbs, and shrubs. Wet-site aspen often have a ground cover dominated by bracken fern. Aspen groves are attractive for camping, but during June and July they may be infested with troublesome insects.

Alpine Tundra

Though it strikes many people as odd, the tundra can be likened to a desert because it receives only minimal precipitation. During the winter, fierce winds prevent snow from accumulating anywhere except in depressions. During the summer, snowmelt drains quickly off the steeper slopes, leaving the vegetation to depend on regular afternoon showers for survival. Despite the harsh conditions, the alpine tundra is quite diverse and includes meadows, boulder fields, fell fields, talus, and both temporary and permanent ponds. The cushionlike meadows are a favorite site for elk herds; boulder fields provide homes for pikas, marmots, and other animals; and protected spaces between the boulders produce beautiful wildflowers. Fell fields are windswept sites from which virtually all the soil has been blown away, leaving behind a "pavement," which despite its austerity supports some plants. Talus fields consist of loose rock and also host some interesting plants and animals. Alpine ponds teem with invertebrates and provide good sites for observing the well-camouflaged ptarmigan.

There's a fascinating world of plant and animal life to be found within Colorado's diverse ecosystems. If you make the effort, perhaps looking closely or waiting patiently, you will undoubtedly witness for yourself the wealth of natural history along the Colorado Trail.

— Hugo A. Ferchau
Thornton Professor of Botany, Western State College

Moonrise above the alpine tundra, San Juan Mountains

The South Platte River flows through Waterton Canyon

◢◣ SEGMENT 1　　16.1 Miles

Kassler to South Platte Townsite　　　　　　**+ 2,224 Feet Elevation Gain**

Location	Mileage	From Denver	Elevation
Waterton Canyon Trailhead	0.0	0.0	5,520
Strontia Springs Dam	5.8		5,800
Bear Creek	8.0		6,200
Ridge above West Bear Creek	10.2		7,200
County Road 97	15.4		6,120
South Platte Townsite	16.1	16.1	6,100

CT Series Maps 1 & 2 (see pages 50-51 & 56-57).

Colorado Trail trekkers sometimes complain about the first 6.2 miles of the CT on the Denver Water Board road up Platte Canyon from the Waterton Canyon Trailhead. Admittedly, this highly used recreation area on a hot summer afternoon can be a discouraging initial experience on the CT, even with the craggy scenery of the canyon as inspiration. However, the canyon takes on a different personality in the pleasant, early morning hours before the crowds appear. Cool breezes sweep the canyon with the fragrant scent of the forests above and nearby riparian vegetation. At this hour, the canyon appears to be your personal domain. You may even be lucky enough to see the local bighorn sheep herd grazing near the river before the multitudes frighten them to the steep slopes high in the canyon. Even so, many consider the "real" trail experience to begin beyond mile 6.2, as the CT leaves the road behind above Strontia Springs Dam.

On your way to Waterton Canyon from the east, notice the hogbacks leaning against the ancient core of the Rampart Range. With little imagination it is possible to visualize these leftover sedimentary rocks crumpling and eroding away through the eons as the Rampart Range forced its way up from below. Beyond the sedimentary layers at the outlet of the canyon, the gorge narrows and reveals its 1.6-billion-year-old metamorphic walls.

Although this canyon was no doubt visited by many Indians and was briefly explored by the Long Expedition of 1820, it was not permanently disrupted until 1877 when territorial governor John Evans built his Denver South Park and Pacific Railroad up the Platte on its way to exploit Colorado's mineral belt. The canyon has known little peace since, and endured a major change in the early 1980s when work began on Strontia Springs Dam. The possibility of the immense Two Forks project just upstream would continue this cycle, as well as inundate a significant portion of the CT in the western end of this segment, requiring a lengthy trail reroute around the massive reservoir.

CT trekkers must abide by the Denver Water Board regulations along the first 6.2-mile section in Waterton Canyon; these include no dogs or camping. This segment of the CT is particularly popular with mountain bikers, and backpackers should be prepared for the columns of bikes speeding by.

Trailhead/Access Points

Kassler-Waterton Canyon Trailhead: There are several routes to the trailhead at Waterton Canyon. Least confusing in to take Interstate 25 south from Denver through the suburbs to Colorado 470. Travel west on Colorado 470 for 12.5 miles to Colorado 121 (Wadsworth Boulevard). Go south (left) on Colorado 121 for 4.5 miles to where the road officially ends at the entrance to the Martin Marietta plant. Turn left off of Colorado 121 and onto a side road marked as "Waterton Canyon." Continue 0.3 mile, following the signs to the large trailhead parking area. Note: If Two Forks Dam is ever built, this access might be closed during construction.

South Platte Townsite: See Segment 2.

Supplies, Services, and Accommodations

Denver and its southern suburbs have the full array of services expected in a metropolitan area. The trailhead at the mouth of Waterton Canyon has limited bus service.

Maps

CT Series: Maps 1 and 2 (see pages 50-51 and 56-57).
USFS: Pike National Forest.
USGS Quadrangles: Kassler, Platte Canyon.

Trail Description

From the Waterton Canyon Trailhead parking area at the old Kassler water treatment plant, begin your Colorado Trail adventure up Platte Canyon on the old railroad grade, now the wide gravel Denver Water Board road. Cottonwoods along the banks of the Platte River provide shade on warm summer days. At 5,520 feet above sea level, this point is the lowest anywhere along the CT, and it serves as a gateway from the eastern plains grasslands to the foothills life zone. Immediately above the shadows of the cottonwoods, the dry rocky slopes of the canyon support little more than yucca, gambel oak and juniper. Higher up on the cooler, more moist mountain slopes, dark patches of ponderosa pine and Douglas fir are visible.

Pass Strontia Springs Dam at mile 5.8 (5,800) and continue straight ahead (south) on the dirt road, which steadily steepens. The public must exit the road at a switchback to the right, 0.3 mile beyond the dam. Here, a short, dead-end spur road to the left (south) leads to a portal of multicolored, metamorphic boulders at mile 6.2 (5,920), and the start of your aesthetic trail experience. A sign here reads "Colorado Trail #1776, Bear Creek-1.6, South Platte Townsite-10.0." Perhaps another entry should be added to the sign stating "Junction Creek Trailhead, Western Terminus 462 miles."

The comfortable trail switchbacks up through a shady Douglas fir forest, offering intermittent glimpses to the north of the rocky summit called Turkshead. From the saddle at mile 7.3 (6,560), a side trail goes east via Stevens and Mill gulches to the summit of Carpenter Peak within Roxborough State Park. Please note that bicycles and equestrians are not allowed in the park, which is open for day use only. Descend from the saddle and cross Bear Creek at mile 8.0 (6,200). Bear Creek is the last reliable point for water until you reach South Platte townsite 8.0 miles beyond.

A barely visible path can be seen descending alongside the creek here. This was an old logging road built by C. A. Deane, who had a sawmill at the confluence of Bear Creek and the South Platte River. Besides providing ties to the DSP&P Railroad during its construction, Deane later expanded his profitable operation by adding a hotel and the whistle stop became known as Deansbury.

Continue 0.1 mile on the CT to the crossing of West Bear Creek. At mile 9.0 (6,640) the CT shares its route with Motorcycle Trail #692 for 0.5 mile, until just after the second crossing of West Bear Creek. Here the trail diverges from the motorcycle trail and proceeds uphill and to the right. Ascend another 0.6 mile to the ridge at mile 10.1 (7,200), where the motorcycle trail crosses the CT a final time. The trail continues a climb in and out of several side drainages to its high point on the northern exposed slope of Platte Canyon. Rock outcrops provide convenient perches for rest stops, where the reservoir below and the foothills to the north and west can be viewed.

At mile 13.0 (7,280) the trail rounds an elevated valley and passes along a ridge, then begins a switchbacking descent into the valley. Pass below the shoreline of the proposed Two Forks Reservoir, then join up with County Road 97 at mile 15.4 (6,120). A widened roadway here provides plentiful parking for this unmarked trailhead point. Long-distance trekkers will have to share the route north on the road for the next 0.7 mile with sometimes inconsiderate motorists. This road was originally graded for the DSP&P Nighthawk Branch. Cross the South Platte River on a wide bridge and enter the historic railroad junction where the boarded-up South Platte Hotel recalls memories of another era. The first CT segment ends here at mile 16.1 (6,100).

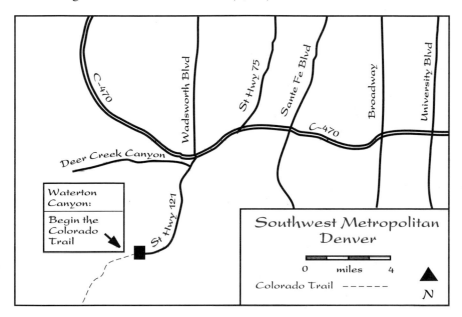

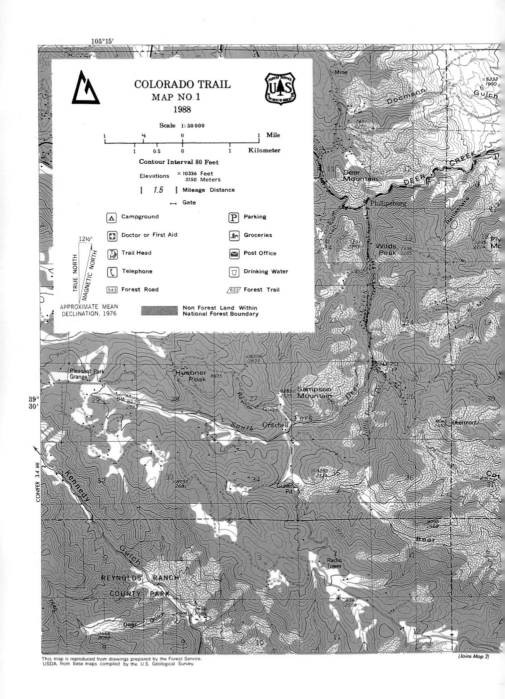

COLORADO TRAIL
MAP NO. 1
1988

Scale 1:50 000

Contour Interval 80 Feet

Elevations ×10336 Feet
3150 Meters

| 1.5 | Mileage Distance

↔ Gate

△ Campground   P Parking

✚ Doctor or First Aid   Groceries

H Trail Head   Post Office

(Telephone   Drinking Water

543 Forest Road   637 Forest Trail

APPROXIMATE MEAN
DECLINATION, 1976

Non Forest Land Within
National Forest Boundary

This map is reproduced from drawings prepared by the Forest Service,
USDA, from base maps compiled by the U.S. Geological Survey.

(Joins Map 2)

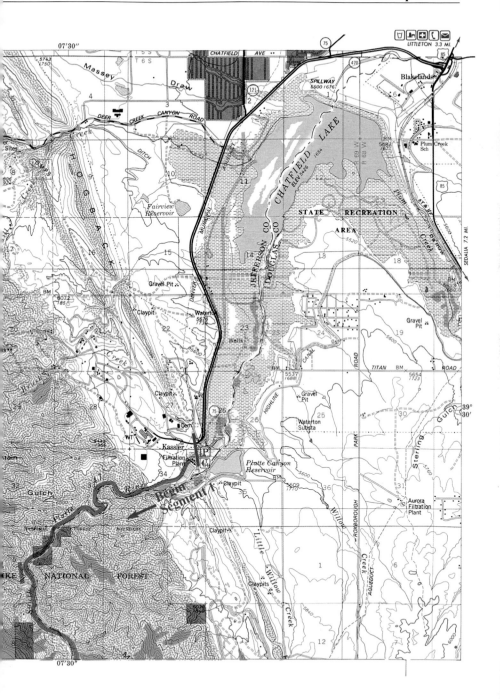

Granite outcrops, Pike National Forest

◭ SEGMENT 2　　9.4 Miles

South Platte Townsite to County Rd 126　　**+1,958 Feet Elevation Gain**

Location	Mileage	From Denver	Elevation
South Platte Townsite	0.0	16.1	6,100
Forest Service Road 538	5.4		7,760
Top of the World Campground	7.1		7,680
County Road 126	9.4	25.5	7,600

CT Series Map 2 (see pages 56-57).

During its heyday, the town of South Platte saw many trains pass by the confluence of the South Platte River and its North Fork. Today the shuttered South Platte Hotel serves as a lone reminder of that age. If constructed, Two Forks Reservoir will submerge this historic junction as well as significant portions of the canyon itself, which is popular with anglers, kayakers, hikers, and rock climbers.

Except along the South Platte River at the outset, the CT route in this segment is completely without water. Even Top-of-the-World Campground is waterless, so pack plenty if you wish to make use of the many potential campsites along the way. This segment parallels, and crosses at its mid-point, FS-538. Side roads and trails leading from this Forest Service road intersect the CT. The views from Top-of-the-World, a ridge the trail traverses on its east side, are the highlights of this segment.

This trail segment makes the transition from the Rampart Range to the Kenosha Mountains, and along the way are splendid examples of the rounded outcrops of the Pikes Peak batholith, formations that take on dramatic, fortress-like appearances. The pink coloration of this billion-year-old granite is disguised by a covering of green and black lichens.

This segment ends at the CT crossing of County Road 126 approximately 3.5 miles south of the town of Buffalo Creek. The Forest Service has provided a parking area here.

Trailhead/Access Points

South Platte Townsite Trailhead: Travel approximately 32 miles west from Denver on US-285 to Pine Junction. Go left (south) on Pine Valley Road (County Road 126), following the signs to Pine and Buffalo Creek. Continue on County Road 126 for 9.4 miles to the outskirts of Buffalo Creek. Turn left onto County Road 96, which parallels the North Fork 10.6 miles to the trailhead at the boarded-up South Platte Hotel. Ample parking is provided here. This trailhead is also accessible from US-24 at Woodland Park by traveling north on Colorado Highway 67 to Deckers. Continue down the Platte River on County Roads 67 and 97 approximately 14 miles to the trailhead. This trailhead is subject to closure if work commences on Two Forks Dam.

Top-of-the-World Campground: At Buffalo Creek, from the instructions above, continue on County Road 126 approximately 2.5 miles and go left onto FS-538, which is marked "Top-of-the-World Campground." It is approximately 1.5 miles to the campground, on a spur that takes off to the right as FS-538 continues ahead. Drive to the cul-de-sac at the end of the campground and park at the small area provided. Follow a short side trail that crosses the road down to the CT, heading east just below the long ridge where the campground is located.

Jefferson County Road 126: See Segment 3.

Supplies, Services, and Accommodations

There is a Forest Service work center and a small general store in Buffalo Creek. Services here are quite limited.

BUFFALO CRK. SERVICES   Distance from Trail: 3 miles

Bank	None
Bus	None
Dining	None
Gear	None
Groceries	J.W. Green Mercantile Co. 17706 County Rd. 96 (303) 838-5587
Information	None
Laundry	None
Lodging	None
Medical	Crow Hill Health Center Hwy. 285 (in Bailey) (303) 838-7653
Post Office	J.W. Green Mercantile Co. 17706 County Rd. 96 (303) 838-5587
Showers	None

Maps

CT Series: Map 2 (see pages 56-57).
USFS: Pike National Forest.
USGS Quadrangles: Platte Canyon, Deckers.

Trail Description

From the confluence of the South Platte River and the North Fork, the CT temporarily follows a Forest Service road around the old hotel's right side and then heads south across the North Fork on a rickety, one-lane bridge. This crossing provides the last reliable water for almost 13 miles. A few hundred feet beyond the bridge, the trail leads right at a well-marked junction and switchbacks uphill through a forest of ponderosa pine and Douglas fir. Several miles up the trail is a large outcrop of pink Pikes Peak granite. This formation makes a leisurely afternoon's destination and affords views of Pikes Peak, Devil's Head, and the Platte Canyon.

At mile 3.8 (7,360) the CT crosses a jeep road. About 0.5 mile beyond, the trail follows an old road for a brief distance. Continue your ascent north of Raleigh Peak through a Douglas fir forest to a ridge at mile 4.7 (7,760), where Chair Rocks are visible to the west. Descend from the ridge to a dry gully, then ascend to mile 5.4 (7,760) and FS-538 at a three-corner intersection. Follow the road west 0.1 mile to where the road turns south. The trail resumes here to the left (south) and heads through a mostly ponderosa pine forest with an occasional juniper. The CT continues to bear south, paralleling FS-538 and crossing several old, abandoned roads — some of which now serve as secondary trails from the Forest Service road into the many side canyons below.

On this section along the Top-of-the-World ridge, striking vistas to the east justify a pace slow enough to allow you to fully appreciate Raleigh Peak, Long Scraggy, and Pikes Peak's rarely seen northwest profile. Pass the short unmarked side trail up to Top-of-the-World Campground at mile 7.1 (7,680). If you have a few minutes to spare, ascend the short distance to the appropriately named campground where a 360-degree panorama reveals the Pikes Peak massif, the entire Rampart Range, and the southern end of the Front Range. Also visible to the west are the Kenosha Mountains and Windy Peak, where you will be headed if you stay on the trail. At this time, there is no water available at the campground.

South of the campground, the trail continues in and out of several shallow gullies which, depending on their orientation, are forested by either ponderosa pine or Douglas fir. At mile 9.0 (7,520) the trail heads in a more westerly direction. Continue to the crossing of Country Road 126 at mile 9.4 (7,600), which is the end of this segment. The town of Buffalo Creek is approximately 3.2 miles north from this point, and the Forest Service trailhead parking area is on the west side of the highway.

Notes

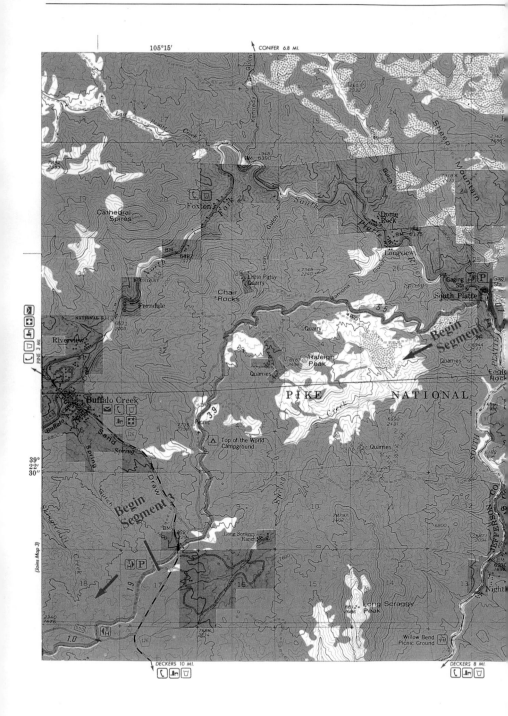

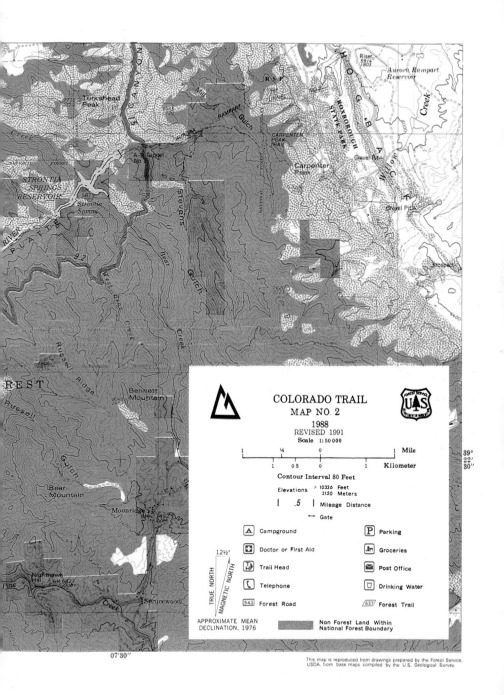

COLORADO TRAIL
MAP NO. 2
1988
REVISED 1991
Scale 1:50 000

Contour Interval 80 Feet

Elevations × 10336 Feet
3150 Meters

| .5 | Mileage Distance

↔ Gate

⌂ Campground   Ⓟ Parking

✚ Doctor or First Aid   🛒 Groceries

🚶 Trail Head   ✉ Post Office

☎ Telephone   ⛉ Drinking Water

543 Forest Road   637 Forest Trail

TRUE NORTH / MAGNETIC NORTH 12½°

APPROXIMATE MEAN
DECLINATION, 1976

Non Forest Land Within
National Forest Boundary

This map is reproduced from drawings prepared by the Forest Service,
USDA, from base maps compiled by the U.S. Geological Survey.

The Front Range and Mount Evans, Pike National Forest

⚠ SEGMENT 3   13.4 Miles

County Rd 126 to Forest Service Rd 543   **+ 1,450 Feet Elevation Gain**

Location	Mileage	From Denver	Elevation
County Road 126	0.0	25.5	7,600
FS-550	1.9		7,840
FS-543 (first crossing)	9.5		7,400
FS-543 (second crossing)	13.4	38.9	8,280

CT Series Maps 2 & 3 (see pages 56-57 & 62-63).

Squeezing between two parcels of private property, the CT begins this segment at County Road 126 approximately 3.2 miles south of the town of Buffalo Creek. The Forest Service has conveniently provided a parking area 0.3 mile south of the trail crossing on County Road 126. This segment crosses several streams in its middle section and has many potential campsites, including the Forest Service's Buffalo Campground. (Meadows Group Campground is available through reservation only). You will pass through the heavily used Buffalo Creek Recreation Area in this segment.

The original trail just west of Tramway Creek was obliterated by logging activity and has since been rebuilt by the Forest Service. The new tread winds above the logged area, at times just skirting it and providing views to the north.

The area through which the CT passes west of County Road 126 is a mountain biker's paradise. Recognizing this, the Forest Service has provided many marked mountain bike routes, several of which use portions of the CT as part of their links or loops. Hikers, equestrians, and animal packers should expect heavier than normal mountain bike traffic in this segment, especially on weekends.

The CT crosses FS-543 twice in this segment. The second crossing is the end of the segment, where a trailhead parking area is provided. Mountain bikers continuing west should note that they need to exit at the first crossing of FS-543 to detour around Lost Creek Wilderness (refer to the Mountain Bike Detours).

Trailhead/Access Points

Jefferson County Road 126 Trailhead: Travel approximately 32 miles west from Denver on US-285 to Pine Junction. Go left (south) on Pine Valley Road (County Road 126), following the signs to Pine and Buffalo Creek. Continue approximately 3.2 miles south of Buffalo Creek on County Road 126 to where the CT crosses the highway. This is the start of this segment, but you can't park on the shoulder, so continue 0.3 mile south to the trailhead parking area on the right (west) side of the road. The CT is about 0.2 mile to the west, beyond the gate, on a Forest Service road closed to motorized traffic.

FS-550 Trailhead: From Buffalo Creek using the driving directions above, continue south on Country Road 126 approximately 4.0 miles and go right (west) on FS-550. Drive barely 0.1 mile to the parking area on the north side of the road. An abandoned road going north from the parking area has been barricaded by a fence. Follow it a few hundred feet to a point where the CT continues west and north.

FS-543 Trailhead: See Segment 4.

Supplies, Services, and Accommodations

Limited services available at Buffalo Creek (see Segment 2).

Maps

CT Series: Maps 2 and 3 (see pages 56-57 and 62-63).
USFS: Pike National Forest.
USGS Quadrangles: Deckers, Green Mountain, Windy Peak.

Trail Description

Cross County Road 126 and continue through a ponderosa pine forest to mile 0.3 (7,720), where you join an abandoned road that leads south, paralleling the highway. The trail leaves the abandoned road to the right (west) at mile 1.3 (7,800), just a few hundred feet north of the FS-550 trailhead parking area. Follow the trail west, and then south, as it curves around an impressive and massive granite outcrop to the crossing of FS-550 at mile 1.9 (7,840).

Beyond FS-550, the trail traverses through ponderosa pine and Douglas fir forests to mile 3.0 (7,800), where it assumes a more southerly bearing into the canyon of Morrison Creek. The Shinglemill bike path descends to the right. Pass under a huge mass of granite blocks on the steeply descending north ridge of Little Scraggy Peak and continue to mile 4.1 (7,760), where the trail seems to end at a jeep road. Bear to the right on the road, cross over the creek, and in a few steps leave the road as the trail resumes at left and ascends 0.2 mile to the crest of the ridge. An old ridge road, which is reverting to nature at its own deliberate pace, crosses the trail at right angles here. Before continuing, study the massive granite outcroppings across the valley to the east. Can you identify the peculiar formation that has been unofficially named "Cantilever Rock"?

Descend from the ridge and cross a small tributary to the east of Morrison Creek on a corduroy bridge. Head up the west side of this tributary to mile 5.0 (7,960), where a sharp right will take you out of this particular gulch and to a gentle traverse in and out of several side gullies. The CT joins and descends an old road beginning at mile 5.8 (8,000) and then crosses Tramway Creek 0.5 mile further on.

On the north side of a clearing at mile 6.7 (7,680), the trail picks up again at a sharp left as the old road continues a descent as the Tramway bike path. At mile 7.2 (7,600) the CT crosses an old logging road that now serves as the Green Mountain bike path. Continue a traverse with some descent as the trail winds in and out of small gullies forested with ponderosa pine and Douglas fir. An expansive logged-over area is visible below from time to time. The trail descends and crosses the log road at mile 9.0 (7,560), then continues 0.2 mile to a stream crossing and a gentle rise to Meadows Group Campground.

The CT, Buffalo Creek, and FS-543 (first crossing) converge at mile 9.5 (7,400). The trail ascends, steeply at times, 0.7 mile west of FS-543 to a broad, rounded ridge. The Castle's granite bulwark is visible to the south through a ponderosa pine forest. On the ascent, be careful not to prick yourself on the nearby yuccas. Indians once wove the yuccas leaves into moccasins and pounded the roots to make soap.

The trail crosses the Buffalo Creek Gun Club Road at mile 11.0 (7,920), then continues west on a gentle ascent. Descend into a small gully at mile 13.1 (8,160), where you may notice a crossing with an old forgotten road. The trail then ascends slightly and drops down to the second crossing of FS-543. A parking area is provided here at the end of this segment at mile 13.4 (8,280).

Notes

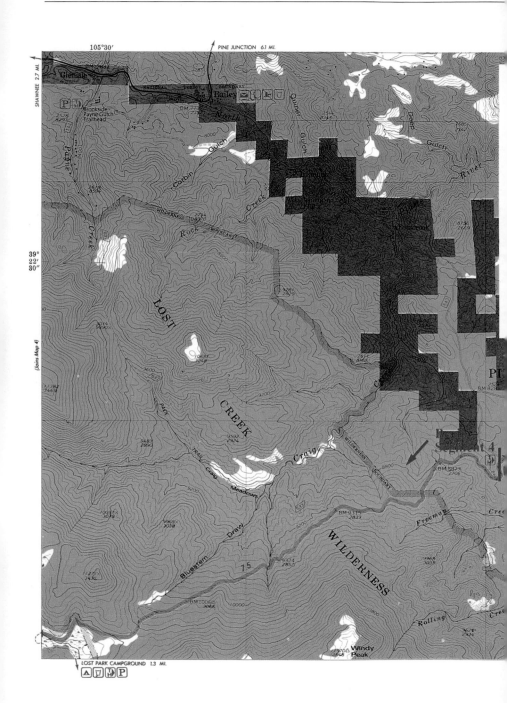

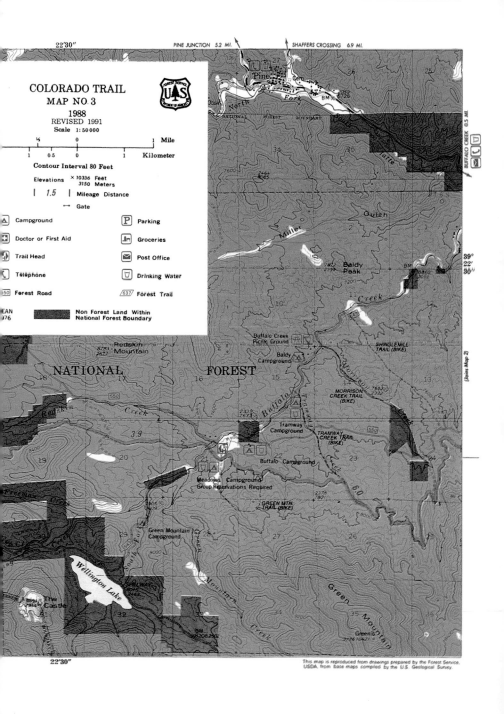

COLORADO TRAIL
MAP NO. 3
1988
REVISED 1991
Scale 1:50 000

Mile

Kilometer

Contour Interval 80 Feet

Elevations × 10336 Feet
3150 Meters

| 1.5 | Mileage Distance

↤ Gate

△ Campground

P Parking

Doctor or First Aid

Groceries

Trail Head

Post Office

Telephone

Drinking Water

Forest Road

Forest Trail

Non Forest Land Within
National Forest Boundary

On top of the Kenosha Mountains, Lost Creek Wilderness

◭ SEGMENT 4   15.2 Miles

Forest Service Road 543 to Long Gulch   **+2,880 Feet Elevation Gain**

Location	Mileage	From Denver	Elevation
FS-543	0.0	38.9	8,280
Lost Creek Wilderness	1.8		9,100
Kenosha Ridge	6.3		10,480
North Fork Saddle	13.2		10,880
Long Gulch	15.2	54.1	10,160

CT Series Maps 3 & 4 (see pages 62-63 & 72-73).

If traveling westbound, you will gain substantial elevation in this segment as you climb to the rounded ridges of the Kenosha Mountains. The exposed Precambrian crest of this range is largely hidden from view by thick lodgepole pine and aspen forests until you travel farther west. Backpackers will find several reliable sources of water, but heavy cattle grazing may taint the supply.

Most of this segment of the CT follows an old logging road that was built between 1885 and 1887 by W. H. Hooper for $1,700. The cost was higher than expected because of several marshy stretches that needed corduroy treatment. Hooper also ran a sawmill operation in Lost Park that was eventually shut down by the Department of Interior for persistent illegalities.

Mountain bikers must detour around the Lost Creek Wilderness (see the Mountain Bike Detours).

Trailhead/Access Points

FS-543 Trailhead: Travel west from Denver on US-285 about 39 miles to Bailey. Go left on Park Country Road 68, which becomes FS-543. Continue approximately 8 miles from Bailey to where the CT crosses the road. A smaller parking area is provided here.

Lost Park Campground: Travel west from Denver on US-285 approximately 58 miles to Kenosha Pass. Continue on the highway another 3.2 miles to the turnoff marked Lost Park Road (FS-127). Turn left (east) onto the dirt road and drive 19.4 miles to the end of the road at Lost Park Campground. A somewhat indistinct and unmarked trail goes north from the campground 1.7 miles and joins the CT.

Longs Gulch Trail Access: See Segment 5.

Supplies, Services, and Accommodations

Limited supplies are available in the town of Bailey, 8 miles west of the trailhead on FS-543.

Maps

CT Series: Maps 3 and 4 (see pages 62-63 and 72-73).
USFS Maps: Pike National Forest.
USGS Quadrangles: Windy Peak, Topaz Mountain.

Trail Description

From the trailhead parking area on FS-543, the CT ascends a Forest Service road to mile 0.3 (8,360), where a gate closes the road to vehicles. At this point, Rolling Creek Trail bends to the left and the CT leaves the road and continues to the right. Observe the wilderness regulation sign here. At mile 0.9 (8,560) the CT joins up with the old road built by Mr. Hooper and begins a steady ascent bearing generally southwest. Pass through a gate a half mile farther on and enter Lost Creek Wilderness at mile 1.8 (9,100). The wilderness boundary is marked by an inconspicuous little metal sign. In a few places it is possible to get a glimpse of Mount Evans to the north through the thick stands of lodgepole pines. The only other vista along here is of nearby Windy Peak when it aligns itself with the swath cut for the old Hooper Road.

At the fork at mile 2.3, continue to the left on the more prominent Hooper Trail. At mile 3.1 (9,320) the Craig Creek Trail descends to the right. The CT

66

BAILEY SERVICES		Distance from Trail: 8 miles	
Bank	None		
Bus	None		
Dining	Crow's Foot	60629 Hwy 285	(303) 838-5298
	Mountain View Cafe	157 Main	(303) 838-9545
Gear	Knotty Pine	60641 Hwy 285	(303) 838-5679
Groceries	Bailey Country Store	149 Main	(303) 838-2505
Information	Chamber of Commerce	P.O. Box 476	no phone
Laundry	Bailey Laundromat	Hwy 285	(303) 838-2768
Lodging	Glen Isle Resort	Hwy 285	(303) 838-5461
	Moredale Lodge	Hwy 285	(303) 838-5918
Medical	Crow Hill Health Center	Hwy 285	(303) 838-7653
Post Office	Bailey Post Office	24 River Rd.	(303) 838-4181
Showers	None		

continues its ascent southwest on the old Hooper Trail, alternately passing through lodgepole pine and aspen forests. Cross a small stream at mile 4.5 (9,360), where the carcass of a long-forgotten truck recalls the enterprising days of this road before the area was designated as a wilderness.

The CT detours to the left off of the old road at mile 5.7 (10,160) and stays high on a ridge. This area was rerouted in late 1994 to avoid the marshy areas that caused Hooper to exceed his budget. The trail rejoins Hooper Road half a mile farther, above the soggy stretch. Pass over a low, forested ridge of the Kenosha Mountains at mile 6.3 (10,480), then descend to the broad, elongated meadow of the North Fork of Lost Creek 1.1 mile beyond and exit the wilderness area. Intersect the Brookside-McCurdy Trail at mile 7.8 (10,200), following it south 1.7 miles to Lost Park Campground. From this trail intersection, you can notice the ruins of an old sawmill to the south across the creek. Could this be the remains of Hooper's operation?

Begin a slow ascent northwest, paralleling the north side of the North Fork's broad grassy valley. A contingent of curious cattle will most likely be observing your progress. In a few places, the craggy, metamorphic ridge of the Kenosha Mountains comes into view.

Top the saddle at the head of the North Fork at mile 13.2 (10,880). Here, the more obvious CT bears slightly to the left as it leaves the old Hooper Trail, which becomes faint and eroded as it descends steeply. The CT contours west beyond the North Fork saddle for 0.2 mile. then takes a sudden turn south, where a westerly exposure offers westbound hikers their first glimpse of the Continental Divide. The trail loses elevation quickly as it switchbacks down to a stream crossing in an area of washed-out beaver ponds at mile 15.2 (10,160). Two short spur trails on either side of the stream lead down to an unofficial but popular parking area and trail access point at the end of a short side road, a spur on the Lost Park Road in Longs Gulch.

Notes

On the way to Kenosha Pass, Kenosha Mountains

◣ SEGMENT 5   14.0 Miles

Long Gulch to Kenosha Pass   **+1,520 Feet Elevation Gain**

Location	Mileage	From Denver	Elevation
Long Gulch	0.0	54.1	10,160
Black Canyon Saddle	2.1		10,520
Rock Creek	7.1		9,520
Johnson Gulch	8.2		9,520
Unamed Ridge	11.3		10,400
Kenosha Pass	14.0	68.1	10,000

CT Series Maps 4 & 5 (see pages 72-73 & 80-81).

You will most likely encounter grazing cattle in this segment, especially during those few times water is available at both Rock Creek and Johnson Gulch. Water can be pumped during the summer from a well located in Kenosha Campground at the end of this segment.

A popular day hike starts at Kenosha Pass and travels east to any one of the many observation points that reveal panoramas of nearby South Park and the Mosquito Range. This easy outing is especially rewarding in autumn when the extensive aspen forests light up the cool days with an energetic golden brilliance. This segment is also popular with mountain bikers until they reach the Rock Creek to Black Canyon stretch, which is within the Lost Creek Wilderness and off limits to mountain bikes.

Trailhead/Access Points

Long Gulch Trail Access: Travel west from Denver on US-285 approximately 58 miles to Kenosha Pass. Continue on US-285 another 3.2 miles to the turnoff marked "Lost Park Road" (FS-127). Turn left (east) onto the dirt road and travel 11.8 miles to an inconspicuous side road that branches left and is only about 0.2 mile long. This short side road has been marked in the past as FS-817, but it may receive a different numerical designation in the future. Park your car at the end of this short road and hike up either of two connecting side trails a few hundred feet to the CT.

Kenosha Pass Trailhead: See Segment 6.

Supplies, Services, and Accommodations

The town of Jefferson is about 4 miles from Kenosha Pass on US-285. Here you will find a small general store with basic provisions.

Maps

CT Series: Maps 4 and 5 (see pages 72-73 and 80-81).
USFS: Pike National Forest.
USGS Quadrangles: Topaz Mountain, Observatory Rock, Mt. Logan, Jefferson.

Trail Description

From either one of the two short access trails, the CT continues west, and enters Lost Creek Wilderness. Ascend to a densely forested saddle at mile 2.1 (10,520), then descend slightly into upper Black Canyon and cross the seasonally flowing stream, a tributary of Rock Creek. The trail descends on the north side of the canyon, winding in and out of several side drainages with intermittent flows. Cross Rock Creek at mile 7.1 (9,520), just downstream from the Rock Creek Cow Camp. Here the trail vanishes momentarily in thick, shrubby cinquefoil which conceals the wooden-timber creek crossing.

On the west side of Rock Creek, follow the old road 0.1 mile downstream (southeast) and be alert for the trail, which veers to the right off the road and immediately enters a spruce forest. Ascend 0.1 mile and pass through a red gate, then make a sharp right turn onto another old road. Continue an ascent 0.3 mile west-northwest on the abandoned road and look for the trail to resume on the left as the road begins to level out. Cross FS-133 at 7.7 (9,720), then descend through a grassy clearing to Johnson Gulch and cross the tiny seasonal flow on a wooden timber at mile 8.2 (9,520).

JEFFERSON SERVICES — Distance from Trail: 4 miles

Bank	None		
Bus	None		
Dining	Jefferson Store (fast food)	38600 Hwy 285	(719) 836-2389
Gear	Jefferson Store	38600 Hwy 285	(719) 836-2389
Groceries	Jefferson Store	38600 Hwy 285	(719) 836-2389
Information	Jefferson Store	38600 Hwy 285	(719) 836-2389
Laundry	None		
Lodging	None		
Medical	None		
Post Office	Jefferson Store	38600 Hwy 285	(719) 836-2317
Showers	None		

From the Johnson Gulch stream, follow the trail about 300 feet west then south-southwest as it ascends to the lower portion of a grassy rise. The trail here barely grazes the edge of an old jeep road at left, the former trail route, which heads northwest up a shallow, dry tributary gully to Johnson Gulch. From this point, a new section of trail bears right (north-northwest to northwest) and ascends to the rounded ridge just north of the gully. Follow this new trail section as it slowly climbs northwest in an intermittent forest of aspen and bristlecone pine. This new route is an improvement from the original because of the shade the trees provide and for ever-expanding views as you gain elevation. The trail ascends to a lofty panorama point at mile 10.0 (10,000), where South Park and the Continental Divide are visible to the west, with the Kenosha Mountains and Black Canyon to the east.

After descending through a forest of aspen, bristlecone pine, and spruce, the trail abruptly opens into another grassy expanse at mile 10.5 (9,960). Proceed 0.2 mile north-northwest on the faint footpath, which may be overwhelmed at times by thick grass, to the base of a grassy hill. The CT ascends the southwest side of the hill, passing through stands of aspen and stately bristlecone pine, to mile 11.0 (10,200), where it makes a left turn onto an old jeep road. Bear generally north to mount a broad, forested unnamed ridge, and then begin a traverse at about the 10,400-foot level.

Descend to a junction with another old road at mile 12.4 (10,240) and go right (north). Continue for just 300 feet on this old road before rejoining the trail to the left. Resume your descent through an aspen forest, and go left where the trail adopts another old road at mile 13.5 (10,080), and left again where the jeep road forks 0.2 mile farther on. In a few more steps you will enter the large, open saddle at Kenosha Pass. Proceed to the trailhead on the east side of US-285 at mile 14.0 (10,000).

Notes

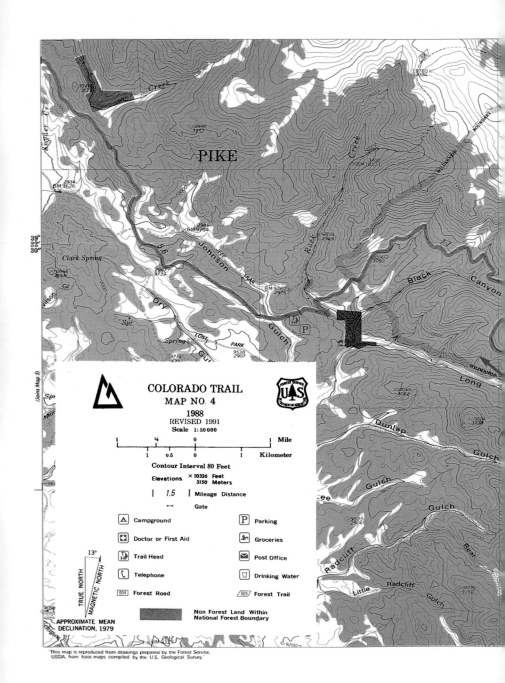

PIKE

COLORADO TRAIL
MAP NO. 4
1988
REVISED 1991
Scale 1:50 000

Contour Interval 80 Feet

Elevations × 10336 Feet
            3150 Meters

| 1.5 | Mileage Distance

↤   Gate

Ⓐ Campground   Ⓟ Parking

▣ Doctor or First Aid   Groceries

Trail Head   ✉ Post Office

Ⓛ Telephone   Drinking Water

004 Forest Road   009 Forest Trail

Non Forest Land Within
National Forest Boundary

TRUE NORTH   MAGNETIC NORTH
13°
APPROXIMATE MEAN
DECLINATION, 1979

This map is reproduced from drawings prepared by the Forest Service,
USDA, from base maps compiled by the U.S. Geological Survey

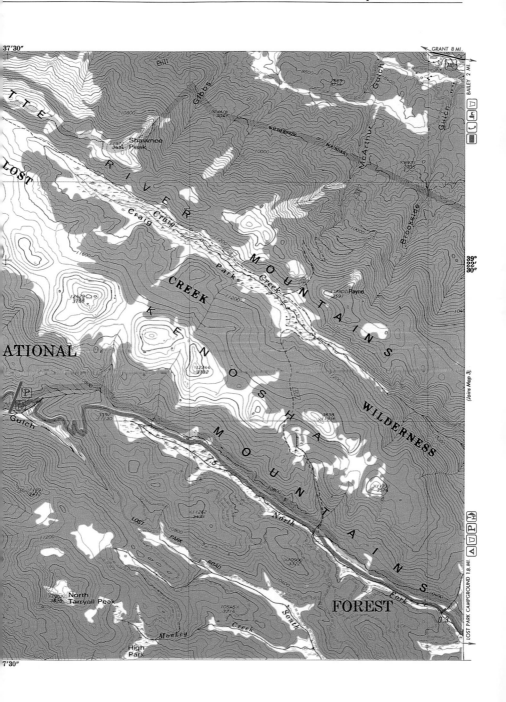

Sunset below Georgia Pass, Jefferson Creek Loop Trail

⚠ SEGMENT 6   25.4 Miles

Kenosha Pass to Gold Hill Trailhead   **+2,560 Feet Elevation Gain**

Location	Mileage	From Denver	Elevation
Kenosha Pass	0.0	68.1	10,000
Jefferson Lake Road	5.8		10,000
Glacier Ridge Road	11.9		11,800
Middle Fork Swan River	16.7		10,160
Gold Hill Trailhead	25.4	93.5	9,200

CT Series Maps 5 & 6 (see pages 80-81 & 86-87).

The CT has its first crossing of the Continental Divide in this segment. You will top out about 0.5 mile east of, and 300 feet higher than, historic Georgia Pass. Water and basic Forest Service facilities are available during the summer at the campgrounds at Kenosha Pass and Jefferson Lake Road. Beyond Jefferson Lake Road, there is no reliable water supply until the trail drops down into the headwaters of the Swan River on the west side of Georgia Pass. Camping within Jefferson Creek Recreation Area is restricted to established campgrounds only.

The Swan River drainage, in the second half of the segment, is the site of past and present private enterprises. Many of the mining operations here are still active, so please behave accordingly. Since 1988, volunteers have been building a new trail that will bypass the original CT route, which follows a Forest Service jeep and county roads from the top of Georgia Pass to Colorado Highway 9 near the end of this segment. By August of 1994 this new trail was complete from the Glacier Ridge Road to the Gold Hill Trailhead.

Kenosha Pass had long served as an Indian trail into the fertile hunting grounds of South Park and was crossed by white parties as early as 1830. Colonel John C. Fremont crossed the pass in the mid-1840s, and when miners began streaming into the Blue River drainage, they paralleled the old Indian trail and then veered west over Georgia Pass, approximating the route of today's CT.

In 1860, a 25-year charter was given by the Kansas Territorial Legislature to John McIntyre, Major Bradford, and Judge Steke to build and maintain a toll road from Denver to California Gulch (future Leadville) using, in part, the Kenosha Pass route. The following year, a stage line began operating over the road. It was Clark Herbert, a driver for the line, who named the pass after his hometown of Kenosha, Wisconsin. Twenty years later, Governor Evans built his DSP&P Railroad over the pass. The DSP&P chugged to Breckenridge and eventually to Gunnison.

At the same time the California Gulch stage line was being built, a group of southern miners were working Georgia Gulch west of the divide and defending their claims as others poured over Georgia Pass. The energetic town of Parkville developed at the mouth of the gulch, but mining activity was so great that by the 1880s the town had been inundated by the tailings of its own prosperity.

A more drastic means of recovering the gold was introduced in the early 1900s by Ben Stanley Revett. His efficient but destructive dredge boats recovered gold from deep within the valley floor, but at the same time they created enormous piles of rock which still run parallel to the Swan and Blue rivers.

Mount Guyot (13,370 feet) is a prominent landmark in this segment and was named in honor of Princeton geography professor Arnold Guyot, who was grateful for having his name attached to a peak on the same connecting ridge of the fourteeners named for his well-known colleagues John Torrey and Asa Grey. Interestingly, a "guyot" is also a geologic term denoting an underwater volcano. Colorado's Mount Guyot is neither submerged nor a volcano, but an igneous intrusion somewhere in the neighborhood of 40 to 72 million years of age, much younger than the granite knobs and metamorphic rocks of the Rampart Range and the Kenosha Mountains.

Trailhead/Access Points

Kenosha Pass Trailhead: Travel on US-285 approximately 58 miles west from Denver to the summit of Kenosha Pass. The trail crosses the highway at Kenosha Campground. The Forest Service requests that you do not park within the campground; parking is available at the trailhead several hundred feet east of the highway on the Forest Service access road.

Jefferson Lake Road Trail Access: From Kenosha Pass, continue for 4.5 miles on US-285 to Jefferson. Turn right on the side road marked "Jefferson Lake Road." Drive 2.1 miles, then turn right again at the sign that marks the way to Jefferson Lake. Continue 3.1 miles to where the CT crosses the road. Just 0.1 mile farther there is temporary parking at Beaver Ponds Picnic Ground. More permanent backpacker parking is available 0.6 mile up the road, near the entrance to Jefferson Creek Campground.

Georgia Pass Trail Access: From Jefferson on US-285, turn right on the side road marked "Michigan Creek Road." Follow the Michigan Creek Road approximately 12 miles to the top of Georgia Pass. The last mile is rough and is best traveled with a high-clearance vehicle. Continue 0.2 mile up the Glacier Ridge Road to the CT crossing.

Gold Hill Trailhead: See Segment 7.

Supplies, Services, and Accommodations

Available in Jefferson (see Segment 5).

Maps

CT Series: Maps 5 and 6 (see pages 80-81 and 86-87).
USFS: Pike National Forest, Arapaho National Forest.
USGS Quadrangles: Jefferson, Boreas Pass, Keystone, Frisco.

Trail Description

West of US-285, the CT passes through the southern portion of Kenosha Campground. Once inside the campground, bear to the left twice and proceed a few steps until the road passes through a gate. The trail resumes to the right, just beyond the fence and climbs northwest through a forest of aspen and lodgepole pine. In July, the understory is thick with golden banner, paintbrush, and columbine. At mile 0.7 (10,400) the noise of US-285 disappears as the trail passes over a ridge and begins a descent through inclined meadows and aspen groves. Expansive South Park extends to the horizon, bounded to the west by the Mosquito Range, the Thirtynine Mile Mountains to the south, and the Puma Hills to the east. As you make your way down through the clumps of aspen trees, notice where ravenous wildlife have stripped large patches of bark off the tree trunks.

Cross an old road at mile 1.4 (10,280) and continue west along a minor ridge with more views of South Park. At mile 2.3 (10,120), the trail opens onto an area of shrubby cinquefoil. The trail continues west, marked by cairns, although it may be difficult to find here. Pick up a reliable trail in 0.1 mile and resume a descent through open areas. Cross FS-809 at mile 2.9 (9,880) and continue ahead on a faint trail obscured by cinquefoil. Enter an aspen grove 150 feet beyond the road and then pass over Guernsey Creek, which is spanned by a huge timber.

The CT exits the aspen groves a hundred feet beyond the creek and crosses an indistinct old road just north of a primitive but popular car camping spot. The trail bears west-southwest, then west. Avoid the forks that leads to FS-809, which runs several hundred feet to the south. The CT continues west in the open to mile 3.4 (9,880), where the trail begins an ascent west to west-northwest through pleasant, alternating pockets of aspen and meadow. At mile 3.8 (10,000) the trail rises to and briefly parallels an old irrigation ditch for 0.2 mile. Bear to the right off of the ditch route and ascend 0.3 mile in an aspen forest to a cluster of gnarled bristlecone pines where you cross FS-427. Continue 0.1 mile beyond, then go right onto an old abandoned road just before crossing Deadman Creek. There is a large timber over the creek a few steps downstream from the ford. Continue a slight ascent north to north-northwest. Bear to the left (west) on the trail 400 feet past the creek crossing; a faint overgrown path continues ahead. Go right (north-northwest) onto a jeep road at mile 4.7 (10,160).

In just 0.2 mile, and as the road assumes a more westerly bearing and crosses a small stream, look carefully for the trail to resume at left (south-southeast). This section of trail passes through a rather dismal, logged and recently burned-out section of forest that is slowly reseeding itself. Reenter the unharmed lodge-pole pine forest beyond, and ascend to a saddle that extends north from Jefferson Hill at mile 5.2 (10,200). Pass through a gate here, then descend 0.5 mile and cross another old road. Continue 0.1 mile on the trail to mile 5.8 (10,000), where you will cross Jefferson Lake Road. Beaver Ponds Picnic Ground is only a few steps north on this road.

Continue on the trail 0.1 mile, then cross Jefferson Creek on a wide timber foot bridge and begin a gradual ascent. Exchange the trail for an old road at mile 6.1 (10,000) and proceed 250 feet north-northwest to where the trail resumes on the left. Continue up switchbacks that ease the ascent. The CT becomes wider when it adopts an old abandoned road at mile 6.5 (10,350) near the head of the elevated gully that you have been ascending. Continue 0.4 mile west to the crossing of a seasonal stream, then continue an ascent west to west-southwest on the trail to mile 7.4 (10,400). Join up with another old road here and follow it north 250 feet to where it curves left. Proceed straight ahead; in 150 feet you will cross another log road and then continue on the trail through several gentle switchbacks on the southeast side of this broad, forested ridge, which is an extension of the Continental Divide. The CT heads northwest through a lodgepole pine forest along an old road for about 300 feet at mile 9.0 (10,880). Admire the little niche of bristlecone pines at the head of Ohler Gulch. As the trail approaches timberline, spruce becomes the dominant tree.

At mile 10.5 (11,400) the trail enters the krummholz zone, the interesting transition between forest and tundra. The prevailing wind pattern is immortalized in the postures of these stunted trees. The trail continues into the tundra at mile 11.1 (11,600). Here, the West Jefferson Trail takes off to the right (northeast) at a well-marked junction for a return into the valley at Jefferson Creek Campground. This side trail provides a pleasant round-trip day hike from Jefferson Creek Road. The CT continues west-northwest from this junction, following posts and cairns to the grassy ridge of the Continental Divide ahead.

Mount Guyot is prominent beyond the divide as a rocky cone almost due west. When you cross a jeep track in about 0.5 mile, you will be approaching a shallow saddle between two minor humps on the divide. The posted route will align more north-northwest as you attain this saddle. On the west side of the divide, follow a rocky trail that descends north from the saddle. This short trail continues 0.2 mile to the Glacier Ridge Road at mile 11.9 (11,800).

At this point, the original and new routes of the CT diverge as mentioned earlier. The new trail continues north to northeast beyond the road. The original CT route descends west-southwest on the road 0.2 mile to Georgia Pass, then continues north and northwest on the 4WD road down the Swan River South Fork. The new trail route is completed from this point to the Swan River Middle Fork. It is more aesthetic and comfortable than the steep and rocky 4WD road that descends from Georgia Pass and, therefore, is described here. However, if you choose to follow the original CT route down the 4WD road into the South Fork, which is shorter than the new route, you follow the South Fork Road from the pass for 4.4 miles and join the route described below at mile 18.7.

Continuing north-northeast from mile 11.9 on the new CT route takes you across a faint section of alpine trail marked by rock cairns just below and parallel to the Glacier Ridge Road. Enter an upper limit spruce forest 0.4 mile beyond and pick up a reliable trail that bears generally north. From time to time there are outstanding views down the valley of the Tenmile and Gore Ranges. At mile 14.8 (10,960), you will cross an old road at a right angle. Continue descending on this well-built new trail for 0.4 mile where you will cross an old, but well-defined, trail at an angle. In another 0.5 mile, and after turning through a few switchbacks, you will pass a scummy pond to your right. Don't be tempted to get water here; the clear flowing Middle Fork is only a mile away. From the pond, the trail descends to a comfortable crossing of Missouri Gulch Creek and, 150 feet north, the Swan River Middle Fork.

Go east for 150 feet on the Middle Fork Road and then enter the forest on the left (west) on a new trail completed in 1994. The trail parallels the road for a few hundred feet before veering off into dense woods with talus slopes on the uphill sides. Heading in a northerly direction, the CT crosses the North Fork of the Swan River in an open, willow-covered meadow. Road access is possible from the Swan River road for resupplying. There are also many fine campsites in the meadow and along the ridge. Signs of the short-lived hamlet of Redford are visible along this stretch. In another quarter mile the trail heads in a westerly fashion with views of the north face of Keystone Ski Area to the north. In the near future there will be a connecting spur trail to the ski area.

For the next 3.0 miles the well-marked trail is crossed numerous times by old mining roads, which are often overgrown. Staying high on the ridge above Keystone Ranch, the trail offers magnificent views of Gurgot Peaks, the Tenmile Range, an the broad Keystone Valley and Dillon Reservoir. After passing through a dense, spindly lodgepole pine forest, the trail makes an abrupt turn to the west at the headwaters of Horseshoe Gulch. After 3.0 new miles of descending trail, you will reach the edge of a private subdivision. Please respect the owner's privacy and stay on the trail. You will cross the Blue River before ascending the ridge out of the river bottom to the Gold Hill parking area on the west side of Colorado Highway 9. The segment ends on the other side of this busy highway.

Notes

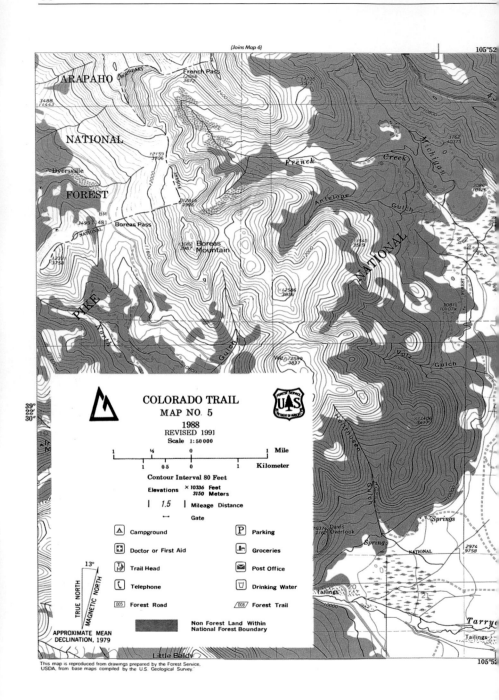

(Joins Map 6)

COLORADO TRAIL
MAP NO. 5
1988
REVISED 1991
Scale 1:50 000

Contour Interval 80 Feet

Elevations ×10336 Feet
3150 Meters

| 1.5 | Mileage Distance

→ Gate

△ Campground   P Parking

✪ Doctor or First Aid   ⬛ Groceries

⛺ Trail Head   ✉ Post Office

✆ Telephone   ⬚ Drinking Water

005 Forest Road   008 Forest Trail

Non Forest Land Within
National Forest Boundary

TRUE NORTH
MAGNETIC NORTH
13°
APPROXIMATE MEAN
DECLINATION, 1979

This map is reproduced from drawings prepared by the Forest Service,
USDA, from base maps compiled by the U.S. Geological Survey.

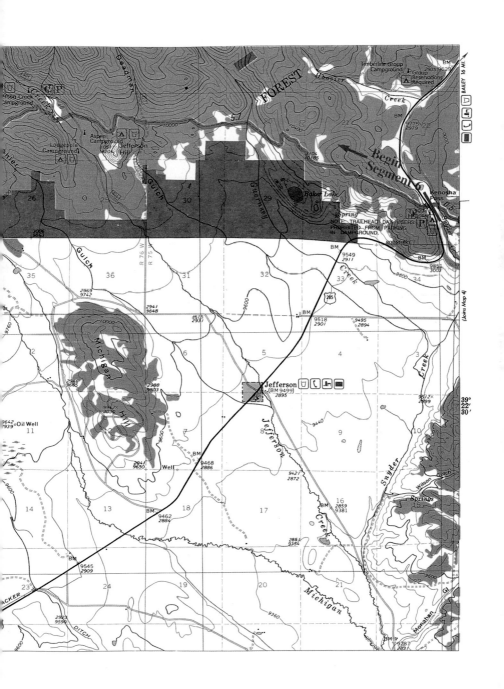

Sunrise on the Tenmile Range, above the town of Breckenridge

◢◣ SEGMENT 7   13.1 Miles

Gold Hill Trailhead to Copper Mountain   **+3,680 Feet Elevation Gain**

Location	Mileage	From Denver	Elevation
Gold Hill Trailhead	0.0	93.5	9,200
Rocky summit	2.3		10,240
Peaks Trail	3.2		9,920
Tenmile Range crest	7.8		12,440
Copper Mountain	13.1	106.6	9,720

CT Series Maps 6 & 7 (see pages 86-87 & 96-97).

This portion of the CT, which makes its way over the Tenmile Range, is steep and strenuous. The alpine section has a narrow trail and has not been well marked in the past. The steep, alpine mountainsides here will challenge even the seasoned hiker, and inclined snowfields may linger well into July. The logging roads and clear-cuts that intercept the trail in several places along the first 2 miles make the going a little confusing, and the blue diamond markers on tree trunks in the initial portion of this segment identify cross-country ski trails and not the CT.

Mountain bikers may not want to attempt this section, but instead use the detour around the Tenmile Range as described in the Mountain Bike Detours. Less experienced hikers may also want to consider this detour, which follows the Tenmile Bike Path to Frisco and up Tenmile Canyon to Wheeler Flats at Copper Mountain.

The alpine tundra traversed along the crest of the Tenmile Range is exquisitely carpeted with flowers in late July and early August and provides a scenic foreground for these ancient metamorphic summits. This linear mountain range connects the southern end of the Gore Range with the northern end of the Mosquito Range. It is named for the creek on its western boundary and is known for its sequentially numbered peaks.

A trail access point on Miners Creek, reached via Frisco and Rainbow Lake (beginning on County Road 1004), is mentioned here only in passing because it is extremely rough and rocky, even for 4WD vehicles.

Trailhead/Access Points

Gold Hill Trailhead: Travel west from Denver approximately 73 miles on Interstate 70 and take the Frisco/Breckenridge/Colorado Highway 9 exit. Proceed approximately 5 miles south of Frisco on Colorado Highway 9 toward Breckenridge. Gold Hill Trailhead will be on your right (west) at the intersection with County Road 950. There is parking for several cars here. If you are coming in from the south on Colorado Highway 9 over Hoosier Pass, continue north approximately 4 miles beyond Breckenridge. Gold Hill Trailhead will be on your left (west).

Wheeler Flats Trailhead: See Segment 8.

Supplies, Services, and Accommodations

Breckenridge is 4 miles south of the Gold Hill Trailhead on Colorado Highway 9. The town has a variety of overnight accommodations and a large grocery store. There are also sporting goods and hardware stores.

Maps

CT Series: Maps 6 and 7 (see pages 86–87 and 96–97).
USFS: Arapaho National Forest.
USGS Quadrangles: Frisco, Copper Mountain, Vail Pass.

Trail Description

Begin at the convenient trailhead just off Colorado Highway 9. The trail starts just opposite the small, informal parking area called the Gold Hill Trailhead and continues through an alternating landscape of sagebrush meadows

BRECKENRIDGE SERVICES		Distance from Trail:	4 miles
Bank	First Bank	200 Ski Hill Rd.	(303) 453-1000
Bus	Summit Stage	Bell Tower Mall	(303) 453-1339
Dining	The Prospector		(303) 453-6858
Gear	Mountain Outfitters	112 S. Ridge	(303) 453-2201
Groceries	City Market	400 N. Park Ave.	(303) 453-0818
Information	Chamber of Commerce	309 N. Main	(303) 453-6018
Laundry	Village Norge	105 S. French	(303) 453-2426
Lodging	Breckenridge Central Reservations		(800) 221-1091
Medical	Breckenridge Medical Ctr	555 S. Park Ave.	(303) 453-9000
Post Office	Breckenridge Post Office	300 S. Ridge Rd.	(303) 453-2310
Showers	Breckenridge Rec. Center	880 Airport Rd.	(303) 453-1734

and lodgepole pine forest with an understory of lupine. The trail appears to end at a confusing three-way logging road intersection at mile 1.0 (9680), but actually it bears to the left (southwest) from this intersection. The CT steadily gains elevation in a lodgepole pine forest, bearing generally south to south-southwest, then takes a more westerly direction before it crosses a logging road at mile 1.6 (9,960). Continue 700 feet uphill, then bear right (north) as the trail joins another old road. Go right (north) at the intersection with still another old road at mile 1.9 (10,120). Continue 200 feet further to a clear-cut. Proceed north across the clear cut on a short section of connector trail. In a few hundred feet, you will pick up the old road again in the forest at the opposite edge of the clear-cut. Go left (west) as the road forks again in another 250 feet. The road leads generally west and slowly takes on a more trail-like character as it ascends to a somewhat rounded, rocky summit at mile 2.3 (10,240). A sparse lodgepole pine forest allows glimpses of the crest of Tenmile Peak to the west.

Descend 0.4 mile from the rocky summit and cross the last logging road. At mile 3.2 (9,920) you join up with the Peaks Trail. Go left (south) and uphill on the Peaks Trail for 0.3 mile, then bear right (west) onto the Miners Creek Trail. The wide, rocky trail ascends to the southwest, paralleling a tributary stream of Miners Creek for 0.6 mile, then abruptly leaves the drainage and climbs to a 0access point on Miners Creek at mile 4.8 (10,560). Continue west from the small parking area, proceeding 200 feet to a point where you will encounter a barricade on the original trail. Go right (west-northwest) here, onto a newly constructed trail, and, after a few steps, cross over Miners Creek on a bumpy corduroy bridge. The trail ascends, steeply at times, through a spruce forest, then veers southward near timberline. At mile 5.5 (11,120), the CT breaks out momentarily into a finger of alpine tundra that reaches down from a glacial cirque on Tenmile Peak.

Ascend steeply beyond timberline to a small saddle at mile 6.6 (11,840). From this point, a narrow trail ascends diagonally across the range, heading for the shallow Peak 5 and 6 saddle ahead. Several cairns along the way on the steep mountainside confirm your route. After about a mile of this alpine section of trail, and as it climbs toward the crest of the range, the CT maneuvers steeply through several switchbacks to avoid a precipitous, rocky area ahead. Mount the Tenmile Range at mile 7.8 (12,440) on the long, shallow saddle that connects Peaks 5 and 6. Here the sketchy trail ends; follow the broad saddle south toward Peak 6 while enjoying the abundant views. Mount of the Holy Cross can be seen far to the west.

After a 0.5-mile walk along the saddle, the cairned route bears slightly to the right (south-southwest) as it approaches Peak 6 and begins a steady descent on the west side of the mountain range. The route bears more westerly as it approaches timberline, picking up a definite trail just inside the trees at mile 9.6 (11,640). Continue descending for 0.4 mile to the intersection with the Wheeler Trail at mile 10.0 (11,240). (The Wheeler Trail is specific to the Tenmile Range; it starts near Hoosier Pass at the south end of the range and continues to Wheeler Flats Trailhead at the end of this segment.) Descend in a northerly direction on the Wheeler Trail and cross several small streams along the way. The steep terrain in this area is a definite impediment to camping.

Intersect an old jeep road which parallels the east side of Tenmile Creek at mile 12.1 (9,760). At mile 12.6 there is a wooden bridge crossing Tenmile Creek. There are many good campsites on the west side of the creek, or you can continue north from this point and follow the road to the paved Tenmile Bike Path at mile 13.1 (9,720) near the confluence of Tenmile and West Tenmile creeks. Go left on the bike path a few steps to the end of this segment at the Wheeler Flats Trailhead parking area at Copper Mountain.

Notes

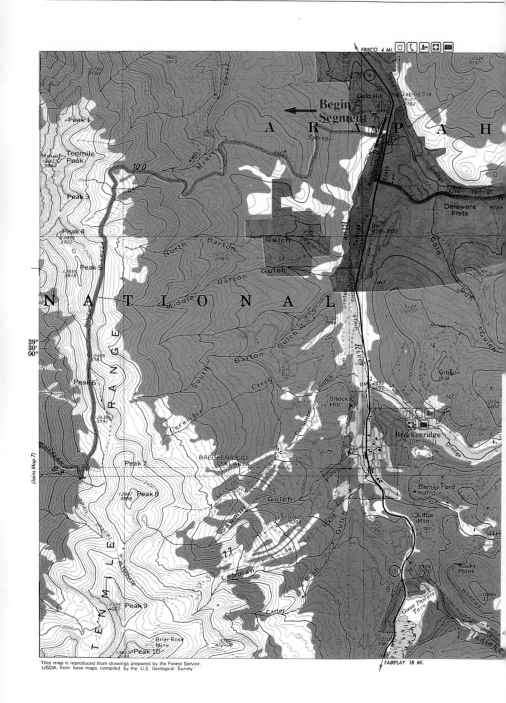

This map is reproduced from drawings prepared by the Forest Service, USDA, from base maps compiled by the U.S. Geological Survey

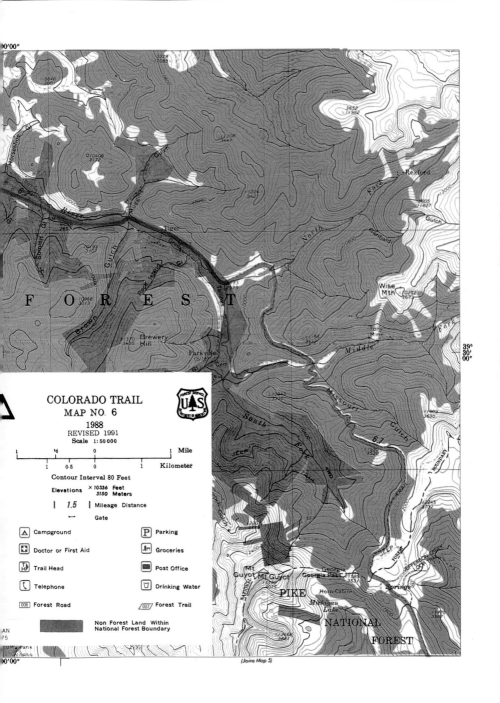

COLORADO TRAIL
MAP NO. 6
1988
REVISED 1991
Scale 1:50000

Contour Interval 80 Feet

Elevations × 10336 Feet
                3150 Meters

| 1.5 | Mileage Distance

←→   Gate

△ Campground   P Parking

✚ Doctor or First Aid   Groceries

Trail Head   Post Office

Telephone   Drinking Water

006 Forest Road   007 Forest Trail

Non Forest Land Within
National Forest Boundary

(Joins Map 5)

The peaks of the Tenmile Range, from Searle Pass

⛰ SEGMENT 8   24.1 Miles

Copper Mountain to Tennessee Pass   **+3,660 Feet Elevation Gain**

Location	Mileage	From Denver	Elevation
Copper Mountain	0.0	106.6	9,720
Searle Pass	8.6		12,040
Elk Ridge	11.2		12,280
Camp Hale	17.9		9,320
Tennessee Pass	24.1	130.7	10,424

CT Series Maps 7 & 8 (see pages 96-97 & 104-105).

The DSP&P Railroad once had a whistle stop known as Solitude on its Tenmile Canyon line near present-day Copper Mountain Resort. Unfortunately, with the activity of the ski area and busy Interstate 70, the isolation of the valley is a thing of the past. As recently as 1970, before the ski area was built and the highway widened, this valley was still known as Wheeler Flats, a throwback to the days when Judge John S. Wheeler would drive his stock over the Tenmile Range to graze in the valley's lush, boggy meadows. A little settlement developed here and served the Tenmile Mining District. The ski resort in this valley typifies the state's economic shift from mining to recreation, a transformation particularly noticeable throughout Summit County.

Copper Mountain is the only developed area through which the CT passes, which is indeed a paradox for a wilderness trail. Some hikers might be persuaded to linger in the comfort of civilization, while others might pass quickly through, attempting to ignore the metamorphosis from obscure mining community to chic ski resort. Whatever your inclination, the resort does provide weary backpackers the opportunity to recharge their batteries before submerging themselves again in the wilderness.

Elk Ridge provides a spectacular perch from which to view the Climax Molybdenum Mine and the immense tailing ponds that have completely inundated the historic mining towns of Robinson and Kokomo. The Tenmile Mining District got its start when Leadville businessman George B. Robinson grubstaked two miners who subsequently discovered ten mines in the headwaters of Tenmile Creek. Robinson's namesake town had the distinction of being Colorado's highest incorporated town, and for a time threatened Leadville for dominance in the area. The little community of Kokomo, named by Indiana miners for their hometown, developed just downstream from Robinson.

Both the D&RG and the DSP&P railroads felt confident enough about the upstart mining district to lay tracks into the valley. Merchant Robinson gained enough influence to emerge as Colorado's lieutenant governor in 1880, but unfortunately he enjoyed only one month of his term before being gunned down in a shoot-out involving the ownership of the Smuggler Mine. Captain J. W. Jacque, for whom Jacque Ridge, Jacque Creek, and Jacque Mountain apparently were named, was also involved in the fatal dispute.

As hikers descend into the headwaters of the Eagle River, they pass through Camp Hale, one of Colorado's most fascinating ghost towns. Construction of this army outpost, named for Brigadier General Irving Hale, began in 1942 and it served as the training base of the 10th Mountain Division during World War II. By 1944, the camp housed some 15,000 men who trained summer and winter in the surrounding mountains. Cooper Hill Ski Area on Tennessee Pass was originally constructed as part of the camp, and at the time had the world's longest T-bar. The troops were eventually attached to the 5th Army and sent to fight in Italy's Apennine Mountains. After the war Camp Hall was largely abandoned, although sporadic use continued until 1963, when it was completely dismantled. Trail crews working there in 1987 unearthed hundreds of spent ammo rounds while building trail in the vicinity of the shooting range.

Portions of the CT above Camp Hale follow the narrow-gauge railroad grade that the D&RG abandoned in 1890, when the line was realigned and widened to standard gauge. This segment ends on Tennessee Pass, which was first crossed in 1845 by Colonel John Fremont.

Except along the first two miles of this segment through Copper Mountain Resort, backpackers have an abundant selection of campsites from which to choose. The exposed, high-altitude section from Searle Pass to Kokomo Pass, along which you are likely to find grazing domestic sheep, has only skimpy water supplies. Snowfields here may linger well into July. This same area has several abandoned vertical mine shafts, some of which are disturbingly close to the CT and partially camouflaged by low, bushy willows. Backpackers wandering on a somewhat independent course through here near dusk would be putting themselves at risk.

The Forest Service requests that horses and pack animals not use the Tenmile Bike Path, which serves as the CT route, between Copper Mountain and Guller Creek. Those traveling with stock should use a short bypass through the lower end of the Union Creek Base area. This bypass, outlined at the end of the trail description, is provided in order to avoid a direct confrontation between skittish animals and mountain bikers zooming down from the top of Vail Pass.

Trailhead/Access Points

Wheeler Flats Trailhead: Go west from Denver approximately 79 miles on Interstate 70 to the Copper Mountain/Leadville/Colorado Highway 91 exit. Take the exit and cross over the freeway on an overpass, then drive just a few hundred feet and turn left onto the side road just opposite the entrance to Copper Mountain Resort. Continue down the side road 0.4 mile to where it dead ends at the Wheeler Flats Trailhead parking area.

Camp Hale (Eagle Park) Trailhead: From the top of Tennessee Pass, descend north on US-24 for 2.5 miles to the point where the CT crosses the highway. Then continue another 0.5 mile and go right on FS-726. Gradually descend on FS-726 for 3 miles to where it joins up with FS-714. The CT follows FS-714 for a short distance here as it skirts around a deep road cut, but don't park here to catch the trail. There is a primitive trailhead parking area about 1 mile west of this point on FS-714.

Another route to this trailhead begins from the intersection of FS-702 and US-24 on the north end of Eagle Park near the railroad overpass. Follow FS-702 (Resolution Road) 1.0 mile, then go right onto FS-714 and continue at the eastern edge of the park 2.2 miles to the trailhead.

Tennessee Pass Trailhead: See Segment 9.

Supplies, Services, and Accommodations

The CT passes through Copper Mountain Resort at the start of this segment. Numerous accommodations are available here, but it might be wise to make reservations if you know your schedule in advance.

Maps

CT Series: Maps 7 and 8 (see pages 96-97 and 104-105).
USFS: Arapaho National Forest, White River National Forest.
USGS Quadrangles: Vail Pass, Copper Mountain, Pando, Leadville North.

COPPER MTN. SERVICES   Distance from Trail: 0 miles

Bank	None		
Bus	Summit Stage		(303) 453-1339
Dining	Several in resort		
Gear	None		
Groceries	Corner Grocery	Village Square Bldg.	(303) 968-2882
Information	Copper Mtn. Resort	West Lake Lodge Bldg.	(303) 968-2882
Laundry	Only available with lodging		
Lodging	Central Reservations		(800) 458-8386
	Carbonate Real Estate	35 Wheeler Place	(303) 968-2073
Medical	Nearest in Vail		(303) 476-5695
Post Office	Copper Mtn. Post Office	West Lake Lodge Bldg.	(303) 968-2882
Showers	Only available with lodging		

Trail Description

The CT follows the paved road 0.4 mile from Wheeler Flats Trailhead parking area past the Amoco station to the stop sign at Colorado Highway 91. Carefully cross the highway to the main entrance of Copper Mountain Resort and continue on the busy street, which is named Copper Road. Stay on Copper Road as it slowly bends around the north end of the resort to mile 1.5 (9,760), where the road crosses West Tenmile Creek on a wide bridge. Go right here on the paved bike path, which continues west, paralleling the creek.

In 0.3 mile you will pass the cutoff to Union Creek Base building where horse and pack animals should detour off the bike path (refer to the Horse and Pack Animal Bypass at the end of this segment). Hikers can continue west on the path, which runs close by I-70, but should still but mindful of the many mountain bikers you will most certainly encounter. At mile 2.6 (9,960), leave the bike path at a bridge crossing over West Tenmile Creek. Bear to the left (southeast) on the trail for a hundred feet and then cross Guller Creek on a wide bridge. The well-established trail then angles right (south then southwest), paralleling the east bank of Guller Creek. Be careful not to be confused by the many directional posts and markers that identify winter cross-country ski trails in this area. Cross under the eastbound Interstate 70 bridge. Continue another 800 feet and cross to the west side of Guller Creek on a double-split log bridge.

From the log bridge at Guller Creek, go about 600 feet to mile 3.0 (10,040), where the horse and pack animal bypass descends from the east and joins the official trail. The trail slowly ascends through occasional wet spots and willow patches following Guller Creek as it trends generally southwest. Cross over to the east bank at mile 3.9 (10,400) on a log bridge and cross Jacque Creek, a tributary of Guller, 150 feet beyond on a similar log bridge. There are several potential camping spots on the grassy, rolling meadow below Jacque Ridge.

The CT bears to the right as the trail forks 300 feet beyond the Jacque Creek crossing, then in just a few more steps it crosses back over to the west side of Guller Creek. At mile 4.7 (10,600), enter a linear meadow that extends along Guller Creek almost to timberline. The CT stays near the edge of the spruce forest, though at times it breaks into the elongated meadow, where there are more good campsites. Guller Creek, always nearby, is usually hidden in a mass of thick willows. The trail makes several switchbacks as it nears timberline and exits the trees at mile 7.4 (11,600).

Above timberline, the route is delineated mainly by posts and cairns. Cross the small, upper headwaters of Guller Creek and continue past two switchbacks marked with cairns. Searle Pass, at mile 8.6 (12,040), is a notch that tends to channel and increase the wind to bothersome levels, but try to take time to admire the fine vistas it gives of the Tenmile and Gore ranges. From the pass, the route makes a traverse, bearing generally south at approximately 12,000 feet and wandering in and out of many little side drainages. Exposed campsites abound in the soft alpine grasses.

Approximately 2.4 miles beyond Searle Pass, the trail becomes more obvious as the CT ascends through several switchbacks to the rocky southern end of Elk Ridge. At mile 11.2 (12,280) the trail levels out on the ridge, which offers commanding views of the unsightly remains of Bartlett Mountain, once 13,555 feet high but now largely reduced to huge pile of tailings visible below.

Descend 0.5 mile along the trail, which is cut deeply into the side hill in places, to 12,000-foot Kokomo Pass. Follow a short but steep ravine as it descends north-northwest from the pass down into a rolling alpine meadow at the headwaters of Cataract Creek. Cross a small tributary stream as the trail nears the forest and then descend to the left 0.1 mile beyond as an obscure animal trail continues ahead. The CT enters the trees and descends through three long switchbacks, then assumes a westerly heading parallel to and slightly above the creek. Continue descending in a spruce forest to an abandoned sawmill site near the creek at mile 13.5 (11,000). For the next 2.4 miles, the CT follows an old logging road down the steepening gorge of Cataract Creek.

Follow the road through a switchback to the left at mile 15.1 (10,200), avoiding the faint continuation of another road that climbs straight ahead. There is a challenging ford of Cataract Creek 400 feet beyond, but a recent log bridge just upstream keeps hikers' feet dry. Avoid the ascending fork which branches left 600 feet beyond the creek, and continue straight ahead on the logging road. The final pitch of the road descends steeply to the upper end of a long meadow (or park) on the East Fork Eagle River. From here, a jeep track descends south 0.1 mile to FS 714, but don't take it. From this point, leave the old logging road and ascend to the right (north) on a trail a few hundred feet to mile 15.9 (9,680), where a cute little arched bridge spans Cataract Creek just a few feet downstream from the falls that name it. There also a rest bench here.

Continue along the trail in a meadow of fragrant sage and cinquefoil with views west toward the upper end of Eagle Park, which not so long ago bustled with the wartime activities of Camp Hale. The trail joins up temporarily with FS-714 at mile 16.7 (9,400). FS-726 peels off to the south here and continues on to US-24. Continue 800 feet west on FS-714 and look for the obscure trail route which veers off into the meadow north of the road. The CT heads west here, paralleling FS-714 for 0.6 mile, after which it again joins the road at the Camp Hale (Eagle Park) Trailhead. Continue approximately 600 feet west on FS-714 and then go left (south) on an intersecting road that takes you past a series of earthen mounds that were part of the Camp Hale shooting range.

Sunset, Searle Pass

Cross the East Fork River on a bridge at mile 17.9 (9,320) just beyond the shooting range and near a line of dilapidated concrete bunkers. For the next 400 feet, the trail nearly disappears into thick, marshy meadow grasses, but it is visible on the hillside ahead. The route bears southwest and is marked by periodic cairns of crumbling concrete piers taken from long-forgotten military buildings. Regain the trail as it enters a lodgepole pine forest and begins an ascent. Turn through two short switchbacks and continue west to southwest for 0.5 mile, then exit briefly onto the upper end of the old "B" slope ski run, which is slowly being reclaimed by the forest. This vantage point gives one of the nicest views possible of the site of Camp Hale.

The CT now reenters the lodgepole pine forest, heading in a more southerly direction and crosses FS-726 at mile 18.8 (9,680). The trail resumes on the opposite side of the road and continues in a southerly direction, at times closely paralleling the Forest Service road below. Jim Miller and his maintenance crew reworked this trail in 1990. They thoughtfully provided a viewing point and bench at a rock outcrop about 0.4 mile up from the road crossing. Follow the trail to US-24 at mile 20.7 (10,000) and carefully cross the busy highway. Pass through a gate and proceed 200 feet on a railroad maintenance driveway. Cross the railroad tracks and continue ahead (west) 400 feet on the faint, elevated grade of an abandoned railroad siding to a small stream crossed via a dirt-fill bridge. Continue along the grade, which fades away as the trail bears to the right (northwest). At this point a well-defined trail, marked by posts, hugs the edge of the meadow, just inside of the trees.

At mile 21.0 (9,920), the CT, marked by rock cairns and wooden posts, turns south-southwest up an expansive meadow encompassing Mitchell Creek. In about 0.3 mile, you follow a definite trail as it enters a lodgepole pine forest at the edge of the linear meadow on your right. Before the trail begins a slow ascent away from the creek in another 0.5 mile, you might want to observe any waterfowl that may be nesting in the many beaver ponds of this marshy meadow. At mile 22.2 (10,200), the trail joins a jeep road deep in the forest. This road is the abandoned narrow-gauge route of the D&RG. Head east-northeast on the road a short distance, then assume a more southerly bearing for a mile. Follow the road as it slowly bends to the east and passes the remains of several large coking ovens. Continue on the jeep road to Tennessee Pass at mile 24.1 (10,424), where this segment ends on the west side of US-24 at the trailhead parking area.

Horse and Pack Animal Bypass

Follow the regular trail description through Copper Mountain Resort on Copper Road to a point just before the intersection with the bike path at mile 1.5 (9,760). Turn right on Beeler Place, which leads to the stables. Proceed on the road to a parking area cul-de-sac and continue ahead toward the Union Creek Base building on the ski area maintenance road. Bend around the base building and cross under the "H" and "K" ski lifts, then proceed 200 feet further to a switchback. Follow the ascending side road that takes off to the right at this switchback and continue for 0.5 mile to the base of "L" lift. An obscure trail forks to the right (west) off the ski maintenance road. Continue on this meandering trail through alternating meadows and lodgepole pine forest for another 0.5 mile, until an abrupt descent is made to the east bank of Guller Creek. Ford the creek and pick up the official CT at mile 3.0 (10,040).

Notes

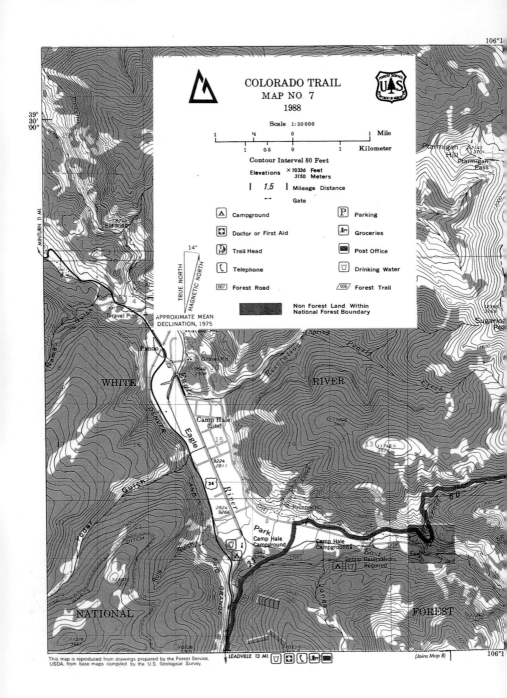

COLORADO TRAIL
MAP NO. 7
1988

Scale 1:50 000

Contour Interval 80 Feet

Elevations ×10336 Feet
3150 Meters

| 1.5 | Mileage Distance

↔ Gate

△ Campground

✚ Doctor or First Aid

🄷 Trail Head

📞 Telephone

007 Forest Road

P Parking

Groceries

Post Office

Drinking Water

006 Forest Trail

Non Forest Land Within
National Forest Boundary

TRUE NORTH
MAGNETIC NORTH
14°
APPROXIMATE MEAN
DECLINATION, 1975

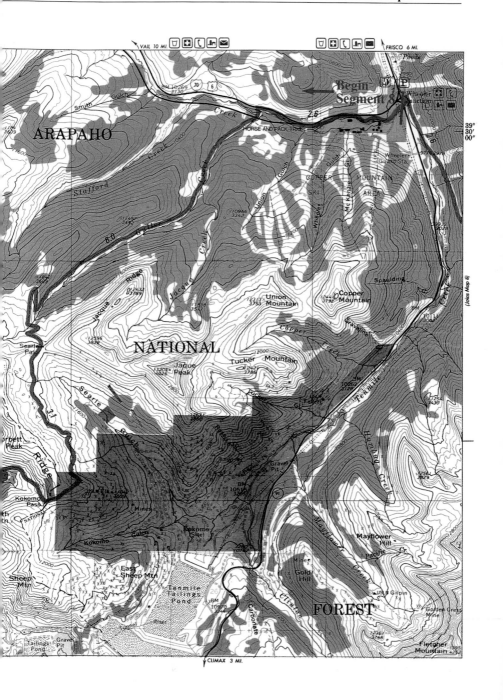

Ski tracks heading toward Homestake Peak, San Isabel National Forest

⚠ SEGMENT 9   14.9 Miles

Tennessee Pass to Hagerman Pass Road   **+1,160 Feet Elevation Gain**

Location	Mileage	From Denver	Elevation
Tennessee Pass	0.0	130.7	10,424
North Fork W. Tennessee Cr.	3.4		10,320
Porcupine Lakes	7.4		11,480
Lake Fork	13.1		10,040
Hagerman Pass Road	14.9	145.6	10,360

CT Series Maps 8 & 9 (see pages 104-105 & 110-111).

At Tennessee Pass, the CT enters the skyscraping Sawatch Range and begins a trek southward along its eastern flank. The Sawatch Range includes some of the highest elevations in Colorado, including that state's highest peak, 14,433-foot Mount Elbert. There are many grand, glacier-scoured valleys leading into the range, and lovely, lake-filled basins as well. Much of the CT route follows the old Main Range Trail, which began as a Civilian Conservation Corps project in the 1930s.

This segment passes through a corner of the Holy Cross Wilderness, where backpackers will find many campsites with backdrops of the Continental Divide's glaciated walls. Mountain bikers must detour around the wilderness areas in Segments 9 and 10 (see the Mountain Bike Detours). A series of blue diamond markers, beginning at Tennessee Pass, identify cross-country ski routes, many of which are part of the Tenth Mountain Trail Association ski system.

Toward the end of this segment, the trail rounds the western edge of Turquoise Reservoir, a water storage basin for the immense Fryingpan-Arkansas Project. The original Turquoise Lake, which received its name from the precious stone mined in the area by early Indians and later collectors, was greatly enlarged when impounded by Sugarloaf Dam. This reservoir is one of six in the system, whose purpose is to divert water from the Western Slope's Fryingpan River and pipe it under the Continental Divide to Eastern Slope users via the Arkansas River. The trail parallels the project and passes Clear Creek and Twin Lakes reservoirs farther south as well as the Mount Elbert hydro-station, all links in the long chain of the Pan-Ark Project.

This segment ends on the road where John J. Hagerman's Colorado Midland Railway once struggled to cross the Continental Divide at the lofty Hagerman Tunnel. Tennessee Pass, a somewhat inconspicuous but no less important crossing, was discovered by Colonel John C. Fremont in the summer of 1845 during his journey to California. The D&RG built a narrow-gauge railroad over the pass in 1881, then standardized the line and built the tunnel under the pass in 1890. It is still in use today.

Trailhead/Access Points

Tennessee Pass Trailhead: Travel north from Leadville on US-24 approximately 9 miles to the top of Tennessee Pass. A parking area on the left (west) side of the road provides adequate parking here. A trailhead bulletin board marks the CT. Don't be misled by other trails, mostly cross-country ski routes, which also start here.

Wurtz Ditch Road (FS-100) Trail Access: Travel north from Leadville on US-24 approximately 7.5 miles to Wurtz Ditch Road (FS-100), which leaves the highway on the left (west). Go 1 mile on the dirt road and bear to the right as the road forks. Proceed 0.3 mile farther, to a point where the CT crosses the road. There is room for only a few small cars here.

St. Kevins Gulch Trailhead (FS-107): This isolated portal into the Holy Cross Wilderness is ideal for those wanting to escape the crowds along most sections of the CT in the Sawatch Range. A high-clearance or 4WD vehicle is recommended on FS-107 once you leave the paved reservoir road. Although there are quicker and more direct routes to Turquoise Reservoir from Leadville, the most straight forward starts approximately 3.5 miles south of town on US-24. Turn right (west) onto Colorado Highway 300 and proceed 0.5 mile on the

LEADVILLE SERVICES

Distance from Trail: 9.5 miles

Bank	Commercial Bank	400 Harrison Ave.	(719) 486-0420
Bus	Bee Hive (shuttle service)	506 Harrison Ave.	(719) 486-2339
Dining	High Country	2nd & Harrison	(719) 486-3992
Gear	Bill's Sports Shop	225 Harrison Ave.	(719) 486-0739
Groceries	Safeway	1900 Hwy 24	(719) 486-0795
Information	Chamber of Commerce	809 Harrison Ave.	(719) 486-3900
Laundry	Laundromat	Poplar Ave.	no phone
Lodging	Timberline	216 Harrison Ave.	(719) 486-1876
Medical	Leadville Medical Center	4th & Washington	(719) 486-1264
	St. Vincent's Hospital	4th & Washington	(719) 486-0230
Post Office	Leadville Post Office	130 W. 5th	(719) 486-1667
Showers	Laundromat	Poplar Ave.	no phone
	Sugar Loafin' Campgrnd	3 mi. west of town	(719) 486-1031

paved road. Turn right (north) onto a road that is marked as the way to Turquoise Reservoir. Drive 1.8 miles north to a skewed three-way intersection. Go left onto the intersecting paved road, which ascends 0.8 mile west to the reservoir, and go right onto the intersecting road. Follow this winding, paved road 5.0 miles until you come to the somewhat obscure FS-107, which takes off to the right (north). Avoid the side roads and respect the nearby private property as FS-107 passes through the old St. Kevins mining district. Continue ahead a total of 2.4 miles on the rough, steep road until it ends at a small parking area at the edge of the Holy Cross Wilderness. Pick up the trail as it passes through this parking area.

Hagerman Pass Road (FS-105) Trail Access: see Segment 10.

Supplies, Services, and Accommodations

Available in Leadville.

Maps

CT Series: Maps 8 and 9 (see pages 104-105 and 110-111).
USFS: San Isabel National Forest.
USGS Quadrangles: Leadville North, Homestake Reservoir.

Trail Description

From the parking area on the west side of Tennessee Pass, traverse just below the Continental Divide bearing generally west to southwest. Note the blue diamonds high up in the lodgepole pines, which are markers for skiers during deep snow. In a few places the thick forest allows views to the south of the upper Arkansas Valley. Cross the sturdy Wurtz Ditch footbridge at mile 2.5 (10,400). This artificial creek bed, which might be either gushing with water or completely dry, is a conduit that diverts water from the west side of the divide to the Arkansas River via Tennessee Creek.

Ascend 0.2 mile further to the Wurtz Ditch road, where the somewhat obscure trail continues on the opposite side, trending generally to the southwest. Pass through a clear-cut to Lily Lake Road at mile 3.0 (10,350). Cross the road on an east-west diagonal, then continue a few steps on a side road that leads to a better road heading south toward a meadow. Before the meadow, the trail temporarily leaves the road to the right to avoid private property and it then bears south-southwest in the lodgepole pine forest. When you intersect the road again at the west edge of the meadow, go right (west-southwest) and continue a few steps to the crossing of the North Fork West Tennessee Creek at mile 3.4 (10,320). There is a double-log bridge just downstream of the road crossing. Proceed 200 feet to the deep ford of West Tennessee Creek. In the past, a couple of downed trees several hundred feet upstream provided a drier, but precarious, crossing.

Just beyond West Tennessee Creek, as the road makes a bend to the left, the trail very obscurely leaves the road and continues ahead (south-southwest) at a "Closed To All Vehicles" sign. The trail curves around to a westerly heading and joins an old road at mile 3.7 (10360). The road becomes more trail-like as it ascends steadily in a westerly, then southwesterly, direction, paralleling West Tennessee Creek through a lodgepole pine forest. At mile 4.7 (10,760) you will join up with another old road (its unused portion has been barricaded to prevent confusion). Proceed bearing generally southwest to west. Cross over a broad ridge at mile 5.1 (10,840), then descend slowly through a lodgepole pine-spruce forest. Enter the elongated meadow of Longs Gulch 1.0 mile beyond, where you will ascend west-southwest toward the very impressive head of this alpine cirque, passing the ruins of an old cabin.

A sign announces your entrance into the Holy Cross Wilderness at mile 6.5 (10,920). At the south side of the creek 400 feet beyond, begin a steep ascent to the southwest. Top a broad saddle at mile 7.4 (11,480), where the ponds of upper Porcupine Creek are nestled into spectacular alpine scenery. Descend 0.3 mile on the sometimes faint trail and cross Porcupine Creek. Follow the trail through a spruce-fir forest, then switchback up to tundra at 11,600 feet and enjoy views east and north of the Tenmile and Mosquito ranges. Reenter the trees at mile 8.5 (11,680) and descend to an old road. Continue the descent southward 0.6 mile, following an unnamed drainage that opens into a meadow.

Briefly leave the wilderness at mile 9.4 (11,240) where FS-107 ends at the primitive trailhead parking area. A sign here marks the wilderness boundary. Cross the small stream behind the sign, reenter the wilderness, and proceed northwest on an abandoned road at the edge of the meadow. In 800 feet, the old road becomes a rocky trail as it enters the forest and descends into the Bear Creek drainage. The terrain is so rocky around here that the trail seems to vanish at times into the surroundings. The CT passes above Bear Lake at mile 10.1 (11,120) in rugged country which might make a usable but uncomfortable campsite. Continue past the shores of the last picturesque lake and ascend to a timberline ridge at mile 11.0 (11,280), where an impressive panorama of Mount Massive and Hagerman Pass comes into view.

Descend steadily through a lodgepole pine forest to mile 12.4 (10,440) where the trail passes under a power line at the southern boundary of the Holy Cross Wilderness. Pass under the power line again 0.5 mile beyond and continue 600 feet to a convenient bridge at Mill Creek. Descend a few steps west-southwest from Mill Creek to the lower part of a meadow near the Lake Fork at mile 13.1 (10,040), where a bulletin board has been erected for hikers. This junction is 300 feet west of a switchback on the paved reservoir road, just up from May

Queen Campground. It doesn't make a good trail access point, however, because parking is very limited and the road sometimes floods.

From the bulletin board in the meadow, reenter the trees, pick up an old jeep road, and continue to the crossing of the swiftly flowing Lake Fork over a long footbridge. Then continue a few steps uphill on the old jeep road, until the trail resumes at left (south-southwest). Pass under the power line at mile 13.4 (10,120) and continue to Glacier Creek, which is crossed via a corduroy bridge. Traverse southeast beyond the creek in a cool spruce-fir forest. The Charles H. Boustead Tunnel, which channels water from the head of the Fryingpan River, is 150 feet below your feet as you approach Busk Creek. After Busk Creek, the trail ascends to the Hagerman Road at mile 14.9 (10,360). This segment ends here where the dirt road has only been slightly widened for temporary parking.

Uncle Bud's Hut, along the Colorado Trail and
the 10th Mountain Division Trail

Notes

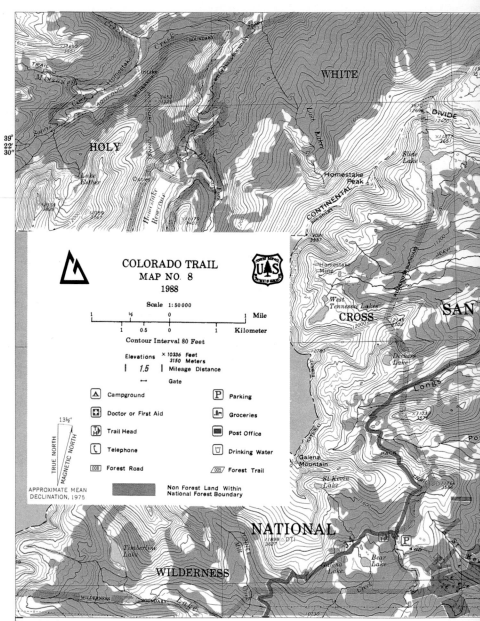

COLORADO TRAIL
MAP NO. 8
1988

Scale 1:50 000

Contour Interval 80 Feet

Elevations ×10336 Feet
3150 Meters

| 1.5 | Mileage Distance

→ Gate

Campground

Doctor or First Aid

Trail Head

Telephone

Forest Road

Parking

Groceries

Post Office

Drinking Water

Forest Trail

Non Forest Land Within
National Forest Boundary

TRUE NORTH
MAGNETIC NORTH
13½°
APPROXIMATE MEAN
DECLINATION, 1975

This map is reproduced from drawings prepared by the Forest Service,
USDA, from base maps compiled by the U.S. Geological Survey.

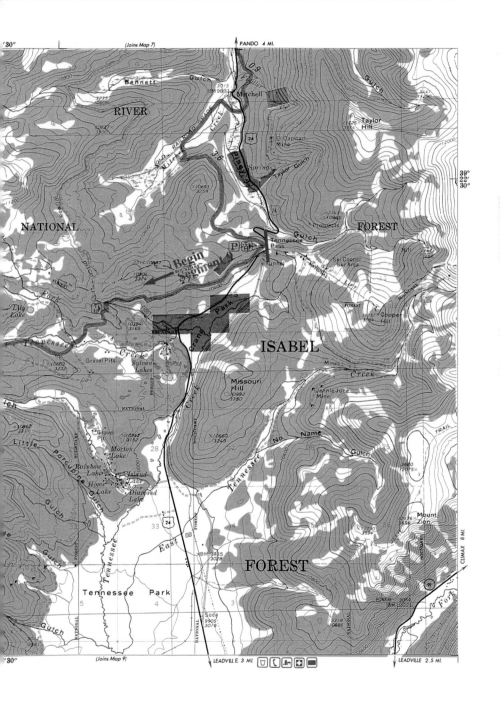

Mount Massive (14,421'), Mount Massive Wilderness

◮ SEGMENT 10   11.4 Miles

Hagerman Pass Road to Halfmoon Creek   **+1,760 Feet Elevation Gain**

Location	Mileage	From Denver	Elevation
Hagerman Pass Road	0.0	145.6	10,360
Sugarloaf Saddle	1.2		11,080
Rock Creek	4.4		10,280
Mount Massive Trail	8.1		11,240
Halfmoon Creek	11.4	157.0	10,080

CT Series Maps 9 & 10 (see pages 110-111 & 118-119).

The Hagerman Pass road is named for John J. Hagerman, builder of the Colorado Midland Railway. His railroad followed this grade to its Continental Divide crossing several miles up the road at 11,528-foot Hagerman Tunnel. The Midland then continued down the Fryingpan River to tap the Roaring Fork's profitable coal fields and silver mines. The right-of-way was abandoned by the railroad in 1920 and has been a dirt road ever since. It even served as an official state auto route in the 1920s, before more adequate highways were built over the Continental Divide.

In the early 1860s, placers flourished in the upper Arkansas country, and Abe Lee is credited with the original discovery of gold in California Gulch, today's Leadville. The gold soon played out, but then silver was discovered in the surrounding hills and by 1879 Leadville was a rip-roaring boomtown which lasted until the demonetization of silver in 1893. In later years, and today as well, the Climax Molybdenum Mine contributed to the local economy. At several points along this trail segment, hikers can view the "Cloud City," its surrounding mine tailings, and Mosquito Pass to the east, over which many of the hopeful filtered into the valley.

This segment travels almost entirely within the boundaries of Mount Massive Wilderness, which takes its name from 14,421-foot Mount Massive, second highest peak in the state, and easily climbable from the CT. Mountain bikers must detour this segment (see the Mountain Bike Detours).

Trailhead/Access Points

Hagerman Pass Road (FS-105) Trail Access: Although there are quicker and more direct routes to the start of this segment from Leadville, the most straightforward starts approximately 3.5 miles south of town on US-24. Turn right (west) onto Colorado Highway 300 and proceed 0.5 mile on the paved road. Turn right (north) onto a road marked as the way to Turquoise Reservoir. Drive 1.8 miles north to a skewed three-way intersection. Go left onto the intersecting paved road and ascend 1.2 miles west to Sugarloaf Dam. Continue on the reservoir road 3.1 miles beyond the dam and turn left onto a dirt road, the Hagerman Pass Road (FS-105). Continue 0.9 mile up the road to the point where the CT crosses it. No parking is provided. If you prefer off-road parking, continue 1.4 miles past the intersection with the Hagerman Pass Road on the paved reservoir road to the fishermen's parking area at the Boustead Tunnel outlet. To find the CT from this parking area, continue on the reservoir road 0.5 mile to a sharp switchback to the right. Leave the road and continue several hundred feet up the rough side road, which is partially flooded by Mill Creek. The CT is marked by a bulletin board in the meadow.

Halfmoon Creek Trailhead: See Segment 11.

Supplies, Services, and Accommodations

Leadville is about 8 miles east from the Hagerman Pass Road trail access point via the reservoir road. The town, which is being restored to its original Victorian grandeur, has grocery, sporting goods, and hardware stores as well as various restaurants and overnight accommodations (see Segment 9).

Maps

CT Series: Maps 9 and 10 (see pages 110-111 and 118-119).
USFS: San Isabel National Forest.
USGS Quadrangles: Homestake Reservoir, Mount Massive.

Trail Description

If it weren't for the sign pointing out the CT intersection on the Hagerman Pass Road, this inconspicuous crossing might be missed altogether. Early in the season, lingering snowbanks also make this point difficult to spot. From the road, the CT climbs steadily through a lodgepole pine forest. Several open areas along the way afford great views to the north of Galena Mountain and the Continental Divide. Reach the saddle below and just west of Sugarloaf Mountain at mile 1.2 (11,080), where the trail crosses a logging road. Continue south of the road and pass underneath a power line into a clear-cut. You may encounter several areas where the trail has suffered severe erosion because of the timbering activity here, although the clear-cut does provide unparalleled views east and south across the upper Arkansas Valley.

Enter Mount Massive Wilderness 700 feet south of the road crossing, then descend slightly and reenter the forest at mile 1.6 (11,040), where the trail crosses a small stream. The trail traverses several small gullies populated by spruce and fir in the cool, damp recesses, and lodgepole pine on the exposed, drier ridges. Top the saddle west of Twin Mounds at mile 3.0 (11,000), then begin a descent south into Rock Creek drainage. Toward the end of the descent, the trail becomes wider, characteristic of an old, abandoned road. Bear to the right (west-southwest) on the trail at mile 3.6 (10,600), as the old road appears to continue ahead. The CT crosses another road 250 feet beyond. Continue ahead (west) as the trail bends around the southern edge of Kearney Park. After briefly leveling out here, the trail continues its southerly descent and enters Leadville National Fish Hatchery property.

The trail descends to the north bank of Rock Creek at mile 4.4 (10,280). Continue on the trail 200 feet beyond the road crossing and cross the creek on a sturdy bridge. The trail ascends 0.3 mile from Rock Creek to South Rock Creek, which is spanned by a corduroy bridge. Leave the hatchery property in a somewhat spooky lodgepole pine forest, where the ground is pitted with large potholes that are likely to be filled with water early in the season.

At mile 6.2 (10,960), the CT intersects the Highline Trail, which continues three steep miles northwest to Native Lake, a popular angler's refuge. The trail proceeds south and crosses North Willow Creek at mile 7.2 (11,040). Ascend to a level spot south of North Willow Creek, beyond which you traverse into a sunny, open area with views east to the Mosquito Range.

Pass the side trail to Mount Massive's summit at mile 8.1 (11,240). On this side trail, it is approximately 3.5 miles and 3,180 vertical feet to the summit of Mount Massive. The CT traverses south from the Mount Massive Trail, then suddenly descends to cross Willow Creek at mile 8.4 (11,000). Cross South Willow Creek 0.6 mile beyond and continue to mile 10.4 (10,600), where a steep cross-country ski trail descends abruptly to the left. Continue ahead on the CT, which gradually descends to the wilderness boundary at the trailhead parking area on Halfmoon Creek Road at mile 11.4 (10,080). The trail continues on the opposite side of the road, south of Halfmoon Creek.

Notes

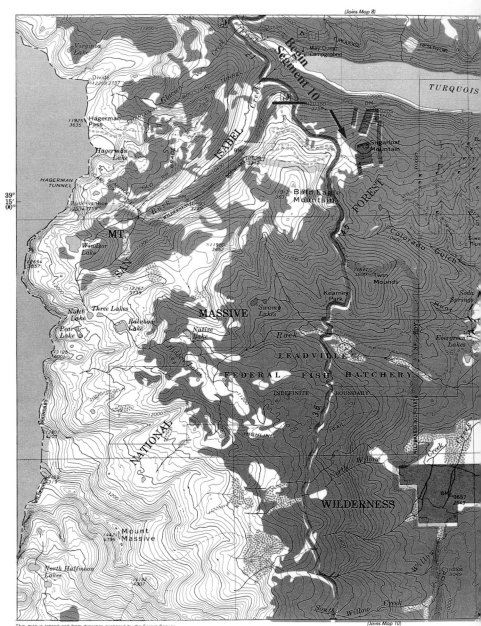

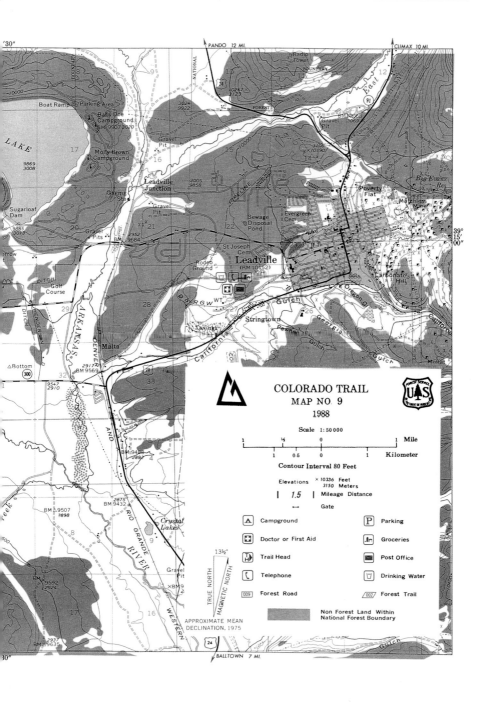

COLORADO TRAIL
MAP NO. 9
1988

Scale 1:50 000

| 1 | ¼ | 0 | | 1 | Mile |
| 1 | 0.5 | 0 | | 1 | Kilometer |

Contour Interval 80 Feet

Elevations	× 10336 Feet
	3150 Meters
| 1.5 |	Mileage Distance
→	Gate

▲	Campground		P	Parking
✚	Doctor or First Aid		🍴	Groceries
🚶	Trail Head		✉	Post Office
☎	Telephone		🚰	Drinking Water
009	Forest Road		002	Forest Trail

Non Forest Land Within
National Forest Boundary

APPROXIMATE MEAN
DECLINATION, 1975

TRUE NORTH
MAGNETIC NORTH
13½°

Old cabin, Twin Lakes

◭ SEGMENT 11   28.9 Miles

Halfmoon Creek to Clear Creek Road   **+4,200 Feet Elevation Gain**

Location	Mileage	From Denver	Elevation
Halfmoon Creek Trailhead	0.0	157.0	10,080
Mount Elbert Trail	1.3		10,560
Lakeview Campground	6.7		9,560
Twin Lakes Dam	10.9		9,200
Hope Pass	20.2		12,520
Clear Creek Road Trailhead	28.9	185.9	8,960

CT Series Maps 10 & 11 (see pages 118-119 & 120-121).

On your way to the trailhead on Halfmoon Creek, take notice of the water diversion structures that are part of the Pan-Ark Project. Twin Lakes Reservoir is also a part of this immense project, which diverts water from the Western Slope under the Continental Divide to the Eastern Slope via the Arkansas River. The reservoir was enlarged in 1972 to serve the Mount Elbert power plant, a pumped-storage station that generates electricity during high-demand periods by using water stored above the plant.

At the head of the reservoir is the village of Twin Lakes, first established as the town of Dayton in the brief but energetic gold placer boom of the 1860s. After the boom, the people of Dayton recognized the town was unique because of its incredible mountain scenery, and by the late 1870s, Dayton and the Twin Lakes had become a popular destination, with a hotel on the south shore of the lower lake. James Dexter acquired the property in 1883 and transformed it into an impressive resort with a dance pavilion and stables as well as the main hotel and an annex. Dexter was so enchanted with the location that he built himself a two-story log cabin with Victorian trim. To fit the mood of the expansion, the isolated retreat was renamed Interlaken. Popular with anglers, tourists, and nature lovers in the late 1800s, the picturesque resort went into a decline after the turn of the century, most likely due to the transformation of the lakes into a reservoir, which flooded the stage road serving Interlaken.

When Twin Lakes Reservoir was enlarged in the 1970s, the Department of Reclamation decided to save the dilapidated buildings from inundation. They were moved slightly uphill from their original locations, stabilized, and given a fresh coat of paint. Today the remains of Interlaken still exist for us to visit and ponder.

Probably no other section of the CT gives such a good look at glacial deposits as the stretch from Twin Lakes to Clear Creek. The parallel ridges bordering the lower valley are lateral moraines — debris deposited by advancing glaciers. The original configuration of Twin Lakes, slightly altered because of its enlargement into a reservoir, was the result of damming by terminal moraines, deposited at the end of glaciers. These unconsolidated deposits, which include gold gouged out of the Sawatch Range and transported into the valley by water and ice, sparked the placer boom of the 1860s. The Arkansas River was pushed against the east side of the valley by ancient ice flows, so that it now runs in a tight channel between the glacial debris and the hard core rocks of the Mosquito Range. Those wishing to inspect the 1.7-billion-year-old Precambrian crest of the Sawatch Range can do so here by following a side trail to the top of 14,433-foot Mount Elbert, the highest point in Colorado.

During the first weekend of August, hikers in this segment share the route with hardy runners participating in the Leadville 100, a torturous mountain marathon held each year.

Trailhead/Access Points

Halfmoon Creek Trailhead: Travel south of Leadville on US-24 approximately 3.5 miles and turn right (west) onto Colorado Highway 300. Drive 0.8 mile and turn left (south) on a dirt road showing the way to Halfmoon Campground. Continue another 1.2 miles and turn right. It is an additional 5.5 miles on the bumpy road to the trailhead parking area, on the north side of the road just beyond an earth-fill bridge.

TWIN LAKES SERVICES   Distance from Trail: 1 mile

Bank	None		
Bus	None		
Dining	Twin Lakes Nordic Inn	6435 Hwy 82	(719) 486-1830
Gear	Twin Lakes General Store	6451 Hwy 82	(719) 486-2196
Groceries	Twin Lakes General Store	6451 Hwy 82	(719) 486-2196
Information	Twin Lakes General Store	6451 Hwy 82	(719) 486-2196
Laundry	Win Mar	Hwy 82 & Hwy 24	(719) 486-0785
Lodging	Twin Peaks Cabins	889 Hwy 82	(719) 486-2667
	Win Mar	Hwy 82 & Hwy 24	(719) 486-0785
Medical	Nearest in Leadville		(719) 486-1264
Post Office	Twin Lakes General Store	6451 Hwy 82	(719) 486-2196
Showers	Win Mar	Hwy 82 & Hwy 24	(719) 486-0785

Lakeview Campground Trailhead/Twin Lakes Reservoir Trail Access: Travel south of Leadville and go west on Colorado Highway 82 for approximately 4.0 miles. Turn right (north) on County Road 24 and ascend 1.0 mile to Lakeview Campground. A trailhead parking area is provided within the campground. You can also park at the Mount Elbert power plant visitors' parking area; the entrance is on the highway 0.5 mile beyond County Road 24. The CT runs right next to the parking area adjacent to the power plant building. Finally, several fishermen parking areas convenient to the CT are located on the north side of Twin Lakes Reservoir.

Clear Creek Road Trailhead: See Segment 12.

Supplies, Services, and Accommodations

Twin Lakes is approximately 1.0 mile west of the CT crossing on Colorado Highway 82. The village has a tavern/inn and a small general store.

Maps

CT Series: Maps 10 and 11 (see pages 118-119 and 120-121).
USFS: San Isabel National Forest.
USGS Quadrangles: Mount Massive, Mount Elbert, Granite, Winfield, Mount Harvard.

Trail Description

From the trailhead parking area, cross the road to the north side of Halfmoon Creek and immediately intercept the CT as it heads south through a lodgepole pine forest. This trail is popular because it is one of the most direct routes up Mount Elbert, named for territorial governor Samuel Elbert. Ford Elbert Creek at mile 0.4 (10,160), and notice how the creek has been diverted from its original streambed as shown on the topographical map. Terminate your ascent at mile 1.0 (10,600) and begin a gradual descent. In 0.3 mile, you will pass a side trail to the right that leads to the summit of Mount Elbert. Continue downhill 0.5 mile to Box Creek, then proceed beyond an old intersecting road that crosses the CT on a diagonal. Cross Mill Creek in a marshy area at mile 2.0

(10,280). The trail joins an old road 0.3 mile beyond and begins an ascent to the south-southeast. This old road splits at mile 2.8 (10,400); the right fork is barricaded, so follow the left fork. The CT becomes more trail-like as it descends quickly into the Herrington Creek drainage. Ford the creek at mile 3.1 (10,320), ascend steeply to the old road continuation on the left (east-southeast), then continue on a southerly ascent. At the upper end of the road, enter the west edge of an elongated meadow and continue to a broad saddle at 3.8 (10,600), where, if you look closely, Turquoise Reservoir is visible to the north.

Descend from the saddle through an aspen forest to a meadow at mile 4.1 (10,440), where the CT veers to the right (southwest) off the old road and reenters the forest. The trail stays to the right (west) and above several small beaver ponds on Corske Creek. Bear to the right (west) at a trail junction above the ponds at mile 4.5 (10,520) and continue uphill 100 feet to another trail junction. The steep trail ahead is another route to Mount Elbert's summit. The CT leaves the ascending path here squarely to the left (south). Continue south on the CT and bear right (southwest) at a trail junction just after a primitive log bridge crossing. Cross a fast-flowing stream 150 feet beyond at mile 4.8 (10,520) on a log bridge. Pick up a jeep road, which dead ends at this point, and descend on it heading generally southwest through an aspen forest. Recross the creek at mile 5.2 (10,280). Keep descending on the road to mile 6.5 (9,640), where the trail resumes on the right (southeast). Just ahead is County Road 24, which leads from Colorado Highway 82 to the Lakeview Campground. Presently the trail drops through an aromatic sagebrush field that allows views south into the huge glacial basin containing Twin Lakes. (In the near future a new trail will be rerouted along the west side of Twin Lakes.)

Pass the trailhead parking area within Lakeview Campground at mile 6.7 (9,560) and continue descending beyond the campground to mile 7.1 (9,320), where a pedestrian underpass at Colorado Highway 82 ensures safe passage. South of Colorado Highway 82, the trail leads east and dips briefly into a cheerful ponderosa pine grove that blooms with an understory of pasque flowers in June. The trail here was constructed with the help of Governor Richard Lamm in September of 1985. When the trail breaks out of the scattered ponderosa pine, the Mosquito Range and a huge lateral moraine that extends east are visible. The century-old buildings of Interlaken are barely visible on the south shore.

Some CT trekkers have complained about the long trudge around the bare north side of Twin Lakes Reservoir through the fields of sagebrush. Admittedly, this section can seem unbearably long to weighted-down backpackers on warm, sunny afternoons. Better, perhaps, to plan this stretch in the early morning when the fragrant smell of sage is still hanging in the cool air. Also, be aware that this stretch is difficult to follow in places from the power plant to the dam, mostly owing to the fact that it is hard to maintain a trail in the gravelly glacial soils. To make matters worse, many of the trail markers and cairns are continually vandalized. Still, this section of trail can be enjoyable and educational under the right conditions and state of mind, given its uncommon geologic and aesthetic characteristics. Trail maintainer Craig Nelson is particularly enthusiastic about this section of trail from the lake to Hope Pass because of the great variety it offers in its 3,500 feet of elevation change.

Pass the Mount Elbert power plant at mile 7.7 (9,280) and continue east along the treeless north shore, where the reflection of Mount Hope sparkles on the water's surface. Cross the earthen dam at mile 10.9 (9,200) and continue south on the gravel road until you can skirt the southeast edge of the reservoir on a dirt road that goes southwest then west. Follow the winding dirt road 0.4 mile west along the fluctuating shoreline until the trail leaves the road in a field of sage near the forest's edge. The trail on the south shore is in stark contrast to the trail on the north shore. The cool forest, which sharply slopes down to the nearby lapping shoreline, generates a laziness and repose to be remembered. There are a few level campsites along here for those who'd like to stay longer. From the south shore, the recessional moraine across the lake is very obvious. The huge undulations created by the receding glaciers are more fully revealed in the setting sun.

Continue west along the south shoreline, using in part the old historic stage road, to mile 13.9 (9,200), where you pass right through the old Interlaken complex. Take a few minutes to look around at the numerous old buildings. Beyond Interlaken, the CT heads southwest for approximately 0.2 mile, crossing a small sagebrush meadow and gradually distancing itself from the reservoir. The trail becomes faint and difficult to follow at times after it enters a lodgepole pine-aspen forest. Continue 1.5 miles, bearing generally west and southwest, to Boswell Gulch. Follow the obscure trail to a junction made obvious by the "Closed To All Vehicles" sign at mile 16.4 (9,280). Go left (south-southwest) here on an intersecting trail that has the appearance of an old road. Ascend south on the rocky, abandoned road 0.3 mile, and notice that a trail then resumes at left (east). Continue less steeply, with the help of a switchback that returns you to a southerly bearing near the bank of Willis Gulch Creek.

When the trail splits at mile 17.6 (10,280), avoid the right fork and continue straight ahead (south) into Little Willis Gulch. Approximately 0.2 mile beyond, cross a large diversion ditch that clings awkwardly to the steep mountainside and might present some difficulty if water is flowing. The CT breaks out of the trees at mile 19.5 (11,760) near a protected alpine lake at the head of Little Willis Gulch. This lake makes a pleasant camping area. Continue ahead through the tundra, in the shadow of towering 13,933-foot Mount Hope, and top out on Hope Pass at mile 20.2 (12,520). Views to the south are of some of the lesser-known Collegiate Peaks: Oxford, Belford, Missouri, Huron, and Ice Mountain. From the top of the pass, Mount Hope is a steep climb almost due west, with some rock scrambling en route.

From the pass, the CT continues south and drops quickly into the protection of the trees. At the end of its long, steep descent down Sheep Gulch, the trail joins a short dead-end side road. Continue 800 feet ahead (south) and join up with County Road 390 at mile 22.6 (9,880). Bear to the left (east) on the county road and continue 6.3 miles down the valley of Clear Creek to the isolated CT trailhead on the dusty road at mile 28.9 (8,960).

Notes

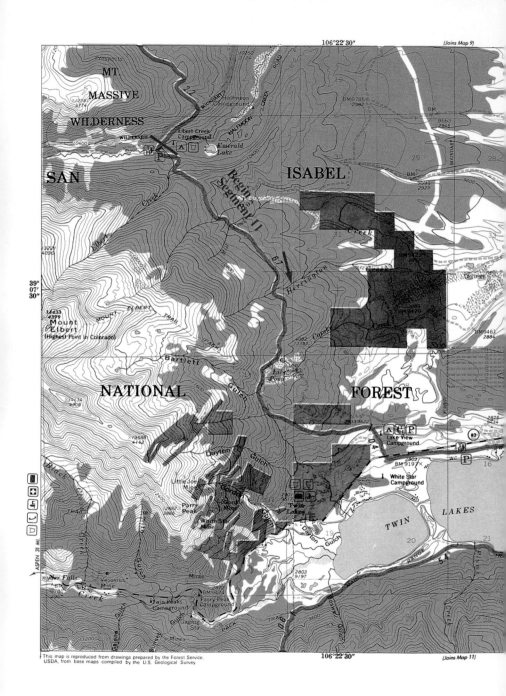

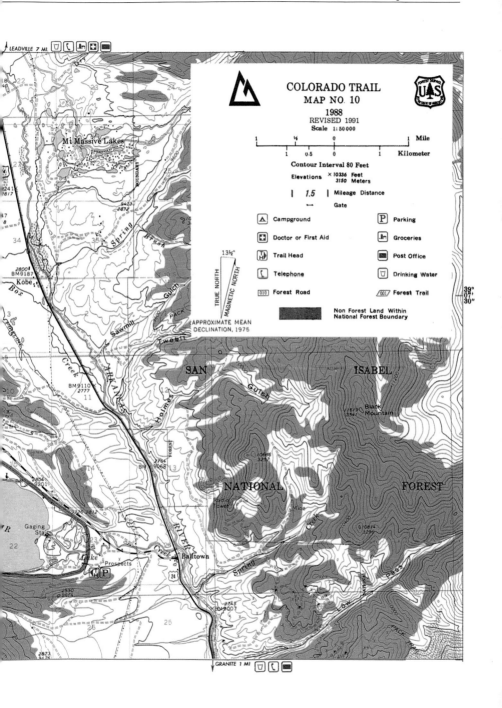

COLORADO TRAIL
MAP NO. 10
1988
REVISED 1991
Scale 1:50000

Contour Interval 80 Feet

Elevations × 10336 Feet
            3150 Meters

| 1.5 | Mileage Distance

→ Gate

△ Campground   P Parking
✚ Doctor or First Aid   Groceries
Trail Head   Post Office
Telephone   Drinking Water
010 Forest Road   001 Forest Trail

Non Forest Land Within
National Forest Boundary

TRUE NORTH
MAGNETIC NORTH
13½°
APPROXIMATE MEAN
DECLINATION, 1975

LEADVILLE 7 MI.

GRANITE 1 MI

SAN   ISABEL

NATIONAL   FOREST

Mt Massive Lakes

Black Mountain

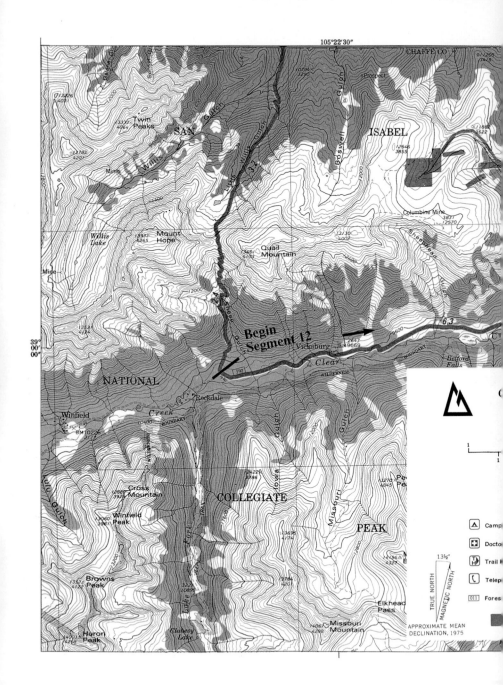

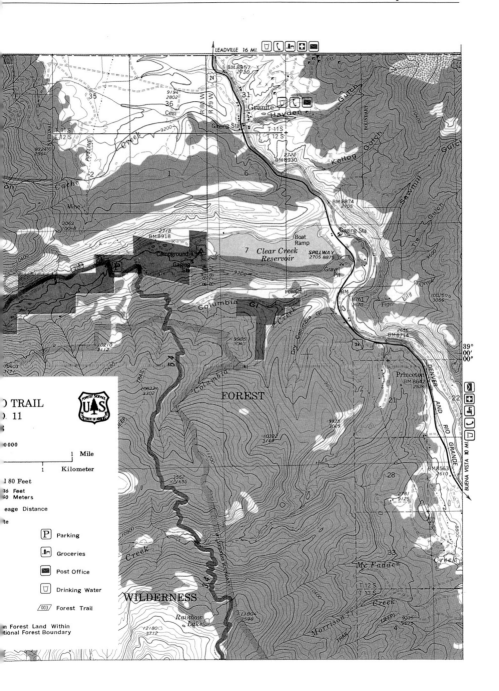

Elephant head wildflowers, upper Pine Creek, Collegiate Peaks Wilderness

▲ SEGMENT 12   18.2 Miles

Clear Creek to North Cottonwood Creek Rd.   **+4,520 Feet Elevation Gain**

Location	Mileage	From Denver	Elevation
Clear Creek Road Trailhead	0.0	185.9	8,960
Waverly Ridge	4.8		11,640
Pine Creek	6.4		10,400
Harvard Ridge	8.8		11,800
North Cottonwood Creek Road	18.2	204.1	9,400

CT Series Maps 11 & 12 (see pages 120-121 & 126-127).

Perhaps the most stately section of the Sawatch Range is the portion known ,
as the Collegiate Peaks, a collection of 14,000-foot mountains rising above
high, extended ridges and deep valleys. The CT continues southward in this segment along the eastern slopes of the Collegiates, ascending and descending this
magnificent terrain. Backpackers will find exceptional campsites all along the
way, as well as side trails leading to alpine lakes and isolated niches. Mountain
climbers will be challenged by several high peaks that rise near the trail, including 14,420-foot Mount Harvard, 14,153-foot Mount Oxford and 14,073-foot
Mount Columbia.

The stunning Collegiate Range was first surveyed in 1869 by a university
team, thus accounting for its unique name. Professor Josiah Dwight Whitney,
the head of the Harvard School of Mining and Geology, led a group of science
students into Colorado Territory to compare the heights of the Colorado Rockies
with those of California's Sierra Nevadas. The group climbed and named Mount
Harvard to honor their institution. Mount Yale was named after Whitney's alma
mater. Mount Columbia didn't join the roster of distinctive of Ivy League fourteeners until 1916, when it was named by Roger Toll, an official of the Colorado
Mountain Club.

This portion of the CT begins on private property along the Clear Creek
road but soon rises out of the valley and enters the Collegiate Peaks Wilderness,
where it remains for most of the segment. Mountain bikers will need to detour
this segment, as well as the north portion of Segment 13 (see Mountain Bike
Detours).

Trailhead/Access Points

Clear Creek Road Trailhead: Travel north from Buena Vista on US-24 and
turn left (west) on County Road 390. Drive 3.0 miles to the informal trailhead
parking area on the north side of the dirt road. The CT goes south from here to
North Cottonwood Creek. To find the CT where it heads north to Twin Lakes,
proceed west up County Road 390 an additional 6.3 miles to where the road
makes a wide bend just beyond the restored town of Vicksburg. A side road goes
right (north) here for several hundred feet, to where the trail begins its steep
ascent to Hope Pass.

North Cottonwood Creek Road Trail Access: See Segment 13.

Supplies, Services, and Accommodations

Available in Buena Vista.

Maps

CT Series: Maps 11 and 12 (see pages 120-121 and 126-127).
USFS: San Isabel National Forest.
USGS Quadrangles: Granite, Mount Harvard, Harvard Lakes, Buena Vista West.

Trail Description

The CT immediately enters private property at the trailhead on the south side
of County Road 390. Latch the gate behind you and continue through the barn-
yard on the road that crosses to the south side of Clear Creek on a wide bridge.
Pass through a gate, and follow the road as it bends left (east) 400 feet beyond at
mile 0.2 (8,960). Continue east on the road, passing donkeys and cattle that will

BUENA VISTA SERVICES		Distance from Trail: 9 miles	
Bank	World Savings	411 E. Main	(719) 395-8608
	Collegiate Peaks	105 Centennial Plaza	(719) 395-2472
Bus	At Your Service (shuttle)		(719) 395-6438
Dining	Marti's	708 Hwy 24 South	(719) 395-9289
	Loback's Bakery	326 E. Main	(719) 395-2978
Gear	Trailhead Ventures	707 Hwy 24 North	(719) 395-8001
Groceries	Vista Super Market	525 W. Lake	(719) 395-2714
	Circle Super	428 Hwy 24 South	(719) 395-2431
Information	Chamber of Commerce	343 Hwy 24 South	(719) 395-6612
Laundry	Morrison's Laundromat	410 Hwy 24	no phone
Lodging	Cottonwood Hot Springs	18999 County Rd. 306	(719) 395-6434
	Bar VV Cabins & Cmpgd.	40671 Hwy 24	(719) 395-2338
Medical	Mountain Medical Center	36 Oak	(719) 395-8632
Post Office	Buena Vista Post Office	112 Linderman Ave.	(719) 395-2445
Showers	None		

likely be grazing in the field. Just before you would pass under a power line at mile 0.6 (8,960), turn onto the faint road that heads to the right (south). Six hundred feet beyond, top a small, bald rise that conceals a fence from view. Go through the gate, being sure to close it behind you. From this point, continue a few more steps south, then south-southeast to the edge of the trees. Here, you should see to your left (east) a sturdy "Closed To All Vehicles" sign concealed in the trees at mile 0.8 (8,960). This marks where the trail begins its ascent out of the valley.

Pass through a burned-out lodgepole pine forest that is slowly coming back to life and switchback uphill in the vicinity of the power line. Enter the damp, but usually waterless, upper Columbia Gulch at mile 1.9 (9,640), where the CT crosses an old road in a sagebrush meadow encircled by aspen and lodgepole pine. As the trail reenters the trees, it crosses the boundary into Collegiate Peaks Wilderness and resumes its ascent southward in an aspen forest. Lodgepole pine begin to outnumber aspen as the trail rises onto the rocky mountainside above the gulch. The trail switchbacks to the right at mile 2.9 (10,040) and moves into a sunnier exposure. Continue the ascent, crossing several small streamlets that form the headwaters of Columbia Creek. Mount the ridge extending east of Waverly Mountain at mile 4.8 (11,640). From here, Mount Harvard's impressive crest is dominant on the southern skyline.

The CT drops quickly through a lodgepole pine forest to its intersection with the Pine Creek Trail in the valley at mile 6.4 (10,400), where there is a well-established campsite. Follow the Pine Creek Trail 500 feet downstream to a bridge that crosses to the south side of the creek. The fork to the left continues downstream, parallel to Pine Creek, to a trailhead on US-24. Continue straight ahead on the CT and begin a long ascent out of the Pine Creek Valley.

At mile 8.1 (11,520), pass an unmarked and indistinct side trail to the right that leads in 0.3 mile to Rainbow Lake, a delightful camping spot. Continue climbing through a ghost forest and proceed to a windy, exposed point with a line of sight up the Arkansas Valley. Duck back into the trees and climb to a ridge extending northeast from Mount Harvard at mile 8.8 (11,800). For the next mile, the CT traverses through alpine flowers and grasses with stands of spruce and bristlecone pine growing at the upper limits of their life zones. The open tundra provides views across the valley to the Buffalo Peaks, the southernmost mountains in the Mosquito Range.

Descend to the crossing of Morrison Creek at mile 9.8 (11,560). Approximately 0.7 mile beyond, pass the Wapaca Trail, which descends to the left. Continue through a spruce forest to Frenchman Creek at mile 11.8 (10,960) and cross the Harvard Trail 500 feet beyond. Some people head west up this side trail to the head of Frenchman Creek for a climb up Mounts Harvard and Columbia from their eastern ridges. The CT continues southeast from this trail junction and rises slightly to cross a ridge at mile 12.6 (11,160). At mile 14.1 (10,640), you pass above a neglected mine. The operator left in such a hurry he forgot his ore cart!

Just beyond the mine, pass an old road more steeply inclined than the CT. Descend to Three Elk Creek at mile 15.1 (10,280) and, 300 feet further along, pass at a right angle the trail that ascends to a cirque on Mount Columbia's southeast face. Here the trail leaves the wilderness area and continues south to upper Harvard Lake, which is more like a pond, and the lower lake at mile 15.4 (10,280). Descend 0.2 mile from the lakes and ford a stream, then begin a traverse at about 10,000 feet through a lodgepole pine forest that has, in places, a lush understory of purple lupine.

Pass over a ridge at mile 17.5 (9,80) and switchback down into an area of mountain mahogany that allows views west up the Horn Fork Basin to the Continental Divide and east into the Arkansas Valley. End this segment on the North Cottonwood Creek Road in a lodgepole pine-fir forest at mile 18.2 (9,400). If you are continuing on the CT, hike approximately 0.1 mile west down the road and look for the trail where it resumes at left.

Notes

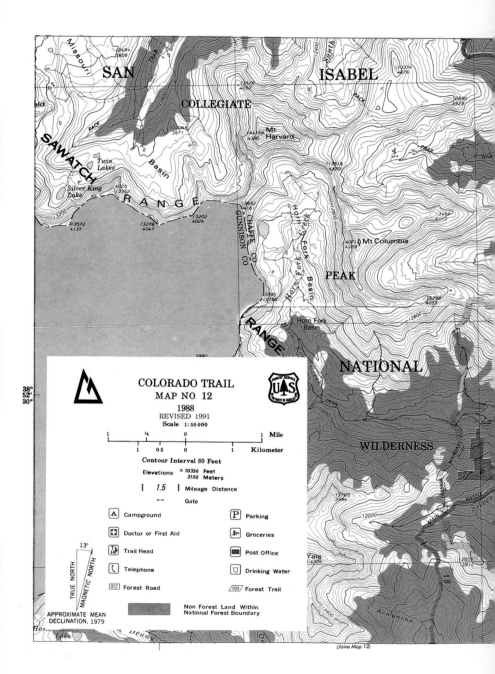

COLORADO TRAIL
MAP NO. 12
1988
REVISED 1991
Scale 1:50 000

Contour Interval 80 Feet

Elevations ×10336 Feet
3150 Meters

| 1.5 | Mileage Distance

← → Gate

[A] Campground

[+] Doctor or First Aid

[TH] Trail Head

[C] Telephone

012 Forest Road

[P] Parking

[Gr] Groceries

[PO] Post Office

[W] Drinking Water

004 Forest Trail

Non Forest Land Within
National Forest Boundary

TRUE NORTH
MAGNETIC NORTH
13°

APPROXIMATE MEAN
DECLINATION, 1979

(Joins Map 13)

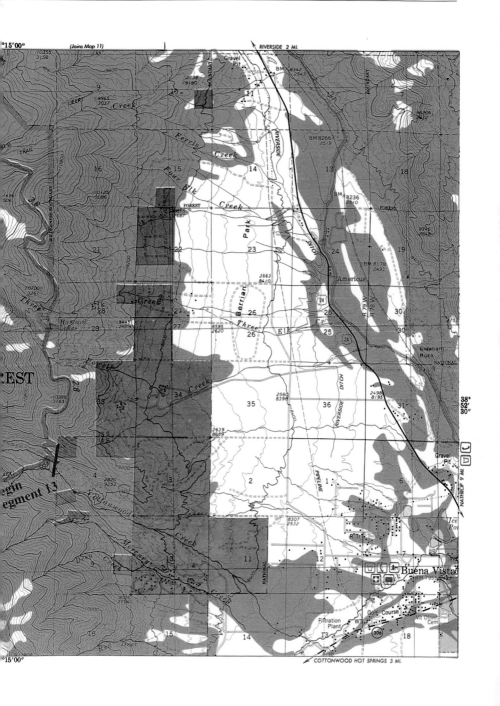

The Chalk Cliffs, Chalk Creek, San Isabel National Forest

⚠ SEGMENT 13   22.2 Miles

North Cottonwood Creek to Chalk Creek Rd.   +3,700 Feet Elevation Gain

Location	Mileage	From Denver	Elevation
North Cottonwood Creek Road	0.0	204.1	9,400
Silver Creek Saddle	3.3		11,880
Avalanche Trailhead	6.6		9,360
Bald Mountain Saddle	11.6		9,880
County Road 162	19.7		8,160
Chalk Creek Trailhead	22.2	226.3	8,360

CT Series Maps 12 & 13 (see pages 126-127 & 134-135).

Near the end of this segment, the CT traverses Mount Princeton's lower eastern flank and descends into Chalk Creek, which was named for the white, crumbly pillars that support the mountain's southeast ridge. This unusual formation is the result of granitic rock that was kaolinized (altered) by hydrothermal solutions rising from cooling magma along fault and fracture zones in the area. Chalk Creek has always been popular for its hot springs and remains well known today. Trail crews working in this location always had plenty of volunteers, who were often released by their team leaders early in the afternoon only to reconvene a few minutes later at the hot springs.

Mount Princeton, which is known for the magnificent symmetrical profile it displays to motorists descending Trout Creek Pass, is a large body of relatively young 30-million-year-old quartz monzonite porphyry intruding into ancient Precambrian metamorphic rocks. It was originally called Chalk Mountain by the Wheeler Survey. Henry Gannett of the Hayden Survey gave the mountain its present name.

Completion of the last 5 miles of this segment is still awaiting the acquisition of right-of-ways. Until that happens, the trail route uses an assortment of county roads to reach the trailhead at Chalk Creek. The trail between North and Middle Cottonwood creeks crosses the southeast corner of the Collegiate Peaks Wilderness and passes within 2 miles and 2,300 vertical feet of 14,196-foot Mount Yale. Mountain bikers must bypass this segment (see the Mountain Bike Detours).

Trailhead/Access Points

North Cottonwood Creek Trail Access: This approach begins with a left turn (west) onto Crossman Street (County Road 350) from US-24 at the north end of Buena Vista. Proceed 2 miles and turn right (north) onto County Road 361. After 0.9 mile, make a sharp left turn (south) onto County Road 365, which may not be suitable for conventional cars. Continue 3.5 miles on this rough road to a small parking area at an obscure trail access point. From here, the CT heads north to Harvard Lakes and, eventually, Clear Creek; 0.1 mile beyond is the trail access point for the southbound CT. Parking at both places is limited.

Avalanche Trailhead (Cottonwood Pass Road): From US-24 in Buena Vista, turn west at the stop light onto Main Street, which becomes County Road 306 as it leaves the city limits. Travel approximately 9.5 miles west from Buena Vista on County Road 306 to Avalanche Trailhead. The CT is marked where it crosses the trailhead area.

Chalk Creek Trailhead: See Segment 14.

Supplies, Services, and Accommodations

Located in the Arkansas Valley, the town of Buena Vista, as might be gathered by its Spanish name, offers stunning views of the Mosquito Range and the towering Sawatch Mountains. Buena Vista is an ideal resupply point for long-distance trekkers because the CT through here is approximately halfway between Denver and Durango. The town has grocery and backpacking stores and overnight accommodations. The most direct way to reach Buena Vista from the CT is to follow County Road 306 for approximately 9 miles east from the Avalanche Trailhead (see Segment 12).

Maps

CT Series: Maps 12 and 13 (see pages 126-127 and 134-135).
USFS: San Isabel National Forest.
USGS Quadrangles: Buena Vista West, Mount Yale, Mount Antero.

Trail Description

This segment of the CT begins approximately 0.1 mile west of the trail access point at the end of Segment 12. Parking here is limited and usually crowded with vehicles of people climbing Mount Yale.

Proceed south from the road, cross North Cottonwood Creek, and sign in at the register. Ascend in a lodgepole pine forest on the north side of Silver Creek, passing outcrops of banded Precambrian metamorphic rock. Continue to a valley meadow, where a large beaver pond backs up Silver Creek at mile 2.2 (11,040). Campers here will be bedding down in the shadow of Mount Yale, which is visible to the southwest. Continue 0.2 mile up the valley and cross to the creek's south side. Ascend the north slope of Mount Yale's eastern ridge, passing through a spruce-fir forest, and enter the Collegiate Peaks Wilderness. Top the saddle between Silver Creek and Middle Cottonwood Creek at mile 3.3 (11,880). From this point, Mount Yale is a steep climb west along a ridge with some rock scrambling along the way. The spruce trees at the saddle are sparse enough to allow a striking and rarely seen view of Mount Princeton and its long, elevated western ridge.

Descend south from the pass through a stately bristlecone pine forest. There is a good campsite on flat ground, situated in a lodgepole pine forest at mile 4.8 (10,640). From there, Hughes Creek is just a short walk down into the gully west. Curve to the left into a dry ravine at mile 5.3 (10,560) and continue descending through a sparse limber pine and Douglas fir forest that allows a view up the valley of Middle Cottonwood Creek. In another 0.4 mile you will drop to an area too exposed and dry for these trees to survive. Here, mountain mahogany clings tenuously to rocky hillside. Notice also the avalanche chutes across the valley on the side of Sheep Mountain.

Exit the wilderness area at mile 6.3 (9,400) and bear to the right, off the barricaded old trail and onto a newer section of tread. After the trail register in 700 feet, go right (west) a short distance beyond on an intersecting old road. Bear left (southwest) off the old road to the Avalanche Trailhead parking area at mile 6.6 (9,360). Continue south-southwest across the large parking area and pick up the trail on the opposite side. In a few steps, the trail reorients east for 200 feet, paralleling County Road 306, before it crosses to the south side of the paved road and continues another 200 feet down an obscure side road. This leads to an informal car camping area on the north shore of Middle Cottonwood Creek. Head to the left here, toward the east end of the car camping area, and pick up the CT, which parallels the creek before crossing it on a bridge at mile 6.8 (9,320). The trail is carved deeply into the side of the steep, south bank of Middle Cottonwood Creek and fireweed grows profusely in the disturbed soil.

Continue east 200 feet beyond the bridge crossing and enter the bottom of an avalanche chute, viewed earlier from the opposite side of the valley. Notice how the aspen have all been knocked down in the direction of the avalanche's

flow. At this point you will also notice a somewhat obscure and overgrown trail that proceeds west above and parallel to the CT and the creek. This old trail was the original route through here, but the CT was rerouted after an avalanche wiped out the trail and a bridge west of the present creek crossing.

The trail ascends and then traverses the north slope of Sheep Mountain, providing views of Rainbow Lake through a cool forest. Descend gradually to the eastern foot of Sheep Mountain, just west of the confluence of South and Middle Cottonwood creeks, where the trail opens up into a sunnier and less dense forest. Fork to the left where the trail splits near the entrance to private property at mile 8.9 (9,000). Continue 400 feet downhill and cross to the east side of South Cottonwood Creek Road (County Road 344). Follow a side road that leads first to an informal car camping site and then to a bridge across South Cottonwood Creek. Turn left immediately after the bridge and parallel the creek downstream. The trail slowly pulls away from the creek and crosses a dirt road at mile 9.6 (8,880), then maneuvers through a series of switchbacks that take you out of the valley.

Cross an old road at mile 10.8 (9,440). About 350 feet beyond, turn right (south) onto another old road. Go uphill through an aspen forest another 350 feet, then fork to the left where the road splits. Proceed another 350 feet past the fork and then leave the old road where the trail resumes to the left (north-north-east) at mile 11.0 (9,560). The trail continues its ascent to a point slightly above the saddle west of Bald Mountain at mile 11.6 (9,880) and then begins a long traverse bearing generally southeast, dipping in and out of several drainages. Cross the meager flow of upper Silver Prince Creek at mile 13.3 (9,840) and continue a half mile further to the trickle in Maxwell Creek.

The trail descends gradually through a varied forest of fir, pine, and aspen to a jeep road crossing and, 0.1 mile beyond, a comfortable log bridge across Dry Creek at mile 15.5 (9,600). This creek, contrary to its name, usually has a good, swift flow. Continue on the CT to a switchback on FS-322 at mile 16.7 (9,480). An information board here explains the route the CT will follow on county roads for the next 5.5 miles.

Descend at left for 0.9 mile on the rough dirt road. Where FS-322 splits, continue straight ahead (east), avoiding the right fork which leads to private property. The Forest Service road becomes County Road 322 approximately 0.2 mile beyond. Follow the graveled county road 0.6 mile east to where it makes a bend to the left (north). Continue in a north-northeast direction on this road approximately 0.2 mile to black-topped County Road 321. Follow this road south, east, west then south again approximately 1.3 miles as it makes a winding descent to the intersection with County Road 162 at mile 19.7 (8,160). For those requiring a pause to soak their bones before continuing, Mount Princeton Hot Springs is immediately south across the road.

Proceed 1.4 miles west and southwest on paved County Road 162, then veer to the left (west-southwest) onto County Road 291. Continue 1.1 miles down this quiet, tree-lined road to the trailhead parking area on Chalk Creek. This segment ends here at mile 22.2 (8,360), where the trail resumes its southerly course at the footbridge over the creek.

Notes

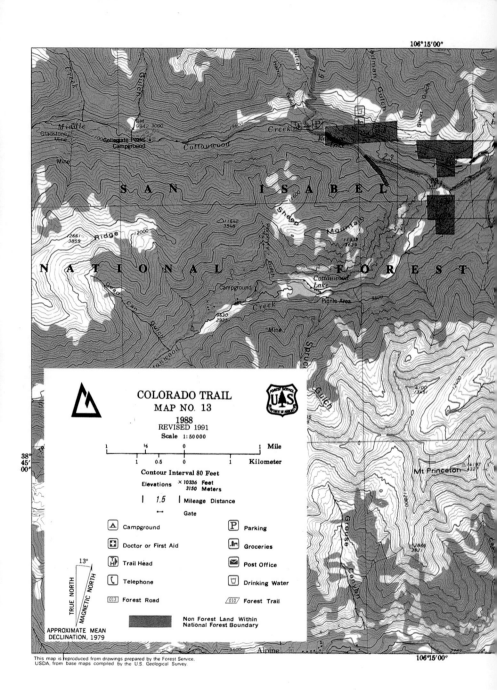

COLORADO TRAIL

MAP NO. 13

1988
REVISED 1991

Scale 1:50 000

Mile

Kilometer

Contour Interval 80 Feet

Elevations × 10336 Feet
3150 Meters

1.5 Mileage Distance

Gate

Campground

Doctor or First Aid

Trail Head

Telephone

Forest Road

Parking

Groceries

Post Office

Drinking Water

Forest Trail

Non Forest Land Within
National Forest Boundary

TRUE NORTH
MAGNETIC NORTH
13°

APPROXIMATE MEAN
DECLINATION, 1979

This map is reproduced from drawings prepared by the Forest Service,
USDA, from base maps compiled by the U.S. Geological Survey.

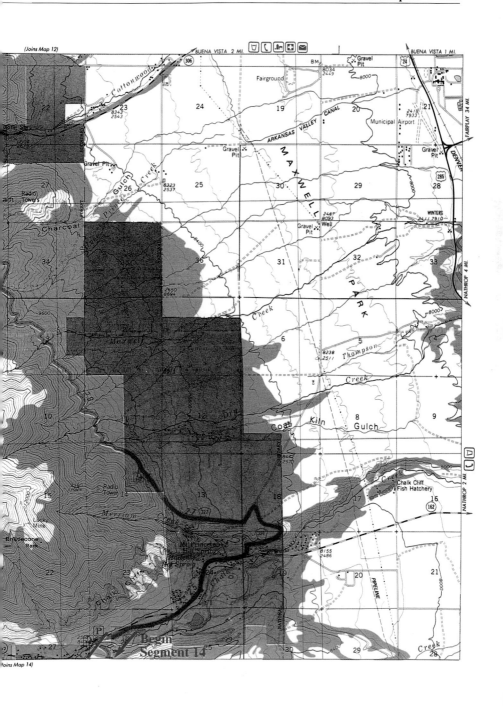

Mounts Etna, Taylor, Tabeguache (14,155'), and Shavano (14,225')

⚠ SEGMENT 14   20.0 Miles

Chalk Creek to US Highway 50   **+ 3,100 Feet Elevation Gain**

Location	Mileage	From Denver	Elevation
Chalk Creek Trailhead	0.0	226.3	8,360
Eddy Creek	2.2		9,000
Browns Creek Trail	6.4		9,600
Mount Shavano Trail	12.7		9,880
Angel of Shavano Trailhead	14.9		9,160
Lost Creek	17.8		9,400
US Highway 50	20.0	246.3	8,840

CT Series Maps 13, 14, & 15 (see pages 134-135, 142-143, & 148-149).

The southernmost peaks of the Sawatch Range honor the memory of the once-mighty Ute Indian nation. Starting at Chalk Creek, the trail rounds the eastern flank of 14,269-foot Mount Antero, which is named after a Ute chief of the Utah-based Unitah band. The trail then continues south to 14,229-foot Mount Shavano, named for a medicine man and chief of the Ute Tabeguache band. On the southern horizon rise Mount Ouray and Chipeta Mountain. These landmarks are named for the last great Ute chief, a diplomatic spokesman for the Ute nation, and his wife, Chipeta.

Mount Antero and its neighbor to the south, 13,667-foot Mount White, are popular with the rockhounding crowd. Gemologists have been flocking to the peaks ever since Nathaniel Wannemaker discovered aquamarine near the 14,000-foot-level on Mount Antero in the 1880s. The crest of the mountain was designated as Mount Antero Mineral Park in 1949. The bronze plaque set on that date still greets mountain climbers just below the summit.

As with previous segments in the Sawatch, this section subjects hikers to a fair amount of elevation gain, but it also has long stretches of mostly level walking. Your efforts are rewarded with grand panoramas of the lower Arkansas Valley and the northern Sangre de Cristo Range. Backpackers will find many potential campsites, as well as gushing streams to satisfy thirsts produced by the warmer temperatures of the lower elevations. A good side trail leads to Mount Shavano.

Trailhead/Access Points

Chalk Creek Trailhead: Travel south from Buena Vista on US-285 to Nathrop. Go right (west) onto County Road 162. Proceed approximately 6 miles and bear to the left on County Road 291. Continue up the tree-lined dirt road 1.1 miles to the trailhead parking area near the footbridge over Chalk Creek.

Browns Creek Trailhead: Travel south from Nathrop on US-285. Go right (west) on County Road 270 and proceed 1.5 miles up this dirt road. Continue straight ahead on County Road 272 as County Road 270 bears to the right. Drive ahead on County Road 272 approximately 2 miles and bear to the left (south) at an intersection. From this intersection it is 1.6 miles further south on County Road 272 to Browns Creek Trailhead. From here, follow the trail west 1.4 miles to where it joins up with the CT.

Angel of Shavano Trailhead: From the intersection of US-285 and US-50 at Poncha Springs, go west approximately 6 miles on US-50 to County Road 240 (North Fork South Arkansas River Road). Go right (north) on County Road 240 and proceed along the dirt road 3.8 miles to the trailhead parking area opposite Angel of Shavano Campground.

US-50 Trail Access: See Segment 15.

Supplies, Services, and Accommodations

Available in Salida.

Maps

CT Series: Maps 13, 14, and 15 (see pages 134-135, 142-143, and 148-149).
USFS: San Isabel National Forest.
USGS Quadrangles: Mount Antero, Maysville.

SALIDA SERVICES — Distance from Trail: 13 miles

Bank	Bank One	146 G St.	(719) 539-3501
Bus	Greyhound	731 Blake	(719) 539-7474
Dining	Country Bounty	413 W. Hwy 50	(719) 539-3546
	Laughing Ladies	128 W. First	(719) 539-6209
Gear	Headwaters Outdoor	228 North F St.	(719) 539-4506
Groceries	Safeway	323 G St.	(719) 539-3513
	Don's Food Town	248 W. Hwy 50	(719) 539-7500
Information	Chamber of Commerce	406 W. Rainbow Blvd.	(719) 539-2068
Laundry	Band Box	119 F St.	(719) 539-2426
Lodging	Super 8	525 W. Hwy 50	(719) 539-6689
	Budget Lodge	1146 E. Hwy 50	(719) 539-6695
Medical	Regional Medical Center	1st & B Streets	(719) 539-6661
Post Office	Salida Post Office	310 D St.	(719) 539-2548
Showers	Salida Hot Springs	410 W. Hwy 50	(719) 539-6738

Trail Description

Hikers going north from this trailhead point should note that a temporary detour will have them walking on county roads for the next 5.2 miles. From the bridge over Chalk Creek at the trailhead parking area, the trail resumes for southbounders and begins a gradual ascent out of the broad valley. Just up from the stream, a side trail branches left to Bootleg Campsite. Surrounded by private property, this little oasis is thoughtfully provided by the Forest Service for back-packers who might otherwise have difficulty finding a place to camp.

The CT continues 0.4 mile southeast beyond the creek and joins up with an old road. Proceed a few steps up the road and join up with County Road 290, which is the abandoned grade of the DSP&P Railroad. Go right (west) on County Road 290 for just a hundred feet and notice that the trail resumes again to the left on the south side of the road. Follow the trail to a fork at mile 0.7 (8680). Go left to stay on the CT; the right fork continues to an old quarry. The delicate trickle of a small stream can be heard below as you ascend the trail, which clings to the steep side of a ravine. Curve to the left (east) at mile 0.9 (8,840) and enter a small, grassy side canyon that makes a good campsite if the little stream mentioned above is still flowing. Aspen, fir, and spruce grow on the cooler north-facing slope of the canyon, while the sunny, south-facing slope supports piñon pine and mountain mahogany.

Continue east to the head of the canyon and maneuver through a series of gravelly switchbacks. Top the sandy saddle above the canyon at mile 1.3 (9,200) and bear left (northeast) along the ridge line, ascending the sandy trail. In 0.1 mile, you top out on a knoll. Take a few minutes to admire this seldom-seen view of the Chalk Cliffs to the north. Descend from the knoll through two switchbacks, then assume an easterly heading and enter a small, elevated mead-ow. As the trail enters a grouping of aspen, it appears to be funneling down a defined gully. Just beyond the aspen grove, the trail bears to the right and almost imperceptibly pulls away from the drainage of the small gully. Before you know it, you are well above the gully and then descending to an arid bench of piñon and mountain mahogany well above the surrounding country to the east. At mile 2.2 (9,000), orient south and drop steeply on a rocky trail to the broad and usually dry Eddy Creek drainage. Go left (southeast) at a fork in a flat grassy area 0.1 mile beyond, which takes you to the east side of a small fenced-in test plot, an area where the Forest Service is determining the effects of grazing and non-grazing on the forest ecosystem.

For the next several miles, the trail stays at or near 9,000 feet and bears to the south to southeast. This section of trail was rerouted in 1989 to avoid an excessively steep and eroded section further west. It crosses a recently burned area between Eddy Creek and Raspberry Gulch, which provides unparalleled vistas north to Chalk Cliffs and east to the lower Arkansas Valley. Keep in mind that this area is the lowest section of the CT in the Arkansas Valley and afternoon temperatures under skies with no shade can be extremely uncomfortable. There are no reliable water sources from Chalk Creek 7 miles to Browns Creek.

From the test plot, continue in a southerly direction, crossing Eddy Creek road and passing through the burn area. At mile 4.0 (8,960), the trail descends a side hill and crosses Raspberry Gulch Road (County Road 273). Beyond Raspberry Gulch Road, there are few signs of the burn and the trail stays in a sunny area of scattered ponderosa pine. At mile 4.7 (9,000), just after crossing an eroded jeep road, the trail drops into a deep and wide but normally dry gully. In the lowest section of this drainage, the trail adopts an old section of road for only a few hundred feet. Rise to the opposite side of the gully into another opening of scattered ponderosa pine, and continue 0.2 mile to the first in a series of three poorly built switchbacks. Here, the trail begins a long ascent bearing generally west to southwest. Where the trail descends slightly and then orients briefly south at mile 5.6 (9,400), it picks up the route of an old mine road, which is not apparent except for the fact that you now have a wider, and correspondingly more eroded, tread. Just 0.2 mile beyond, thoughtful trail-builders have constructed a detour around a particularly rough and steep section in the old road.

The CT becomes rocky and steep just before a confusing intersection at mile 6.2 (9,720). You want to continue on the CT here to the left (southeast then south), avoiding the forks to the right (north) and straight ahead (south to southwest). Just above the ponds on Little Browns Creek at mile 6.4 (9,600) you will join up with the Browns Creek Trail, up from the Browns Creek Trailhead. Ascend southwest past an old fork to the left, which leads to some beaver ponds, and continue to a trail junction at 6.6 (9,640), where the Browns Creek Trail continues ahead to Browns Lake. The CT goes left at this junction and continues 400 feet to Little Browns Creek. In another 600 feet, you will cross Browns Creek.

Continue on the wide trail 700 feet past Browns Creek to another trail intersection. Go straight ahead here (south) and avoid the fork leading downhill to the left. Ascend slightly and then traverse through a lodgepole pine forest to Fourmile Creek at mile 8.8 (9,680). The trail grazes a jeep road and continues to Sand Creek at mile 10.0 (9,600).

Ascend to a gravelly ridge at mile 11.1 (10,160), then drop down into a damp gully 0.4 mile beyond. The trail then climbs to another high point, where Mount Ouray and Chipeta Mountain can be seen to the south through the fir-lodgepole pine forest. Descend to Squaw Creek at mile 12.2 (9,760) and continue 0.2 mile farther to where the CT joins a jeep road and continues south. The Mount Shavano Trail climbs to the right at mile 12.7 (9,880). This comfortable side trail ascends to within 800 vertical feet of 14,229-foot Mount Shavano. About 0.2 mile beyond the intersection with the Mount Shavano Trail, you will cross a cattle guard and leave the jeep road as it descends to the left. Notice that a rather obscure trail continues ahead (south-southwest) through a grassy meadow ringed with aspen. Pick up an obvious trail in 400 feet on the opposite side of the meadow and cross a jeep road at mile 13.2 (9,800). About 0.4 mile beyond, pass through a meadow that is often trampled by cattle. The trail might be a little hard to spot here but becomes easier to follow once it reenters the aspen. Not long after reentering the forest, the CT crosses two old roads and descends into a lodgepole pine forest.

Pass through a gate and ascend slightly to a ridge at mile 14.2 (9,640), where the forest stops abruptly. Descend a sunny slope and reenter the trees just before the Angel of Shavano Trailhead parking area on the north side of County Road 240 at mile 14.9 (9160). Continue northwest on the road, toward the entrance of Angel of Shavano Campground. The trail resumes to the left just beyond the campground sign and continues 800 feet to the footbridge over the fast-flowing North Fork. Steer through several switchbacks and ascend to a lodgepole pine forested ridgetop at mile 16.5 (9,760). The trail then descends 0.3 mile in a pronounced ravine, after which it bends to the right and begins a traverse. Join up with a more obscure trail at mile 17.0 (9,600) and continue 600 feet to another obscure trail junction. Continue straight ahead on the CT here. The trail continues around the northwest side of Dry Lake, an isolated pond with no inlet or outlet.

Continue west beyond the pond, staying on the well-blazed main trail and avoiding the several less noticeable spurs that split off to either side. Beyond mile 17.5 (9,560), the trail has been obscured by a logged and burned area. Notice how aspen are coming up to take the place of the destroyed lodgepole pine forest. Bear generally south along the east edge of the burned forest, following a set of jeep tracks. Approach the southern edge of the burned area in 0.1 mile, where the jeep tracks end at an intersection of three dirt roads that lead east, west, and south. Follow an indistinct route that proceeds west-southwest between the roads leading west and south. Follow this obscure spur 150 feet, to a sharp left back onto the CT in a healthy forest.

Descend to Lost Creek at mile 17.8 (9,400) and cross a jeep road just west of the creek. Proceed south and west to a small open area at mile 18.8 (9,360). The sometimes faint trail proceeds 0.1 mile around the north and west perimeter of this open area and then crosses a dirt road. Descend to Cree Creek at mile 19.3 (9,200). Backpackers should note that this is the last decent camping opportunity north of US-50. The trail ascends south from Cree Creek to the edge of the lodgepole pine forest, where the South Arkansas Valley and US-50 come into view. Continue south underneath a power line tower and descend an exposed, south-facing slope on a rocky old road. Cross the abandoned D&RG Railroad grade at mile 19.9 (8,880), then enter a ponderosa pine forest and continue 450 feet to US-50. This trail segment ends here on the highway at mile 20.0 (8,840).

Notes

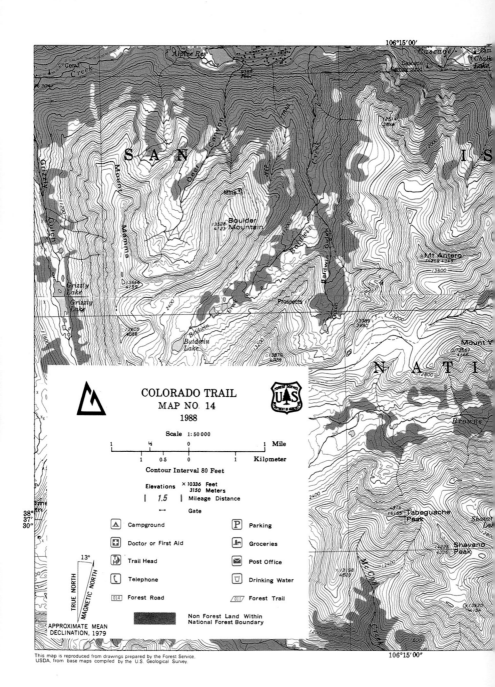

COLORADO TRAIL
MAP NO. 14
1988

Scale 1:50 000

1   ½   0   1 Mile
1   0.5   0   1 Kilometer

Contour Interval 80 Feet

Elevations × 10336 Feet
            3150 Meters

| 1.5 | Mileage Distance

←→   Gate

△ Campground   P Parking

✚ Doctor or First Aid   Groceries

Trail Head   Post Office

Telephone   Drinking Water

014 Forest Road   017 Forest Trail

                        Non Forest Land Within
                        National Forest Boundary

TRUE NORTH   MAGNETIC NORTH
13°
APPROXIMATE MEAN
DECLINATION, 1979

This map is reproduced from drawings prepared by the Forest Service.
USDA, from base maps compiled by the U.S. Geological Survey.

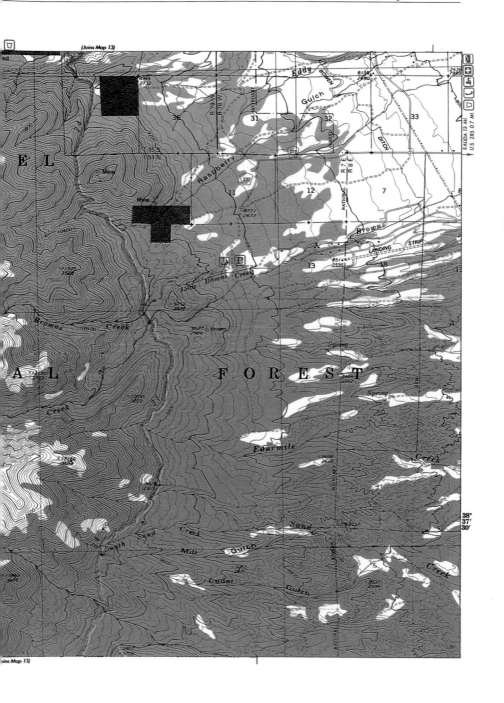

Evening light on Mount Ouray (13,972'), along the Continental Divide

◭ SEGMENT 15   14.0 Miles

US Highway 50 to Marshall Pass   **+ 3,340 Feet Elevation Gain**

Location	Mileage	From Denver	Elevation
US Highway 50	0.0	246.3	8,840
South Fooses Creek Trailhead	2.9		9,560
Continental Divide	8.5		11,920
Marshall Pass	14.0	260.3	10,880

CT Series Maps 15 & 16 (see pages 148-149 & 150-151).

The CT mounts the Continental Divide in this segment and parallels its crest for the next 130 miles, linking up with the Continental Divide Trail. Long-distance hikers will want to make sure they are well supplied before progressing south of US-50. The next supply point is Creede, nearly a hundred miles away. The towns of Saguache and Gunnison can be accessed from segments 16 and 17, although they are considerable distances from the trail.

From the head of South Fooses Creek to Marshall Pass, the CT traverses the first portion of this high-altitude route, with views of the Cochetopa Hills and the Gunnison Basin. Just before the trail drops down to Marshall Pass, it skirts the divide's western ridge, which connects 13,971-foot Mount Ouray and 12,850-foot Chipeta Mountain. The area around Marshall Pass marks the southernmost point of the Sawatch Range, and it is also the junction of three major mountain ranges: the Sawatch to the north, the Sangre de Cristo to the southeast, and the Cochetopa Hills to the southwest.

The rocks in the Mount Ouray area are ancient sedimentary and metamorphic Precambrian, mostly derived from volcanoes. Interestingly, the 1.7-billion-year-old volcanic rocks underlie adjacent 30-million-year-old volcanic rocks southwest of Marshall Pass in the next trail segment.

Trailhead/Access Points

US-50 South Fooses Creek Trailhead: From the intersection of US-285 and US-50 at Poncha Springs, drive west approximately 9 miles on US-50 to Fooses Creek Road (County Road 225). The CT crosses the highway here and follows Fooses Creek Road, which continues southwest from US-50. If you choose to drive up the road, a high-clearance vehicle is recommended. It is 2.9 miles up the rough road to the trail access point on South Fooses Creek. Be aware that the first 0.7 mile is across private property. Take the left fork 0.1 mile in from the highway, and left again at junctions located at miles 1.7, 2.0, and 2.8. The last will take you to the obscure trail access point on South Fooses Creek. There are no facilities here.

Marshall Pass Trail Access: See Segment 16.

Supplies, Services, and Accommodations

Garfield is located approximately 3 miles west of the crossing on US-50. A small general store here has basic items. Salida is about 13 miles east of the CT crossing on US-50. The town has hardware and sporting goods stores, a grocery, and overnight accommodations (see Segment 14). Poncha Springs is located approximately 9 miles east of the CT crossing on US-50. A general store here provides the basics.

Maps

CT Series: Maps 15 and 16 (see pages 148-149 and 150-151).
USFS: San Isabel National Forest, Gunnison National Forest.
USGS Quadrangles: Maysville, Garfield, Pahlone Peak, Mount Ouray.

Trail Description

Starting on US-50 just east of Garfield, follow Fooses Creek Road 2.9 miles to the trail access point. The road crosses private property for the first 0.7 mile. Fork left at 0.1 mile in from the highway, and left again at junctions located at

GARFIELD SERVICES — Distance from Trail: 3 miles

Bank	None		
Bus	None		
Dining	Monarch Lodge & Rest.	Hwy 50	(800) 322-3668
	Yukon Deli & Pub	22455 W. Hwy 50	(719) 539-4065
Gear	Monarch General Store	22455 W. Hwy 50	(719) 539-4065
Groceries	Monarch General Store	22455 W. Hwy 50	(719) 539-4065
Information	None		
Laundry	None		
Lodging	Monarch Mtn. Lodge	Hwy 50	(800) 322-3668
Medical	Nearest in Salida		(719) 539-6661
Post Office	Monarch Mtn. Lodge	Hwy 50	(800) 322-3668
Showers	None		

miles 1.7, 2.0, and 2.8. The trail resumes at mile 2.9 (9,560) where it crosses Fooses Creek. Continue up South Fooses Creek; blue diamonds here mark cross-country ski routes.

Cross over to the east side of South Fooses Creek at mile 3.4 (9,720) and ascend through a lodgepole pine forest. After fording the creek to the west side at mile 4.3 (9,840), continue 0.4 mile to a section of turnpike tread constructed specifically to keep your feet dry in marshy terrain, the result of very labor-intensive trail work.

Cross to the east bank of South Fooses Creek at mile 5.0 (10,160). Continue to a meadow in the shadow of Mount Peck and negotiate a quick double switchback, which helps ease the ascent, at mile 6.2 (10,520). Enter another grassy area 0.4 mile beyond and begin to rise higher on the mountainside. The trail here is rough and rocky at times. As the CT gains elevation, it crosses several streamlets that form the headwaters of South Fooses Creek.

At mile 8.3 (11,600) the trail enters the tundra, where a receding blanket of snow in early summer reveals a field of marsh marigolds. Top out on the Continental Divide at mile 8.5 (11,920). Angle left (southeast), following the sign that points the way to Marshall Pass. Be sure to look closely for tiny alpine forget-me-nots that carpet the gravely ridge. The trail, although obscure for several hundred feet, soon resumes and traverses the southwest slope of Point 12,195, then continues due south on the divide ridge, passing impressive cairns that have been constructed from white quartz. Mount Ouray and Chipeta Mountain can be viewed close-up from here, and farther to the south rises 13,269-foot Antora Peak.

The CT descends through a spruce forest, then opens into a small meadow on the divide at the head of Green Creek at mile 10.1 (11,480). The trail through this meadow is somewhat overgrown with grass. A small lean-to at the edge of the trees might provide shelter from afternoon showers. For those contemplating an overnight stay, the headwaters of Green Creek are less than a 0.3-mile walk from here.

The CT reenters the trees on the east side of the meadow, indicated by a sign for East Agate Creek. Continue south and into tundra at mile 10.4 (11,480).

The trail crosses a small spring here, then passes into a ghost forest. The tundra vegetation is thick and colorful, contrasting sharply with the gray, rocky slopes of Mount Ouray to the east.

The Agate Creek Trail descends to the right at mile 11.2 (11,720). Just beyond, the CT enters a spruce forest and begins a gradual descent. The trail crosses a rockslide in 0.3 mile, where thistles and columbine grow out of the jumbled, rocky terrain. Continue past a small stream and pick up a jeep road (FS-243.2G) at mile 12.6 (11,400). From the site of an old quarry, this road descends south past a miner's cabin and a spring that gurgles out of a pipe. Cross a cattle guard at mile 13.4 (11,000) and continue 0.4 mile through two switchbacks down to the Marshall Pass Road. Ascend 0.2 mile south on the road to the deep roadway cut that is the summit of the pass and the end of this segment at mile 14.0 (10,880). The CT leaves the main pass road just before the cut, and continues south on a side road.

Notes

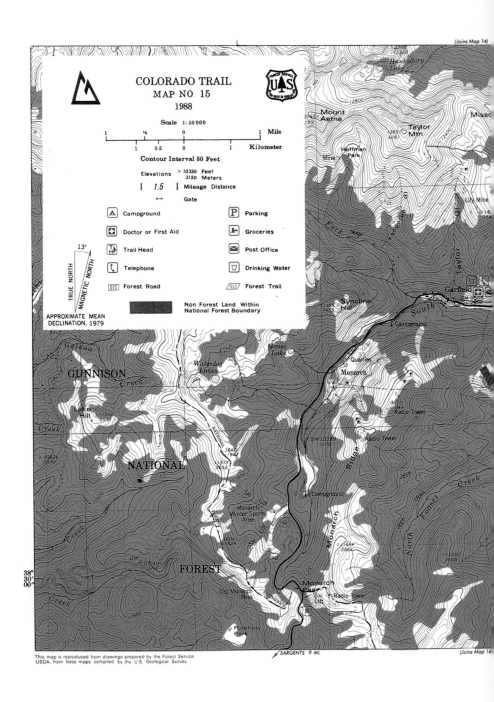

COLORADO TRAIL
MAP NO. 15
1988

Scale 1:50 000

Contour Interval 80 Feet

Elevations × 10336′ Feet
3150 Meters

| 1.5 | Mileage Distance

Gate

△ Campground   P Parking

Doctor or First Aid   Groceries

Trail Head   Post Office

Telephone   Drinking Water

015 Forest Road   012 Forest Trail

Non Forest Land Within
National Forest Boundary

13°
TRUE NORTH
MAGNETIC NORTH
APPROXIMATE MEAN
DECLINATION, 1979

This map is reproduced from drawings prepared by the Forest Service.
USDA, from base maps compiled by the U.S. Geological Survey.

SARGENTS 9 MI.

(Joins Map 16)

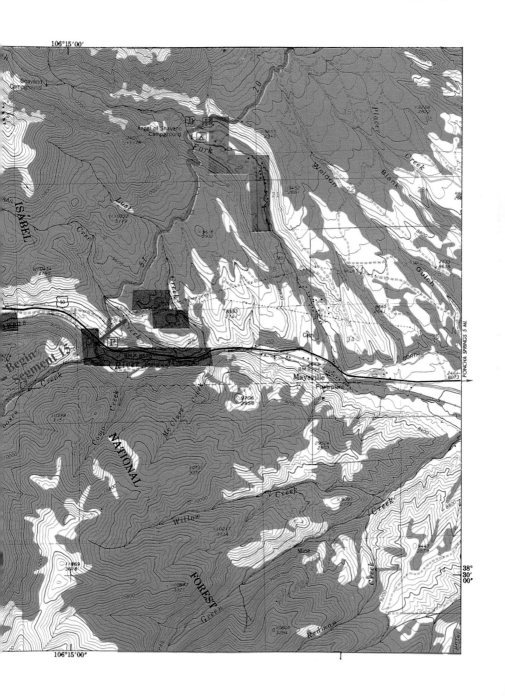

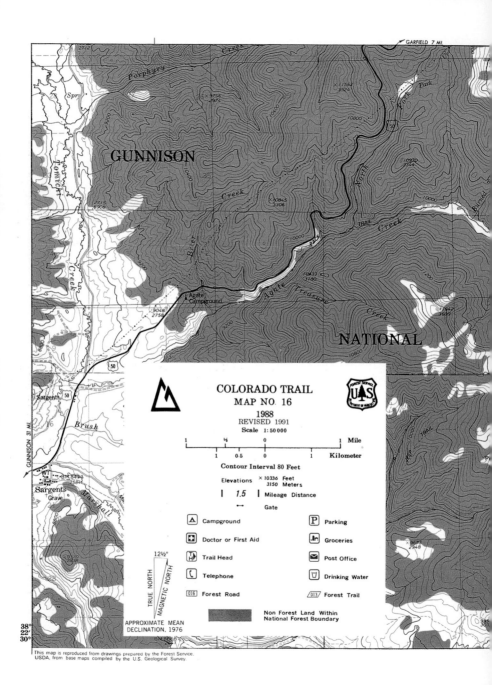

GARFIELD 7 MI.

GUNNISON

NATIONAL

COLORADO TRAIL
MAP NO. 16
1988
REVISED 1991
Scale 1:50000

1 ——— ½ ——— 0 ——————— 1 Mile
1 ——— 0.5 ——— 0 ——————— 1 Kilometer

Contour Interval 80 Feet

Elevations × 10336 Feet
            3150 Meters

| 1.5 | Mileage Distance

↔ Gate

△ Campground   P Parking

✦ Doctor or First Aid 🛒 Groceries

🚶 Trail Head   ✉ Post Office

📞 Telephone   🚰 Drinking Water

016 Forest Road   013 Forest Trail

▇▇▇ Non Forest Land Within
     National Forest Boundary

12½°
TRUE NORTH MAGNETIC NORTH

APPROXIMATE MEAN
DECLINATION, 1976

This map is reproduced from drawings prepared by the Forest Service,
USDA, from base maps compiled by the U.S. Geological Survey.

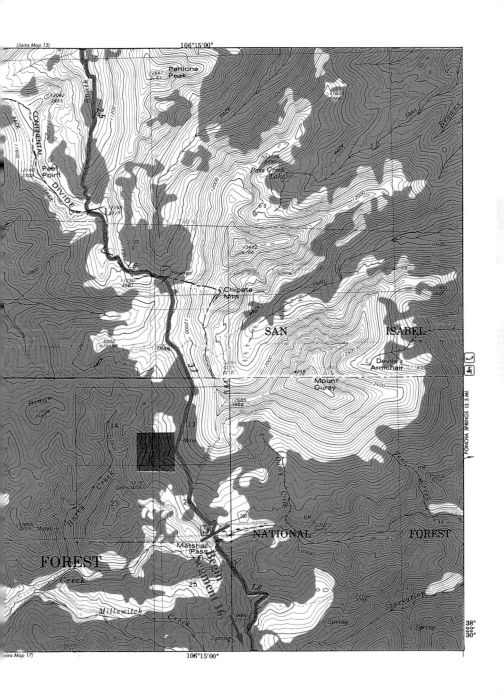

(Joins Map 15)

106°15'00"

CONTINENTAL DIVIDE

Pahlone Peak

PACK

Pass Creek Lake

Peel Point

Shelter

Chipeta Mtn

TRAIL

SAN

ISABEL

PACK

Devils Armchair

Mount Ouray

Ridge

14   13

Mine

Florey Creek

23

26

Marshall Pass

FOREST

NATIONAL

FOREST

Creek

Bean

Begin Segment 16

25

1.8

Millswitch

Creek

Spring

Spring

Spring

PONCHA SPRINGS 13.5 MI.

38° 22' 30"

(Joins Map 17)

106°15'00"

Mount Ouray from Windy Peak (11,885'), Rio Grande National Forest

◭ SEGMENT 16   14.5 Miles

Marshall Pass to Sargents Mesa   **+ 2,840 Feet Elevation Gain**

Location	Mileage	From Denver	Elevation
Marshall Pass	0.0	260.3	10,880
Point 11,862	4.6		11,560
Tank Seven Creek	11.1		10,280
Sargents Mesa	14.5	274.8	11,600

CT Series Maps 16 & 17 (see pages 150-151 & 156-157).

Before making the transition to the dramatic scenery of the San Juans, the CT continues south and southwest from Marshall Pass through the more gentle Cochetopa Hills, providing glimpses of the La Garita Mountains ahead and the Sawatch Range behind. This segment enters Tertiary Age lava flows, volcanic tuffs and breccias of Colorado's southwestern mountains.

Because the trail remains near the crest of the Continental Divide, water can be a concern. The only place you will find running water along this segment is where the trail briefly parallels Tank Seven Creek. It is also feasible to detour into upper Silver Creek, which is closer to Marshall Pass, in order to resupply.

Confusion in the trail route caused by logging operations just south of Marshall Pass and in the vicinity of Cameron Park have been largely eliminated by reroutes and better trail identification. However, you may still encounter some logging activity as well as portions of the trail that might be faint or otherwise difficult to follow. It would be wise to keep a map and compass handy to confirm your location.

The lands west of the divide here made up part of the huge Ute Indian Reservation of 1865, which was moved farther west three years later. Marshall Pass was discovered in 1873 when a bad toothache persuaded Lieutenant William Marshall of the Wheeler Survey to take a short cut from Silverton to the dentist in Denver. Otto Mears built a toll road over the pass and later sold it to the D&RG Railroad. Rails were laid over Marshall Pass in 1881 to connect the mineral-rich Gunnison area to the Eastern Slope.

The Rainbow Trail links up with the CT on the Continental Divide at the head of Silver Creek. This 100-mile trail traverses the east side of the Sangre de Cristo Range from this point southeast to Music Pass, at the head of Sand Creek just north of Great Sand Dunes National Monument. Along the way, there are numerous side trails that lead to isolated lakes and mountaintops within the Sangres. Needless to say, a Rainbow Trail detour would offer a unique diversion. For details about the trail, contact the Salida Ranger District of the U.S. Forest Service.

Trailhead/Access Points

Marshall Pass Trail Access: Travel approximately 5 miles south of Poncha Springs on US-285 and turn right (west) at the Marshall Pass and O'Haver Lake Campground turnoff. Proceed on County Roads 200 and 202 for 13.1 miles to the roadway cut at the top of the pass. The CT bends to the left here, off of the main road and south on a logging road. The trail heading north leaves the pass road 0.2 mile before the roadway cut at the top of the pass, following FS-243.2G.

Sargents Mesa Trail Access (FS-855): See Segment 17.

Supplies, Services, and Accommodations

No convenient supply points. The closest supply point, which is a considerable distance, is the town of Saguache, 33 miles off the trail.

SAGUACHE SERVICES — Distance from Trail: 33 miles

Bank	Bank One	400 4th	(719) 655-2555
Bus	None		
Dining	Dinner Bell	Hwy 285	(719) 655-9935
	The Oasis	Hwy 285	(719) 655-9942
Gear	None		
Groceries	Q Foods	610 Gunnison Ave.	(719) 655-2885
Information	None		
Laundry	Shay's	Hwy 285 & San Juan	(719) 655-2832
Lodging	Saguache Creek Lodging	21495 S. Hwy 285	(719) 655-2264
	Hillside Motel	440 Gunnison Ave.	(719) 655-2524
Medical	Saguache Clinic	405 Denver Ave.	(719) 655-2531
Post Office	Saguache Post Office	350 Denver Ave.	(719) 655-2511
Showers	None		

Maps

CT Series: Maps 16 and 17 (see pages 150-151 and 156-157).
USFS: San Isabel National Forest, Gunnison National Forest,
Rio Grande National Forest.
USGS Quadrangles: Mount Ouray, Bonanza, Chester, Sargents Mesa.

Trail Description

From the east side of the roadway cut at the top of Marshall Pass, the CT bears to the left (south-southeast) temporarily following a side road (FS-203). Avoid the left fork at 300 feet; this descends east into Poncha and Starvation creeks. Continue on the side road another 200 feet, then go left (south-southeast) on a jeep track that has been closed to vehicles and ascend a grassy hill. In 700 feet the trail leaves the jeep track to the right (south) and climbs to a pleasant ridge on the Continental Divide with views east to the Sangre de Cristo Range and west to the Gunnison Basin. From here the trail rambles along the divide, then briefly joins an old logging road as it ascends a ridge jutting east of the divide. There is a switchback to the right (west) at mile 1.2 (11,200), which is notable because you do not want to continue straight ahead on the more obscure trail.

The CT follows mostly on or near the top of the broad divide ridge in and out of the forest to mile 2.5 (11,160), where it intersects an old logging road at a Forest Service directional sign. Bear left (south) here, ascending the old road for about 0.4 mile until it levels out and leaves the logging area behind. The Rainbow and Silver Creek trails descend to the left at mile 3.6 (11,240). If you need water, the head of the Silver Creek is only a short hike down the valley, which also makes a nice camping spot at the foot of Antora Peak. The Silver Creek Trail ends in a few miles while the Rainbow Trail continues along the east flank of the Sangre de Cristo Range.

From the Silver Creek-Rainbow Trail junction, the CT ascends an old jeep track south-southwest then west through a meadow of blue flax. As you approach the trees ahead, be on the lookout for the trail to leave the jeep track at right (west-northwest). The CT then traverses west on the north side of Point

11,862 (which is about 0.8 mile east-southeast of Windy Peak) at about the 11,600-foot level. At mile 4.6 (11,560), you pass through a gate west-northwest of Point 11,862. This marks the Continental Divide and the boundary between the Gunnison and Rio Grande national forests. Continue southwest about 100 feet and join another jeep track that descends to the saddle between Point 11,862 and Windy Peak. From the saddle, continue southwest on the CT about 0.4 mile, then look for an important, although somewhat inconspicuous, sharp right (north) turn that takes you up Windy Peak's forested south ridge to mile 5.3 (11,680). Here the trail bends to the left (northwest) and levels out just below the summit. In 0.3 mile, the trail joins the broad, forested divide ridge west of Windy Peak and begins a westerly descent.

Cross Jay Creek Road at mile 6.6 (10,880) and continue down through a lodgepole pine forest. The trail ends its long descent at mile 7.4 (10,560) and begins a series of minor ups and downs along the crest of the divide, still heading west. Join up with a swath cut through the forest for a natural gas pipeline at mile 8.4 (10,640) and follow the swath 200 feet south to where the trail resumes at right. About 0.2 mile beyond, the CT follows the divide as it makes a rapid turn from west to south and then continues along the broad ridge, climbing over occasional small knobs.

Make a sharp right at mile 10.6 (10,560) and descend to the ford on Tank Seven Creek, which received its unusual name from a D&RG water stop downstream. Tank Seven Creek is the last water until Baldy Lake, 11 miles to the west. Join up with an old road on the west side of the creek at mile 11.1 (10,280). Proceed south and then west up the old road that parallels Tank Seven Creek, to grassy Cameron Park at mile 12.3 (10,800), where the trail levels out briefly and crosses FS-578. A couple of dilapidated cabins here may provide minimal protection in a downpour.

The area around the Cameron Park has been heavily logged, leaving a confusing maze of roads. It is necessary to remain on the trail as close as possible to upper Tank Seven Creek through the elongated meadow so as to not get lost. From FS-578, the trail heads west-southwest, ascending the narrowing upper portion of the park. Cross a logging road at mile 13.2 (11,080) and continue 0.2 mile west, where the trail levels out briefly again as it exits the upper portion of Tank Seven Creek and opens into the lower end of Sargents Mesa. At this point, the mesa is surrounded by a tight formation of spruce with occasional groves, a combination that conceals the true expansiveness of the mesa. The trail bears right here (north-northwest) for several hundred feet to detour a marshy spot. As you proceed, the trail becomes less identifiable until it ties into an old, obscure jeep track (FS-486) at mile 13.5 (11,240) that bears west-southwest. As you ascend on FS-486, a large alpine meadow opens up and reveals views north to the Sawatch Range. Continue south then southwest, ascending on the jeep track until it joins FS-855 at mile 14.5 (11,600). Segment 16 ends at this obscure Forest Service road intersection on Sargents Mesa.

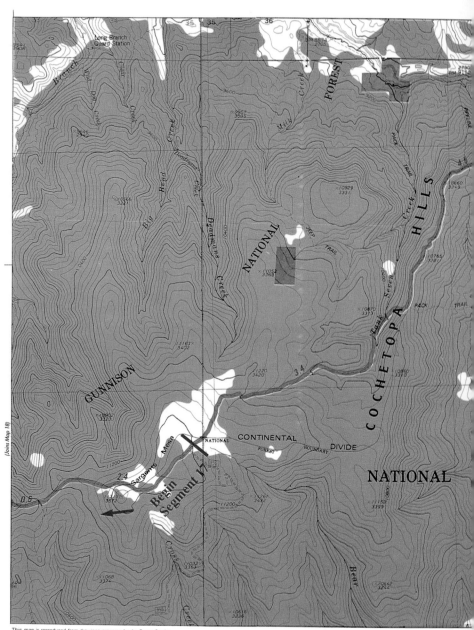

This map is reproduced from drawings prepared by the Forest Service.
USDA, from base maps compiled by the U.S. Geological Survey.

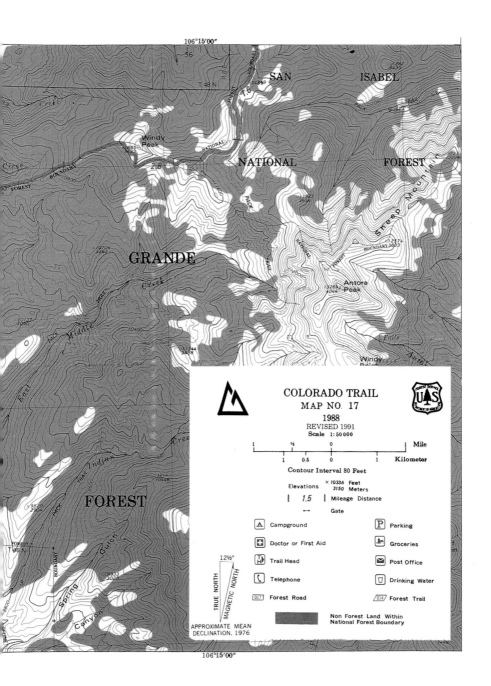

COLORADO TRAIL
MAP NO. 17
1988
REVISED 1991
Scale 1:50 000

Contour Interval 80 Feet

Elevations × 10336 Feet
                    3150 Meters

| 1.5 | Mileage Distance

↔ Gate

Ⓐ Campground   Ⓟ Parking

✚ Doctor or First Aid   Ⓖ Groceries

Ⓗ Trail Head   ✉ Post Office

Ⓒ Telephone   Ⓓ Drinking Water

017 Forest Road   014 Forest Trail

Non Forest Land Within
National Forest Boundary

12½°
TRUE NORTH
MAGNETIC NORTH
APPROXIMATE MEAN
DECLINATION, 1976

Reflections on Baldy Lake, Gunnison National Forest

⚠ SEGMENT 17   20.3 Miles

Sargents Mesa to Colorado Hwy 114   **+ 2,440 Feet Elevation Gain**

Location	Mileage	From Denver	Elevation
Sargents Mesa	0.0	274.8	11,600
Long Branch Trail	2.4		11,160
Middle Baldy	9.2		11,680
Razor Creek	10.7		10,880
Point 11,017	14.4		11,017
Colorado Highway 114	20.3	295.1	9,600

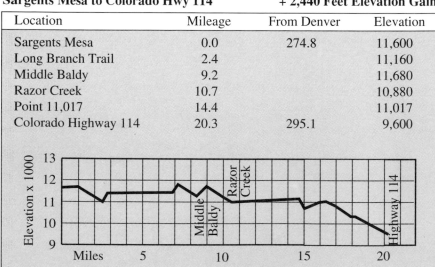

CT Series Maps 17 & 18 (see pages 156-157 & 162-163).

This segment continues through the serene isolation of the Cochetopa Hills and, with the exception of a short bypass into upper Razor Creek, remains on the broad, forested crest of the Continental Divide until reaching Lujan Creek Road. No drinking water is available along the first 7 miles of this segment. Not until Baldy Lake, which is 0.5 mile off the trail, can you be assured of water. Upper Razor Creek (and Park) is an ideal place to camp, although the stream may not be flowing here in the summer. Several parties have reportedly missed the rather obscure CT junction back to the divide at Razor Creek, so be extra attentive here.

The trail in this segment is not as heavily used as other portions of the CT and may be difficult to follow or poorly marked in places. Map and compass readings may be necessary from time to time to confirm your location. The Cochetopa Hills are composed of the relatively recent (Tertiary Age) lava flows, volcanic ash, and breccias that form much of the San Juan Mountains.

Trailhead/Access Points

Sargents Mesa (FS-855) Trail Access: From Saguache on US-285 in the San Luis Valley, drive west on Colorado Highway 114 for 10.5 miles and turn right (north) onto County Road EE38 (also marked as County Road 38FF). Proceed 0.8 mile to a fork and bear to the left, still on County Road EE38. Approximately 5 miles beyond, make a sharp right onto County Road EE38 (also marked as FS-855 at the National Forest boundary). Continue approximately 10 miles, then go left at a fork (the right fork, FS-578, enters a confusing labyrinth of logging roads). Proceed on the left fork 0.4 mile to the end of the improved road. FS-855 continues as a jeep road for another 0.7 mile where it dead ends into FS-486, which is the CT route in the upper park on Sargents Mesa and the start of this segment.

Lujan Creek Road Trail Access: From Saguache on US-285 in the San Luis Valley, drive west on Colorado Highway 114 approximately 30 miles to the summit of North Pass (also called North Cochetopa Pass). Descend 1.1 miles from the pass to Lujan Creek Road (County Road 31CC and FS-785), which ascends to the right (northeast) and is the route of the CT. Follow this dirt road, an impassable quagmire in rainy weather, 2 miles to a switchback to the right. Avoid the side road that forks to the left here. In another 0.1 mile you will top the divide at a cattle guard and then immediately face a fork in the road. Go left and continue east 0.1 mile to where the CT leaves the road to the left (north).

Colorado Highway 114 Trail Access: See Segment 18.

Supplies, Services, and Accommodations

No convenient supply point. The closest supply point, which is a considerable distance, is the town of Gunnison, 38 miles off the trail.

Maps

CT Series: Maps 17 and 18 (see pages 156-157 and 162-163).
USFS: Rio Grande National Forest, Gunnison National Forest.
USGS Quadrangles: Sargents Mesa, West Baldy, North Pass.

GUNNISON SERVICES

Distance from Trail: 38 miles

Bank	First Nat'l Summit	201 N. Main	(303) 641-1621
Bus	TNM&O Bus Lines	303 E. Tomichi	(303) 641-0060
Dining	Cattlemen Inn	301 W. Tomichi	(303) 641-1061
	Mario's Pizzeria	213 W. Tomichi	(303) 641-1374
Gear	Gene Taylor's Spt. Goods	201 W. Tomichi	(303) 641-1845
Groceries	City Market	401 W. Georgia Ave.	(303) 641-3816
	Safeway	112 S. Spruce	(303) 641-0787
Information	Chamber of Commerce	500 E. Tomichi	(303) 641-1501
Laundry	Hi-Country Service	700 N. Main	(303) 641-3894
Lodging	Cattlemen Inn	301 W. Tomichi	(303) 641-1061
	Best Western	Hwy. 50	(303) 641-1131
Medical	Gunnison Valley Hospital	214 E. Denver Ave.	(303) 641-1456
Post Office	Gunnison Post Office	200 N. Wisconsin	(303) 641-1884
Showers	KOA Kampground	Dos Rios Rd.	(303) 641-1358

Trail Description

From the upper end of Sargents Mesa, the CT follows FS-486 both to the left (southwest) and to the right (northeast) from the spot where FS-855 dead ends into it. Bear to the left on FS-486 to start this segment southward. Ascend slightly and almost immediately you will enter a patchy spruce forest as the road trends southwest and levels out on the large, rolling summit of the mesa. The La Garita Mountains are visible ahead, just above the horizon. The road skirts around the north side of a burned-out knob on the west end of the mesa at mile 1.0 (11,640) and descends 1.3 miles beyond to the saddle between Long Branch and Jacks Creek. Here, the CT leaves the road. Continue 800 feet west on a faint trail, across the gravely saddle, to mile 2.4 (11,160), where you will cross another intersecting faint trail. Ascend to the south side of Point 11,547, then begin a stroll northwest along the broad, undulating Continental Divide ridge on a trail that is rocky and sometimes hard to spot, but usually well blazed.

You will intersect the trail to Baldy Lake at mile 6.9 (11,480). The lake, which is located in a cirque below Long Branch Baldy, is 0.5 mile down this side trail to the right (north). From this intersection, ascend 0.4 mile west to a high point south of Long Branch Baldy. Slowly descend 1.2 miles to the saddle, then climb to the large summit of Middle Baldy at mile 9.2 (11,680), where you can see the vast Gunnison Basin from the summit's treeless west side. Descend from the summit. At mile 9.8 (11,480), you will pass a trail descending north into Dutchman Creek.

Just 0.2 miles beyond the Dutchman Creek Trail junction, enter the upper part of Upper Razor Park. Here, the trail disappears in a grassy meadow where the route has been poorly marked in the past. Descend south-southwest across the park, aiming for the funnel formed by the trees in the lower part of the meadow that drops into a distinct draw above the mouth of Razor Creek. A faint trail emerges at mile 10.4 (10,920) and crosses to the left (east) side of the creek in 250 feet. Continue south and ford to the right (west) of Razor Creek at mile 10.7 (10,880). Immediately, a sign directs you back to the east side of the creek and the trailless CT now continues eastward away from the creek 200 feet across a meadow, then enters the trees, where a marker confirms the route. Continue southeast through a swath in the dense forest that has been cleared although no actual trail tread has yet been builtt.

The CT aligns itself again on the wide crest of the Continental Divide, passing a side trail to Razor Creek at mile 12.3 (10,960). Trail conditions improve as you progress south to south-southwest along the divide. Ascend to a minor summit, Point 11,017, at mile 14.4, then descend 0.7 mile to a forested saddle. Climb steeply from the saddle on several recently reconstructed switchbacks to a logging road at mile 16.1 (11,000). The original route of the CT followed the logging road downhill to the right, but in 1988 volunteers rebuilt a neglected footpath, giving hikers the opportunity to remain on trail for another 1.5 miles.

Bear left (south) on the logging road and follow it a few steps to a broad, forested ridge, which is again the crest of the Continental Divide. Here, the old logging road changes into a sometimes difficult to follow trail and begins a descent to the south, still along the Continental Divide. The trail swings through several long switchbacks on its way to Lujan Creek Road at mile 17.8 (10,320), passing through an alternating forest of aspen, lodgepole, and bristlecone pine.

Bear right (west) on the road and continue several hundred feet to a cattle guard, the boundary between Rio Grande and Gunnison national forests. Follow the road approximately 500 feet and head downhill to the left (southwest) at the switchback. Avoid the logging road that continues north from this switchback. Follow the Lujan Creek Road downhill (southwest) and join up with Colorado Highway 114 at mile 20.0 (9,680). Continue 0.3 mile southwest, carefully paralleling the highway, to a widened shoulder on the south side of the highway at mile 20.3 (9,600), where this segment comes to an end.

Notes

162

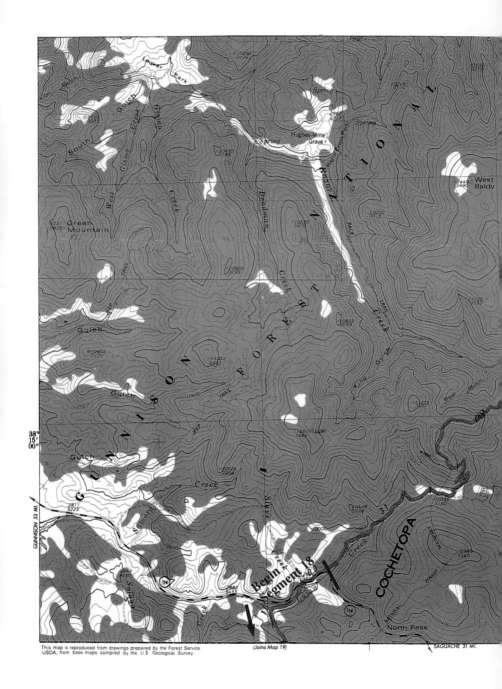

This map is reproduced from drawings prepared by the Forest Service. USDA, from base maps compiled by the U.S. Geological Survey.

(Joins Map 19)

SAGUACHE 31 MI.

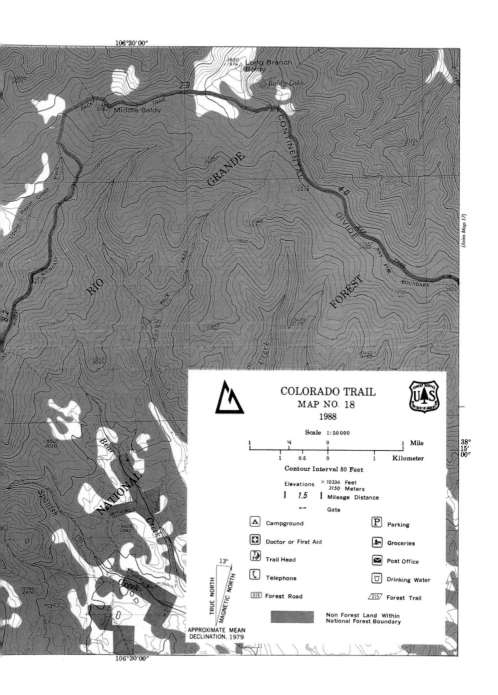

The Cochetopa Hills, Gunnison National Forest

⚠️ SEGMENT 18　12.9 Miles

Colorado Hwy 114 to Saguache Park Rd.　+ 1,210 Feet Elevation Gain

Location	Mileage	From Denver	Elevation
Colorado Highway 114	0.0	295.1	9,600
Lujan-Archuleta Creeks Saddle	3.7		10,240
Los Creek	8.9		9,560
Saguache Park Road	12.9	308.0	9,520

CT Series Map 18 & 19 (see pages 162-163 & 168-169).

The Cochetopa Gap has been used for centuries by wildlife and humans as passage between the San Luis Valley and the Gunnison Basin. Few other Continental Divide crossings in Colorado have such an impressive background, probably because the Cochetopa Gap extends for miles, providing several relatively easy passages rather than a single isolated notch as is characteristic of other passes. To the Utes, their ancestral "Pass of the Buffalo" (as the word Cochetopa is translated) had a significance that today is only hinted at by the three relatively minor Continental Divide auto routes over the gap: North Pass on Colorado Highway 114, South Pass on County Road 17FF, and Cochetopa Pass, the historic route of the Saguache-San Juan toll road, on County Road NN14.

The gap was already well used by the Utes following buffalo herds when the Spanish governor of New Mexico, Juan Bautista de Anza, led his army into the San Luis Valley in 1779. De Anza's object was the renegade Comanche known as Greenhorn, but during his pursuit de Anza did not fail to notice the long, low point in the mountains to the west, which he correctly deduced was the divide between the Rio Grande and the western San Juan country. By 1825, after first entering the San Luis Valley via Mosca Pass in the Sangre de Cristo Range, Antoine Robidoux was leading pack trains over the gap.

Probably the area's most dramatic event took place just southwest of here in the winter of 1848-49 when Colonel John Charles Fremont led a party into the region to explore potential railroad routes. Unfortunately, guide Bill Williams aimed in the wrong direction and the expedition ended up somewhere on the high ridges of the La Garita Mountains. A fierce blizzard resulted in the deaths of 11 of the 35 men. Some of the survivors were accused of cannibalism, although formal charges were never made. A more infamous cannibal, Alferd Packer, made his way over the gap in April of 1874, after having survived the winter by murdering and devouring his five fellow travelers. Packer was later arrested in Saguache.

After the gap was bypassed by the trans-Continental railroad, Otto Mears and Enos Hotchkiss built a toll road from Saguache to Lake City over Cochetopa Pass in 1874. Today, the historic North, South, and Cochetopa passes are rarely used and retain a quiet sense of antiquity.

Backpackers will find meager water supplies along this segment. Lujan, Pine, Archuleta, and Los creeks all have small flows. Special measures may be needed during dry years or in late summer. In emergencies, hikers can detour to a small spring at Luders Creek Campground. The CT in this segment uses a curious assortment of logging, jeep, Forest Service, and county roads. A map and compass might come in handy to help decipher the maze.

Mountain bikers should refer to the chapter in the back of the book for the description of the long detour around La Garita Wilderness that starts on the Cochetopa Pass Road.

Trailhead/Access Points

Colorado Highway 114 Trail Access: From Saguache on US-285 in the San Luis Valley, go west on Colorado Highway 114 approximately 30 miles to the summit of North Pass. Descend 1.1 miles on the west side of the pass to Lujan Creek Road (County Road 31CC), which ascends to the right (northeast) and is the route of the CT in Segment 17. Continue on Highway 114 for 0.3

mile to a widened shoulder of the road that is not graded for parking. The CT continues south from here across the meadow of Lujan Creek. A better trail access point, away from the activity of the highway, is up Lujan Creek Road (County Road 31CC). Refer to Lujan Creek Road Trail Access as described in Segment 17.

Cochetopa Pass Road (County Road NN14) Trail Access: From Saguache on US-285 in the San Luis Valley, go west on Colorado Highway 114 approximately 21 miles and bear to the left on County Road NN14 (FS-750), which is the historic route of the original Cochetopa Pass Road. Follow the road to Luders Creek Campground, then continue approximately 1.8 miles further to the summit of Cochetopa Pass. Descend 1.2 miles west of the pass to FS-876 (Corduroy Road), which leaves the Cochetopa Pass Road to the right (north) and is the route of the CT. From this point, the CT follows the pass road for the next 0.5 mile as it descends through two switchbacks. No parking is provided at this trail access point.

Saguache Park Road Trail Access: See Segment 19.

Supplies, Services, and Accommodations

There are no convenient supply points within this segment.

Maps

CT Series: Maps 18 and 19 (see pages 162-163 and 168-169).
USFS: Gunnison National Forest.
USGS Quadrangles: North Pass, Cochetopa Park.

Trail Description

At the widened shoulder 1.4 miles west of North Pass on Highway 114, proceed southwest through the gate and drop down slightly into the lush meadow of Lujan Creek. Ford the creek at mile 0.2 (9,560) and climb above the marshy lowlands surrounding it. Follow the trailless route, which is marked with carsonite posts that sway in the breeze, in a more westerly direction. Shortly, you will curve to the left (south) and follow the posts into Pine Creek drainage. Join up with an old logging road at mile 0.8 (9,560). Continue south up the valley and avoid the fork to the left 0.1 mile beyond. Cross over to the west side of the creek at mile 1.6 (9,680) and take time to admire the cinquefoil and sego lily wildflowers that adorn the area. Go right at the fork 0.1 mile beyond, where the logging road begins an ascent out of Pine Creek Valley. Continue along the road as it bends around and assumes a northerly direction. Switchback to the left at mile 2.4 (9,920) and resume a southerly bearing.

The logging road ends in a cul-de-sac at mile 3.4 (10,000). Begin a much steeper ascent, still in a southerly direction, from the road end, following a route that has been cleared and bulldozed but is without a tread. Reach the saddle between Lujan and Archuleta creeks at mile 3.7 (10,240) and pass through a gate. Descend 0.1 mile on a cleared route to another old logging road (FS-876). Go left on this logging road that descends south into the upper drainage of Corduroy Creek. Reach the Cochetopa Pass Road at mile 6.4 (9,760).

Follow the pass road downhill to the right 0.5 mile, through two switchbacks, to where a jeep road (FS-864.2A) leaves the graded road to the left (south). Cross over to the south side of Archuleta Creek on a dirt-fill bridge and continue on the jeep road that parallels the pass road and the tiny creek upstream for several hundred feet. Angle slowly to the right as the jeep road heads south up a shallow intersecting valley. At times the road seems to disappear into the lush grasses of the broad meadow. Avoid the fork to the right that cuts up into the hillside, and continue a slow bend to the southwest at the edge of the meadow. Pass through a gate at the indistinct divide between Archuleta and Los creeks at mile 7.7 (9,800) and descend west into the wide, grassy valley. About 0.1 mile beyond the gate, continue west on FS-864.2A, avoiding the fork to the left. In 0.5 mile begin paralleling the main flow of Los Creek. Continue west on the north side of the creek, which is almost hidden by willows and cinquefoil.

Cross Los Creek as it turns north at mile 8.9 (9,560), just upstream from a stock pond. Immediately after the creek crossing, follow FS-787.2A as it ascends west out of the Los Creek drainage. Top a grassy saddle 0.5 mile beyond and descend bearing generally west on the rocky Forest Service jeep track that parallels a fence. A full view of broad Cochetopa Dome dominates the scenery to the north. Level out as the jeep track enters the edge of immense Cochetopa Park at mile 10.4 (9,400). In 0.8 mile, fork to the right just beyond a gate and continue on FS-787.2A to Saguache Park Road (County Road 17FF) at mile 11.4 (9,340). Turn left (south) onto the graded county road and continue to a cattle guard at a wooded saddle. Descend west along the road, then veer back to the south and ascend slightly to mile 12.9 (9,520). This segment terminates here as the CT route joins a jeep track (FS-787.2D) to the right and leaves the Saguache Park Road in a meadow at the edge of the forest.

Notes

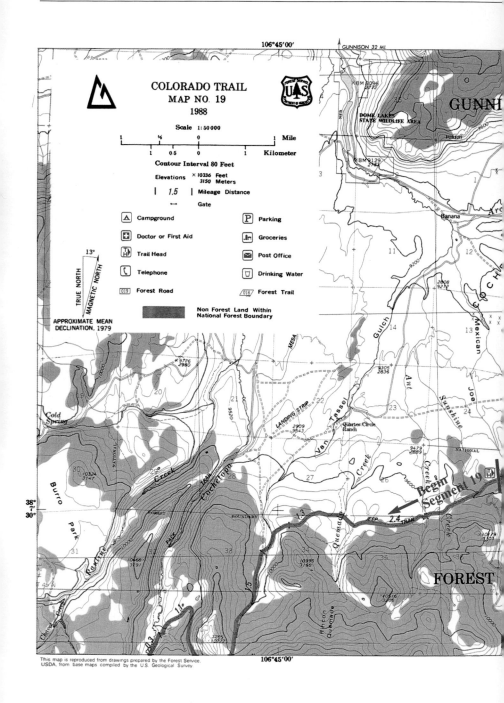

COLORADO TRAIL
MAP NO. 19
1988

Scale 1:50000

Contour Interval 80 Feet

Elevations ×10336 Feet
3150 Meters

| 1.5 | Mileage Distance

Gate

△ Campground

⊕ Doctor or First Aid

🏠 Trail Head

📞 Telephone

019 Forest Road

P Parking

🛒 Groceries

✉ Post Office

🚰 Drinking Water

016 Forest Trail

Non Forest Land Within
National Forest Boundary

13°
TRUE NORTH
MAGNETIC NORTH
APPROXIMATE MEAN
DECLINATION, 1979

This map is reproduced from drawings prepared by the Forest Service.
USDA, from base maps compiled by the U.S. Geological Survey.

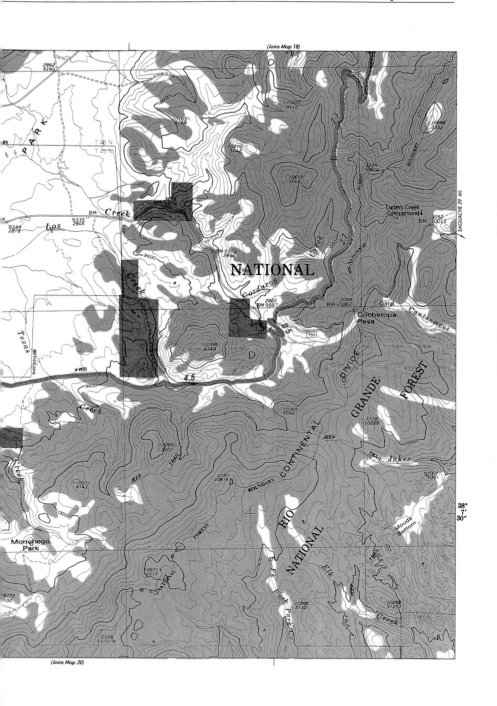

(Joins Map 18)

NATIONAL

GRANDE FOREST

RIO NATIONAL

Cochetopa Pass

Duders Creek Campground

Monchego Park

SAGUACHE 29 MI.

38° 7' 30"

(Joins Map 20)

Ancient pines along Stewart Creek, La Garita Wilderness

◢◣ SEGMENT 19   13.5 Miles

Saguache Park Rd. to Eddiesville Trailhead   **+ 1,660 Feet Elevation Gain**

Location	Mileage	From Denver	Elevation
Saguache Park Road	0.0	308.0	9,520
Van Tassel Saddle	5.4		10,400
Cochetopa Creek	7.0		9,720
Eddiesville Trailhead	13.5	321.5	10,320

CT Series Maps 19 & 20 (see pages 168-169 & 174-175).

In this segment, the CT in this segment crosses several small, and usually dry, drainages while skirting the southern boundary of Cochetopa Park on existing jeep roads. There are campsites in the isolated valley of Cochetopa Creek, but backpackers may experience some aggravating moments if they unintentionally stray off the sometimes obscure trail as it parallels the creek to Eddiesville Trailhead.

The last several miles of this segment take you into La Garita Wilderness, where mountain bikes are not allowed (refer to the Mountain Bike Detours).

Trailhead/Access Points

Saguache Park Road Trail Access: From Saguache on US-285 in the San Luis Valley, go west on Colorado Highway 114 approximately 30 miles to the summit of North Pass. Continue on Highway 114 west of the pass approximately 5.2 miles and go left (south) on County Road 17GG. Continue on the dirt road approximately 5.2 miles around the southwest side of Cochetopa Dome. Go left (east) onto County Road NN14, the Cochetopa Pass Road. Drive 1.1 miles east on the pass road and go right (south) on County Road 17FF (FS-787), the Saguache Park Road. Continue up County Road 17FF to the cattle guard that signals your entry into Gunnison National Forest. The CT takes off immediately to the left (east) at this point, following a jeep track (FS-787.2A). From here, the trail follows the Saguache Park Road (FS-787) as it continues ahead (south) 1.5 miles until it veers to the right (southwest) off FS-787 at another jeep track (FS-787.2D). No parking area is provided at either of these trail access points on the Saguache Park Road.

Eddiesville Trailhead: See Segment 20.

Supplies, Services, and Accommodations

There are no convenient supply points within this segment.

Maps

CT Series: Maps 19 and 20 (see pages 168-169 and 174-175).
USFS: Gunnison National Forest.
USGS Quadrangles: Cochetopa Park, Saguache Park, Elk Park.

Trail Description

At the beginning of this segment, the CT leaves the Saguache Park Road and joins up with a rocky jeep track (FS-787.2D) on the right that proceeds southwest through a meadow. At mile 0.1 (9,520), continue straight ahead, avoiding the right fork. Ascend a gully of scattered spruce, pine, and aspen to a small rise, then descend slightly into the dry gully of Sunshine Creek where fields of sego lily bloom. Climb to a low, open ridge dividing Ant and Sunshine creeks, then drop down to the usually dry Ant Creek at mile 1.2 (9,720). Pass through gates on each side of the creek. Avoid the left fork, which goes south, after crossing Ant Creek and instead continue west at the edge of the forest along the southern boundary of Cochetopa Park. The rounded, smooth profile Cochetopa Dome dominates the foreground, while the Elk Mountains provide a snowy backdrop far to the north.

Descend slowly, entering the Quemado Creek drainage to a confusing junction at mile 2.2 (9760), where several jeep tracks come together. Continue 0.2

mile northwest from this junction on an obscure jeep track, then bear to the left (west) on another set of tracks that takes you over a dirt-fill creek crossing in 150 feet. Climb west out of the drainage to a high point, where you pass through a gate at mile 3.2 (9,960). Descend west and then south into Van Tassel Gulch. Bottom out in the dry gulch at mile 3.7 (9,840) and ascend 500 feet to a jeep road (FS-597). Turn left (south) onto the road and climb the west side of the wide gulch through a sparse aspen forest.

Top the saddle at mile 5.4 (10,400) in a small clearing ringed with aspen, where the jeep road forks. Bear right onto another jeep road (FS-597.1A) that descends and slowly bends to the west. As the road continues to drop, it slowly assumes a more northerly direction and eventually breaks out of the trees and switchbacks to the left (southwest) at mile 6.5 (9,960). Continue 0.2 mile southwest to a pond at another confusing junction of jeep tracks. Follow a sketchy trail as it proceeds between the west shore of the pond and a small knoll. Pick up a jeep track again southwest of the pond and descend steeply to mile 7.0 (9,720), level with the broad valley bottom of Cochetopa Creek. Just above the marshy valley bottom, look for an obscure trail at left; this begins a long, gradual ascent south and southwest up the creek.

Cross a small stream just as the trail leaves the jeep track and continue south on the east side of the valley. Cochetopa Creek meanders through the grassy valley bottom, where there are many spacious campsites. The sometimes obscure trail bears generally south-southwest and begins to take on the character of a jeep track in 0.7 mile. Ascend to a high point above the creek in the surrounding forest at mile 9.5 (9,960), then drop steeply 0.1 mile to a small side stream. Continue on the jeep track beyond the side stream, where the trail then bears to the right (southwest). This short section only goes about a 100 feet before it joins another jeep track and continues southwest on a grassy, elevated bench above and parallel to Cochetopa Creek.

Toward the southern end of this grassy bench at mile 10.2 (9,960), the trail descends quickly to the level of the creek and disappears into a sand bar. Bear to the right through a tangle of willows and carefully ford Cochetopa Creek at a deep, precarious crossing. Once across the creek, head south-southwest to a large cairn on the west bank just above the level of the willows. The trail is indistinct in places until you rise above the creek. Ascend southwest from the cairn to a grassy bench on the west side of the creek at mile 10.5 (10,000). From here, another trail continues downstream (northeast). This junction is obscure and it could be a problem for eastbound CT hikers headed for the Saguache Park Road.

Continue on the trail south-southwest up the west side of Cochetopa Creek and ford the rushing side drainage of Nutras Creek at mile 10.8 (10,000). Just beyond this point, you enter La Garita Wilderness. Ascend near the banks of the creek on a mostly treeless slope with a southern exposure, which can be uncomfortably warm on summer afternoons. The trail levels out on a rolling, grassy bench well above the creek at mile 12.1 (10,240). Take the right fork where the trail splits at mile 13.0 (10,280). Continue to the isolated Eddiesville Trailhead parking area at mile 13.5 (10,320), where the CT briefly leaves the La Garita Wilderness.

Notes

174

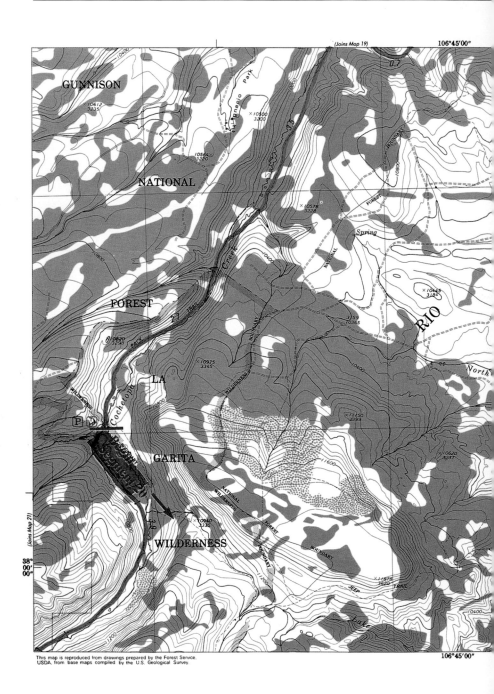

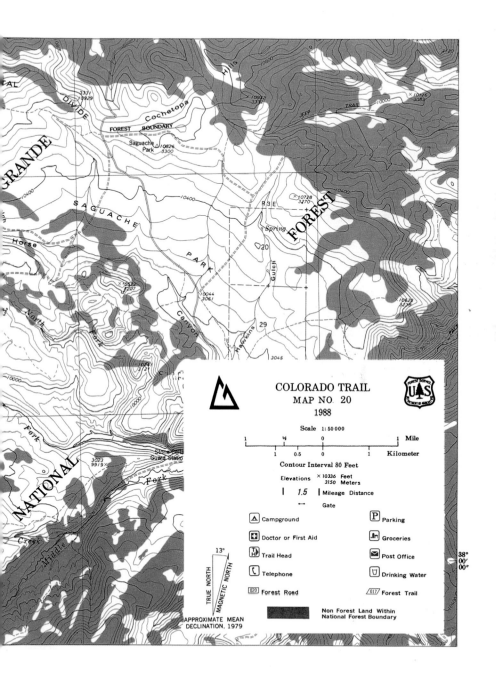

COLORADO TRAIL
MAP NO. 20
1988

Scale 1:50 000

| 1 | ½ | 0 | | 1 Mile |
| 1 | 0.5 | 0 | | 1 Kilometer |

Contour Interval 80 Feet

Elevations   × 10336 Feet
                    3150 Meters

| 1.5 | Mileage Distance

↔   Gate

△ Campground   Ⓟ Parking

✚ Doctor or First Aid   Groceries

⌂ Trail Head   ✉ Post Office

☎ Telephone   ▽ Drinking Water

020 Forest Road   017 Forest Trail

        Non Forest Land Within
        National Forest Boundary

13°

TRUE NORTH

MAGNETIC NORTH

APPROXIMATE MEAN
DECLINATION, 1979

Camped on San Luis Pass, La Garita Wilderness

⚠ SEGMENT 20   12.2 Miles

Eddiesville Trailhead to San Luis Pass   **+ 2,680 Feet Elevation Gain**

Location	Mileage	From Denver	Elevation
Eddiesville Trailhead	0.0	321.5	10,320
San Luis Saddle	8.4		12,600
Spring Creek	10.0		12,080
Continental Divide	11.6		12,360
San Luis Pass	12.2	333.7	11,920

CT Series Maps 20 & 21 (see pages 174-175 & 186-187).

This segment traverses stunning alpine country on the old and appropriately named Skyline Trail. It also has the honor of making the CT's closest approach to a 14,000-foot peak, passing just 1,400 feet below and within 1.3 miles of 14,014-foot San Luis Peak. This mountain was probably christened by members of the Hayden Survey, who were probably influenced by the vast San Luis Valley to the east. At the head of Cochetopa Creek, the trail passes the extreme northwest corner of the La Garita Mountains, a small but unique subset of the immense San Juan Mountains.

Stewart Creek gets its name from Stewart Peak, where the creek begins. The peak, which is not visible in this trail segment, was named by the Wheeler Survey for Senator William M. Stewart of Nevada, who was an advocate of the free coinage of silver. Having Senator Stewart's name attached to a prominent peak is evidence of the strong feelings Coloradans had for a free-silver economy. Stewart Peak also has the dubious distinction of having been demoted from its previous 14,000-foot stature, which occurred when inaccurate early triangulations were superseded by more precise modern survey techniques. Since this rather ignominious demotion, this noble 13,983-foot mountain is now virtually ignored by peak baggers who flock into the area to climb San Luis Peak.

From San Luis saddle west to San Luis Pass, the CT stays at or above 12,000 feet and only once grazes the upper limits of a spruce forest at the head of Spring Creek. With the exception of the last mile approaching San Luis Pass, the trail is generally continuous, although obscured at times by talus or thick tundra grasses. Snowfields often linger well into the summer on the north slopes beyond San Luis saddle.

Backpackers will certainly want to tarry in this segment, which is almost entirely within the wilderness. You can set up camp anywhere along the upper course of Cochetopa Creek or near the headwaters of Spring Creek farther west. The interesting gnome-like figures, or "hoodoos," that decorate the mountainsides through here are eroded out of volcanic ash.

Mountain bikers will have to use the mandatory detour around La Garita Wilderness (see Mountain Bike Detours).

Trailhead/Access Points

Eddiesville Trailhead: From Saguache on US-285 in the San Luis Valley, travel west on Colorado Highway 114 approximately 30 miles to the summit of North Pass. Continue on Colorado Highway 114 west of the pass approximately 5.2 miles and go left (south) on County Road 17GG. Continue on the dirt road approximately 5.2 miles around the southwest side of Cochetopa Dome and go right (west) on Rd-NN14, which is the Cochetopa Pass Road. Drive west 1.3 miles on the pass road and go left on County Road 15GG. Follow this main road, which is marked as "Stewart Creek," approximately 21 miles to the Eddiesville Trailhead parking area near the end of the road.

San Luis Pass Trail Access: See Segment 21.

Supplies, Services, and Accommodations

Available in Creede.

CREEDE SERVICES
Distance from Trail: 11 miles

Bank	First Nat'l. Bank	117 N. Main	(719) 658-0700
	Rio Grande County Bank	116 Creede Ave.	(719) 658-2688
Bus	None		
Dining	Pizza House	on Main St.	(719) 658-2767
Gear	San Juan Sports	137 Creede Ave.	(719) 658-2359
Groceries	Kentucky Bell Market	2nd & Main	(719) 658-2526
Information	Chamber of Commerce	end of Main St.	(719) 658-2374
Laundry	Creede Laundermat	101 E. Fifth	no phone
Lodging	The Blessing Inn B&B	on South Main St.	(719) 658-0215
	Creede Hotel B&B	120 Main	(719) 658-2608
Medical	Health Clinic	Loma Ave.	(719) 658-2416
Post Office	Creede Post Office	100 Creede Ave.	(719) 658-2615
Showers	Snowshoe Motel	Hwy 149 & 8th	(719) 658-2315

Maps
CT Series: Maps 20 and 21 (see pages 174-175 and 186-187).
USFS: Gunnison National Forest, Rio Grande National Forest.
USGS Quadrangles: Elk Park, Halfmoon Pass, San Luis Peak.

Trail Description
From the Eddiesville Trailhead parking area, head south on the road, which dips slightly, to cross Stewart Creek. Leave the road as it enters private property at mile 0.2 (10,320) and continue to the right (southwest) 500 feet on a trail that parallels a barbed-wire fence to a gate. Pass through the gate and briefly cross private property. The trail joins a set of jeep tracks in 0.3 mile and continues south. At mile 1.1 (10,360), a trail separates just briefly from the jeep track to pass through a gate and reenter the La Garita Wilderness. It then immediately rejoins the jeep track and continues south along the west bank of Cochetopa Creek.

The CT assumes a more southwesterly bearing at mile 2.0 (10,400) as the valley makes a wide, slow turn to the west. The trail ascends and enters small clumps of spruce amid the narrowing valley bottom. Pass through a gate at mile 3.5 (10,640) and continue through a forest that breaks into grassy meadows from time to time. At mile 7.2 (11,720) a very obscure side trail ascends to Stewart Creek. Just 200 feet beyond that, you ford the headwaters of Cochetopa Creek. Above timberline, follow the trail through the willows and enjoy the magnificent views of nearby Organ Mountain. The trail is engulfed by tundra grasses just short of the saddle west of San Luis Peak. Continue to this saddle at mile 8.4 (12,600). The summit of San Luis Peak is only a 1.3-mile ridge walk north of this point.

Pick up the trail again on the opposite side of the saddle and traverse south, then west, into a cirque at the head of Spring Creek. Climb slightly to another saddle at mile 9.6 (12,360), then descend on the trail that disappears 200 feet beyond into the grass. A post visible just west of the saddle marks where the trail resumes; follow as it descends slightly into another alpine cirque. An old sign at mile 10.0 (12,080) identifies where the obscure Spring Creek Trail intersects the CT. Cross a small stream 200 feet beyond and continue to mile 10.5 (12,000), where the trail briefly enters a upper-limit spruce forest.

Proceed 0.4 mile on the trail to another small stream and begin a long ascent. Climb steadily to a switchback then ascend west to mile 11.3 (12,200), where the trail becomes indistinct in the thick tundra grasses. Continue northwest and aim to the right (north) of the rocky knob that rises prominently above the smooth, grassy ridge of the Continental Divide. Top the divide north of the rocky knob at mile 11.6 (12,360). The trail is faint or nonexistent for the next 0.7 mile from here to San Luis Pass, and numerous old posts and claim stakes may make the descent confusing. From the divide, descend slowly 0.3 mile to the northwest. Stay above a mass of short but dense willows below. Continue a slow descent until San Luis Pass comes into view as a reference point, then descend steeply west maneuvering around the willows to reach the pass, and the end of this segment, at mile 12.2 (11,920). Creede is about 10 miles distant, first on a side trail, then on a road (FS-503) that heads south down the valley.

Notes

Alpine sunflowers along Mineral Creek, La Garita Wilderness

⚠ SEGMENT 21   14.5 Miles

San Luis Pass to Spring Creek Pass   **+ 2,920 Feet Elevation Gain**

Location	Mileage	From Denver	Elevation
San Luis Pass	0.0	333.7	11,920
East Mineral Creek	2.8		11,720
Middle Mineral Creek	4.2		11,840
Snow Mesa	11.5		12,360
Spring Creek Pass	14.5	348.2	10,898

CT Series Map 21 & 22 (see pages 186-187 & 194-195).

This segment continues a challenging and exceedingly rewarding portion of the CT along the old Skyline Trail. The high-altitude route is sometimes poorly identified and often without noticeable tread. Map and compass readings may be necessary occasionally to decipher your location in this jumbled terrain of valleys, ridges, and mountaintops. North slopes may be snowed in until mid-July. Beware of significant lightning hazard on exposed ridges and Snow Mesa.

Much elevation is gained and lost as the CT mounts high ridges and then drops into the headwaters of East and Middle Mineral creeks, where you can camp in the protection of spruce forests. Snow Mesa is an alpine experience unlikely to be forgotten as the CT makes its way along the historic La Garita Stock Driveway, with its old cairns and posts still standing. Mountain bikers need to detour around La Garita Wilderness as described in the mountain biking chapter at the end of this guide.

There is something magical about hiking through the La Garita Wilderness, something almost spiritual in its primeval isolation. The Spanish term means "the lookout," most likely so named because Indians used the mountains as signal stations. It was probably among the high ridges of the La Garita Mountains farther east that Colonel John C. Fremont's expedition became stranded in a deadly blizzard during the winter of 1848-49, although no one knows for sure from the sketchy records that remain.

Nicholas Creede probably never dreamed of the rowdy town that would spring up after he staked out his Holy Moses Mine on East Willow Creek in 1889. The town of Creede, like other high-spirited mining communities, had its share of riffraff. The most notorious were Soapy Smith and Bob Ford. Ford, the killer of Jessie James, was shot to death while residing in Creede. The town was recorded for posterity by Cy Warman's poem of the day, which could have typified many of Colorado's mining towns:

Here's a land where all are equal
Of high or lowly birth,
A land where men make millions
Dug from the dreary earth,
Here meek and mild eyed burros
On mineral mountains feed,
It's day all day in the day time
And there is no night in Creede.

The cliffs of solid silver
With wondrous wealth untold,
And the beds of the running rivers
Are lined with the purest gold,
While the world is filled with sorrow
And hearts must break and bleed,
It's day all day in the day time
And there is no night in Creede.

Trailhead/Access Points

San Luis Pass Trail Access: Travel on Colorado Highway 149 to Creede and go north on the town's main street. At the north edge of town, proceed into a dramatic, steep-walled canyon. About 0.5 mile beyond Creede, continue straight ahead on FS-503 as a side road forks to the right. Your car will need a strong first gear and a little extra ground clearance to negotiate these steep, rough roads. Follow FS-503 north approximately 6.5 miles to the end of the improved road at the entrance to the Equity Mine. A small parking area is provided here for cars. FS-503 continues on as a 4WD road, which you follow north up the valley for another 1.6 miles — either on foot or in an appropriate vehicle — until it bears to the left (west) and climbs steeply over the high ridge. From here, continue northward on foot along the sometimes obscure side trail in the narrowing valley bottom for another 1.5 miles to San Luis Pass. This access point is popular with people setting off to climb San Luis Peak, so you will probably have some company.

Spring Creek Pass Trailhead: See Segment 22.

Supplies, Services, and Accommodations

It is a 10-mile side trip into Creede from San Luis Pass. Descend on a side trail south along the headwaters of West Willow Creek until you meet FS-503, then continue into town, where there is a backpacking store, grocery and various watering holes that recall the town's rip-roaring past (see Segment 20). A Rio Grande National Forest District ranger station is located here as well.

Maps

CT Series: Maps 21 and 22 (see pages 186-187 and 194-195).
USFS: Gunnison National Forest, Rio Grande National Forest.
USGS Quadrangles: San Luis Peak, Baldy Cinco, Slumgullion Pass.

Trail Description

From the Forest Service signs on the grassy saddle at San Luis Pass, ascend slightly, without aid of any visible trail, a little south of west. After about 500 feet of easy tundra walking, look for a break in a wall of willows that is the start of a short trail section ascending the steep, willow-covered hillside just southwest of the pass. Climb this trail south to mile 0.3 (12,080), where a post marks its end. Make a sharp right (west) and mount the top of a somewhat broad ridgeline that becomes more defined as you gain elevation. Follow the ridge west toward the base of the rocky summit of Point 13,111, at mile 1.1 (12,760). A weathered post here signals the beginning of another short trail segment and your entry into the La Garita Wilderness.

Proceed northwest on the rocky trail to the east side of a long, grassy ridge that extends north from the steep slopes of Point 13,111. The trail disappears here, near a post on the ridge at mile 1.3 (12,840). Massive San Luis Peak dominates the eastern horizon from this vantage point. Continue west over the ridge and descend southwest on the wide, grassy slope following a series of cairns and posts. Bear to the left (south) at mile 1.6 (12,520) and cross a wide erosion course approximately 600 feet beyond. Don't be tempted to follow this channel downhill into East Mineral Creek, but instead cross it and continue south until you pick up the beginnings of a deeply eroded trail at mile 1.8 (12,320).

Follow the trail as it leaves the grassy slopes to descend the steep walls of an amphitheater; it continues to the alpine meadow below. Ford a sporadically flowing upper tributary of East Mineral Creek at mile 2.0 (12,120). Descend gradually another 0.2 mile where the trail becomes poorly defined in a sloppy, wet area. Continue west and pick up a better trail as the soil becomes firmer, then descend slightly to mile 2.4 (11,920), where you will traverse generally southwest across a rock wall with a variety of alpine flowers protruding from every crevice. Enter the trees at mile 2.5 (11,880) and continue several hundred feet on a descending trail to the lower end of a small open area. The trail descends diagonally through the open area on an east-west axis until it re-enters the trees in about 200 feet. Proceed through a spruce forest to mile 2.6 (11,840), where the trail again opens onto a narrow clearing. At the eastern edge of this clearing, an old sign confirms the intersection of the obscure East Mineral Creek Trail with the old Skyline Trail. Continue west 150 feet across the clearing and reenter the trees.

At mile 2.7 (11,800), the trail abruptly leaves the trees again at the edge of a massive rockslide. Bear to the right (north) here and descend steeply to a stream crossing 250 feet beyond. Make a short but steep ascent after the ford and continue around the foot of the rock avalanche to mile 2.8 (11,720). The trail enters the trees and begins an ascent out of the East Mineral Creek drainage. Climbing through spruce forest and then tundra, continue to mile 3.3 (12,160), where the trail fades out just below the saddle. Bear to the right (west-southwest) and head for the post 200 feet beyond. This post marks the saddle between East and Middle Mineral creeks.

From the saddle, descend west through a few willows on a faint trail that gives out after a few hundred feet. Continue the steep descent westward on a grassy slope, following a posted route that enters the trees just before crossing an intermittently flowing stream. Pick up the trail again here and head southwest across the normally dry streambed at mile 3.6 (11,760) and continue descending southwest through a small clearing in the otherwise dense forest.

Proceed through the spruce forest to the edge of larger clearing at mile 3.7 (11,720), where the trail fades away again. Descend diagonally west across this inclined meadow, following a posted route, and cross a small seasonal stream near the middle of the opening. Continue west and enter the trees at mile 3.8 (11,680) where the trail gradually reappears. If you plan to camp, consider using an established campsite just off the trail here.

Cross the main drainage of Middle Mineral Creek 0.1 mile past this point, just downstream from a large beaver dam. A few steps beyond, the trail bears to the right (northwest) near the remains of a long collapsed cabin. Cross another tributary stream and continue to the trail's low point in this valley at mile 4.2 (11,480). Ascend through several switchbacks to the saddle between Middle and West Mineral creeks at mile 4.8 (11,840). Notice the evidence of a forest fire that burned long ago in the vicinity.

Continue southwest across the saddle, keeping a sharp eye out for the faint trail, which is marked by ancient blazes on the trees. From the saddle, the old Skyline Trail, which links up the the CT here, continues to ascend, bearing generally southwest through a spruce forest. Cross a prominent avalanche chute at mile 5.2 (12,000), where a snow field often lingers well into the summer. Continue west 0.1 mile to a point where the trail exits the cool, north-facing spruce forest and reorients to a southerly direction onto a west-facing exposed rock expanse, which can be uncomfortably warm on sunny summer afternoons.

The trail crosses the rocky area just below some impressive cliffs and continues an ascent to the saddle visible ahead. In a north-facing gully just before the saddle, you may find that you have to cross a steep snow field in early summer. Cross over the saddle at mile 5.7 (12,240) and continue on the faint trail that generally follows the contour around an upper side drainage of West Mineral Creek onto another north-facing slope with another potentially steep snow field crossing.

Enter a field of willows at mile 6.0 (12,280) and maneuver between the bushes, bearing generally west-southwest on a vague path that eventually is overwhelmed by the willows. A broken directional sign at mile 6.1 stands alone, protruding above the willows and pointing out the junction of the obscure West Mineral Creek Trail and the old Skyline Trail. From the sign, continue west through the willows to the grassy saddle between West Mineral and Miners creeks at mile 6.3 (12,280). The saddle is marked with a solitary post. Ascend west-northwest on the broad ridge that extends upward from the saddle, following a posted route. Navigate as necessary through the willow patches and pick up a vague footpath again at mile 6.7 (12,480), near the bottom of a talus slope. Bear to the left and continue climbing southward on a reemerging trail marked with an occasional post. As the trail veers to the right (west) and levels out, it fades away again at mile 7.1 (12,680), but a posted route continues through thick alpine tundra just below the crest of the broad Continental Divide ridge.

At mile 7.4 (12,760), pick up a faint but recognizable trail that descends gradually to the west-northwest. The distinctive profile of Uncompahgre Peak is visible through the notch ahead. Look on the opposite side of the valley, to your left and below, for a curious rock formation reminiscent of the Wheeler Geologic Area.

The trail continues a descent, the last part across a rocky area, to the notch saddle at mile 8.1 (12,560). The Skyline Trail descends northwest into Rough Creek, but the CT bends left (south), staying in the upper drainage of Miners Creek. Snowfields often cover the trail here until mid-summer, and water is usually plentiful in the upper basins of the creek just below the trail. The CT continues to bear generally south as it clings to the steep and sometimes rocky mountainside above Miners Creek. Take time to enjoy the panoramas down valley and of Table Mountain to the south. The trail tread comes to an end at mile 9.3 (12,320) at the extreme eastern edge of Snow Mesa, northeast of a small pond that forms the headwaters of Willow Creek. Continue around the east, then the south side of the pond. From the south side, strike out almost due west across expansive Snow Mesa, following infrequent cairns of the old La Garita Stock Driveway and more recent carsonite posts, as you gently dip in and out of several shallow branches of Willow Creek.

If the weather is clear at mile 11.5 (12,360), the CT route and the cairns and posts marking the southern boundary of the stock driveway can be seen to stretch westward in front of you for more than a mile. A large rock cairn, barely visible at the western edge of the mesa, identifies the northern line of the driveway, which should be avoided.

Visible to the south, far beyond the Rio Grande Valley below, are the rugged peaks of the southeastern San Juan Range. These carry the Continental

Divide on a large, meandering "U" that forms the huge watershed of the mighty Rio Grande. Most prominent in the distance is the distinctive profile of the Rio Grande Pyramid.

Continue west, following the southern line of the stock driveway cairns, to mile 12.6 (12,280), where a final cairn marks the approach to the western edge of Snow Mesa. Proceed west-southwest to the head of a prominent drainage that plunges off the side of the mesa. An obscure but important post at mile 12.7 (12,240) signals the beginning of a trail that descends into the drainage. This rocky trail makes a gradual bend to the right (west), then rises a little on the north side of the drainage and enters an area of scattered trees at mile 13.0 (11,840). The trail, marked with old blazes, descends here through a spruce forest bearing generally west to northwest.

The CT then descends a seasonal drainage that is usually flowing only in early summer, but nevertheless causes yearly trail erosion problems. The trail essentially disappears at mile 13.4 (11,640), where it exits the forest and opens up into a gently rolling meadow dotted with a few stands of spruce. Angle to the right here (northwest) and continue across the meadow following a series of carsonite posts and rock cairns. Views ahead are of Jarosa Mesa and the lopsided summit of Uncompahgre Peak. The route enters a stand of spruce at mile 13.6 (11,600), where you begin to pick up a faint trail again. Angle to the right here and take a more northerly bearing for approximately 200 feet as the trail dips slightly into a shallow gully. Then bear to the left (west) and descend into a small clearing ringed with spruce to mile 13.7 (11,560). Enter the trees again and follow the trail as it bears to the right and traverses about 200 feet to the Continental Divide, which is broad and forested here and barely recognizable as the backbone of the continent. Descend along the crest of the divide due west on a trail that might be difficult to spot in places.

As you approach Spring Creek Pass, Colorado Highway 149 is visible below through the spruce and aspen. Exit the trees just above the highway and cross over the buried diversion ditch ahead, which sends water from the headwaters of Cebolla Creek to the Eastern Slope. This segment ends at mile 14.5 (10,898), where Colorado Highway 149 tops the Continental Divide at Spring Creek Pass.

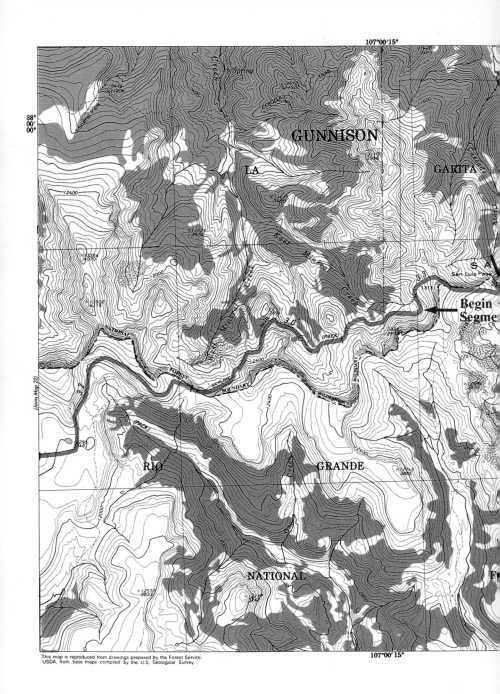

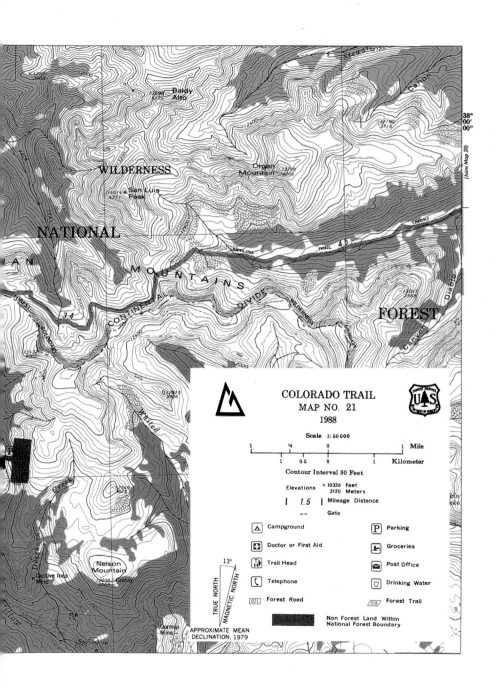

Non Forest Land Within National Forest Boundary

Volcanic cliffs above Jarosa Mesa, Rio Grande National Forest

◭ SEGMENT 22 18.3 Miles

Spring Creek Pass to Carson Saddle   **+ 3,980 Feet Elevation Gain**

Location	Mileage	From Denver	Elevation
Spring Creek Pass	0.0	348.2	10,898
Big Buck Creek	9.8		11,480
Coney Summit	16.6		13,334
Carson Saddle	18.3	366.5	12,360

CT Series Maps 22 & 23 (see pages 194-195 & 200-201).

With an average elevation of more than 12,000 feet, this segment has the distinction of being the loftiest single portion of the CT. Not surprisingly, it also tops out at the trail's high point, 13,334-foot Coney Summit. The trail winds its way along the broad, grassy alpine ridges of the Continental Divide and only once drops down into a suitable camping area at Big Buck Creek. Otherwise the entire route is waterless, but you can descend short distances to the headwaters of either Rambouillet Park or Ruby Creek for water and a more protected campsite.

This segment, like the previous one, follows a challenging alpine route. Although a well-defined jeep road does delineate the CT for the first 10 miles, the next 7 miles to Coney Summit are mostly trailless with only an occasional stock driveway cairn or carsonite post to mark the way. Map and compass readings might be necessary on occasion. Mountain bikers might consider detouring around this segment, for the trail is steep and becomes a quagmire during rains.

Hiking on this segment's grassy, rolling highlands and extensive rock fields is not particularly dangerous in itself, but lingering summer snowfields can turn the route into a threatening obstacle course. Likewise, frequent summer thunderstorms may pose a significant lightning hazard.

On the positive side, this exposed alpine ridge abounds with views nearly every step of the way. To the southwest are the Needle Mountains and Grenadier Range; while to the west, in a confusing jumble of summits, are three popular fourteeners: Handies, Redcloud, and Sunshine peaks. To the north, down the valley of the Lake Fork, is Colorado's second largest natural body of water, Lake San Cristobal.

Although there is some controversy over the naming of the lake, there is no question as to how it was formed. Somewhere between 700 and 350 years ago, the Slumgullion Earthflow, a massive landslide of mud and earth, detached itself from Cannibal Plateau and flowed down to dam the valley, thus creating the emerald green lake. (It is called slumgullion because its brightly colored, mineralized contents reminded New Englanders of the discarded entrails of a slaughtered whale.) The escarpments here were formerly thought to be lava flows extruded on the surface, but are now recognized to have been formed out of airborne ash so hot that it was welded together upon deposition, forming a dense, crystalline rock layer.

The most likely, if not the most romantic, tale of the naming of Lake San Cristobal recalls the H. G. Prout Ute Reservation survey of 1873. It seems one of the engineers, a Cornishman, was a great admirer of Tennyson, and one night around the campfire persuaded his colleagues to bestow on the lake the name of one of the poet's fictional landscapes.

Trailhead/Access Points

Spring Creek Pass Trailhead: This obvious trailhead is located where Colorado Highway 149 tops the Continental Divide at Spring Creek Pass. The pass is approximately 17 miles southeast of Lake City and 33 miles northwest of Creede. There are a few pullouts and picnic tables here, but this is not an official campground and facilities are minimal. A jeep road, FS-550, continues west from the top of the pass near the divide and serves as the CT route for the first several miles of this segment.

Carson Saddle, Wager Gulch Road Trail Access: See Segment 23.

LAKE CITY SERVICES

Distance from Trail: 17 miles

Bank	First Nat'l. Bank	231 Silver	(303) 944-2242
Bus	None		
Dining	Lake City Cafe	310 N. Gunnison Ave.	(303) 944-2733
	Western Belle Lodge	1221 Hwy 149	(303) 944-2415
Gear	The Sportsman	238 S. Gunnison Ave.	(303) 944-2526
Groceries	Lake City Market	951 Hwy 149 North	(303) 944-2332
Information	Chamber of Commerce	3rd & Silver	(303) 944-2527
Laundry	The Wash of Lake City	325 Silver	(303) 944-2655
Lodging	Lake City Resort	307 Gunnison Ave.	(303) 944-2866
	Western Belle Lodge	1221 Hwy 149	(303) 944-2415
Medical	Lake City Medical Center	700 Henson	(303) 944-2331
Post Office	Lake City Post Office	803 Gunnison Ave.	(303) 944-2560
Showers	The Wash of Lake City	325 Silver	(303) 944-2655

Supplies, Services, and Accommodations

It is 17 miles to Lake City on Colorado Highway 149 from Spring Creek Pass. The town has a grocery and a few local pubs as well as some cabins that are usually full during the tourist season.

Maps

CT Series: Maps 22 and 23 (see pages 194-195 and 200-201).
USFS: Gunnison National Forest, Rio Grande National Forest.
USGS Quadrangles: Slumgullion Pass, Lake San Cristobal, Finger Mesa.

Trail Description

Begin at the cul-de-sac pullout parking area on the west side of Colorado Highway 149 at Spring Creek Pass. The CT follows FS-550 as it ascends west from the cul-de-sac, then levels off in a spruce forest punctuated with meandering meadows. Continue on the jeep road and notice the headwaters of Rito Hondo Creek off to the left (south) and below at mile 1.6 (11,040).

Cross a small stream at mile 2.5 (11,320) while ascending toward Jarosa Mesa on the jeep road through a wide corridor in the spruce forest. Notice the old stock driveway posts on tree trunks on either side of this elongated, ascending meadow. Top out on a grassy field at mile 2.7 (11,480) east of the wide, rolling Jarosa Mesa, which appears velvety green because of its extensive covering of willows. Bear to the left (southwest) as the sometimes indistinct jeep track continues around the perimeter of the mesa. Snow Mesa and Bristol Head can be identified to the east, and the Rio Grande Pyramid is visible ahead.

The jeep track penetrates the willows at mile 3.3 (11,520) and continues a traverse around the southeast side of Jarosa Mesa. Exit the willows at mile 4.1 (11,480) as the jeep track gradually ascends west, then northwest. Take the right fork (north-northwest), marked as FS-550, at mile 5.8 (11,840). The summit of Jarosa Mesa east of here appears nearly flat from this perspective. Those considering camping in this area will have to descend into the headwaters of Buck Creek to the south or Rambouillet Park to the north to find water and some protection from the extreme exposure of this alpine highland.

Descend slightly to another jeep track junction at mile 6.5 (11,720), where an unmarked fork goes to the left. FS-550 continues its descent north into the willows and drops into Rambouillet Park. The unmarked jeep track at left continues the CT as it traverses around the south side of Antenna Summit (12,305), so called because of a radio tower at the top. If you want to follow the high divide route over Antenna Summit, head northwest on the grassy tundra between the two jeep tracks toward a very obvious swath cut in the willows. This swath ascends to the smooth, rounded top of Antenna Summit. Climb northwest, then west, to the summit using the convenient corridor cleared through the willows. The photovoltaic antenna array on top seems strangely out of place in this remote location. Five fourteeners are visible from this lofty point. Also clearly visible is the path of the Slumgullion Earthflow.

Bear generally south-southwest from the Antenna Summit and pick up the route of the old stock driveway as it descends to the saddle at mile 8.2 (12,040). Join up here with the jeep track and CT which traverses the south side of Antenna Summit, and follow it 0.2 mile uphill (southwest) to another grassy knob on the divide. Begin a slow descent southwest on the jeep track that follows the rolling highland. As you approach timberline, the jeep track drops more quickly until it levels off at mile 9.8 (11,480) in a gently inclined meadow ringed with spruce on the headwaters of Big Buck Creek. The route here varies greatly from that shown on the USGS Lake San Cristobal map.

Bear to the right (west) on the jeep track and ascend an elevated, marshy drainage. Just before crossing the saddle ahead, leave the jeep track at mile 10.3 (11,720) and bear to the left (south), following a series of posts 600 feet across the grassy marsh. Pick up a jeep track as you enter a spruce forest and continue a sometimes steep ascent, bearing generally south.

At mile 11.0 (12,000), break out of the trees onto the lower end of a broad, slightly inclined, willow-covered ridge that extends west toward the grassy crest of the Continental Divide. Follow the indistinct jeep track in a more westerly direction through the willows. As you progress, an unmistakable swath cuts through the willows and slowly assumes a more southwesterly direction. As the willows becomes patchy and the swath less recognizable, the CT bears west again through the willow thicket. The trail bears to the left (south) as it exits the willows in grassy tundra at mile 11.6 (12,200), and turns through a couple of ill-defined switchbacks. From here, the CT is marked mostly by carsonite posts on a narrow — and momentary — alpine footpath that bears generally south-southwest near the edge of the willows.

The route assumes a more southwesterly direction at mile 12.6 (12,440) as it heads for an indistinct, rocky saddle on the divide 0.5 mile beyond. Pick up a short trail remnant at the saddle, then begin an ascent to the right into a grassy bowl. This impressive cirque forms the main headwater drainage of Ruby Creek. Take advantage of a short section of trail that climbs steeply through several switchbacks to a rocky point on the divide at mile 14.0 (13,040). If it is a clear day, take a few minutes to observe the dramatic surroundings. Follow the route marked with carsonite posts as it bears generally south-southwest, detouring around patches of talus and rock where necessary. At the crest of this huge, rolling highland the views extend all the way to San Luis Peak on the northeast horizon. At mile 14.5 (13,000), the route bends to the southwest, then west, where a saddle becomes visible.

Descend to the saddle at mile 15.0 (12,840) and then immediately begin a diagonal ascent to the south-southwest, crossing an inclined rock field to the gentle slopes of a smaller and rockier alpine highland. This ascent has small sections of trail near its top, marked with a cairn. Contour to the right (southwest), still following the route of the stock driveway. At mile 15.5 (12,960), yet another saddle comes into view to the southwest. Descend to this saddle at mile 15.9 (12,840) and begin climbing generally south-southwest to the CT's high point, 13,334-foot Coney Summit.

Take a few minutes to ponder your route to the summit from here. The route shown on the USGS Finger Mesa map ascends a steep, north-facing talus slope, which levels out a little bit below on the left (east) side of the summit. Early in the season, this route can be blocked by steep and potentially dangerous snow fields. If this route is snowed in, it is possible that a narrow, grassy corridor between the snowfield and a steep drop-off at the very crest of the divide (west of and above the route shown on the USGS map) might be thawed out at an earlier date. However, if this alternative is also snowed in, it is much more dangerous than the route shown on the USGS map because of the steep drop-off west of Coney. In a situation such as this, mountaineering experience is essential.

If there are no snow fields, ascend south-southwest from the saddle at mile 15.9. Head slightly south at the steep talus slope, where you may pick up a short section of trail that takes you to the broad, open summit of Coney at mile 16.6 (13,334). Widely spaced stock driveway markers identify the route shown on the USGS map east of, and slightly below, the high point of this Continental Divide crest. Don't be too alarmed if you meet a rental jeep loaded with flatlanders from Lake City here, Coney is a popular tourist destination.

From the top, an indistinct jeep track begins and descends south-southwest to a grassy saddle at mile 17.1 (13,080), between Coney Summit and Point 13,277. Bear to the right (west-northwest) on an obvious jeep road and descend steeply into the old Carson mining district. Go right (west-northwest) on an intersecting jeep road at mile 18.1 (12,320). Continue to a three-cornered jeep road intersection at a saddle on the divide at mile 18.3 (12,360). This obscure point is given the name Carson Saddle to identify it as the end of this segment. The jeep road that descends northward from Carson Saddle into Wager Gulch eventually ties into Colorado Highway 149 near Lake City. The route of the CT follows the jeep road that bends to the left (south) here and descends into the headwaters of Lost Trail Creek.

Notes

194

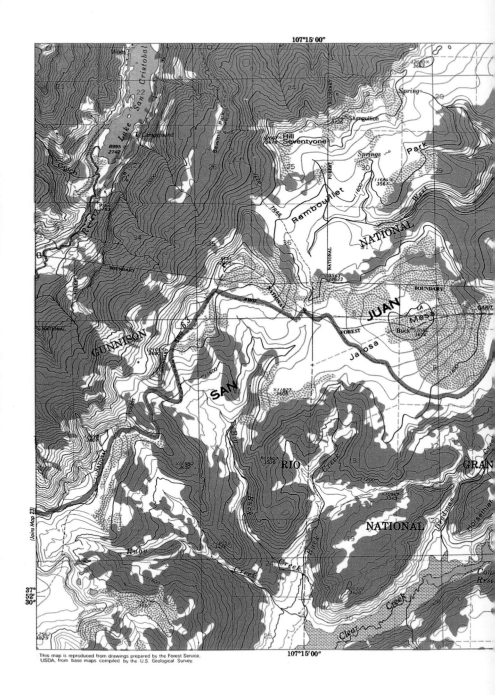

This map is reproduced from drawings prepared by the Forest Service.
USDA, from base maps compiled by the U.S. Geological Survey.

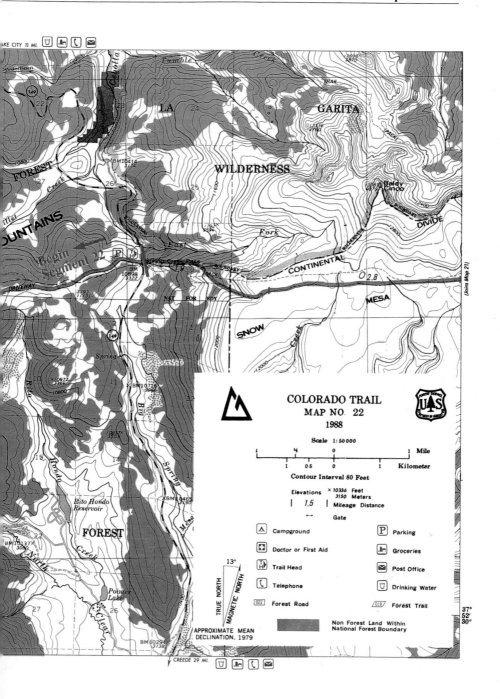

COLORADO TRAIL
MAP NO. 22
1988

Scale 1:50 000

1	½	0	1 Mile
1	0.5	0	1 Kilometer

Contour Interval 80 Feet

Elevations ×10336 Feet
3150 Meters

| 1.5 | Mileage Distance

← → Gate

△ Campground   P Parking

⊡ Doctor or First Aid   🛒 Groceries

🅷 Trail Head   ✉ Post Office

☏ Telephone   🚰 Drinking Water

022 Forest Road   019 Forest Trail

Non Forest Land Within
National Forest Boundary

13°

TRUE NORTH   MAGNETIC NORTH

APPROXIMATE MEAN
DECLINATION, 1979

CREEDE 29 MI.

Eroded volcanic ash along Pole Creek, Rio Grande National Forest

▲ SEGMENT 23   12.0 Miles

Carson Saddle to Rio Grande Reservoir Rd.   + 1,020 Feet Elevation Gain

Location	Mileage	From Denver	Elevation
Carson Saddle	0.0	366.5	12,360
Lost Trail Creek	1.5		12,000
Pass	3.6		12,920
Pole Creek	7.8		11,480
Rio Grande Reservoir Road	12.0	378.5	10,560

CT Series Maps 23 & 24 (see maps 200-201 & 208-209).

The challenging, high-altitude route of the CT continues in this segment, although now it more often follows established trails through more-protected water drainages, which makes the going a little easier. However, you will have to bushwhack through thick and sometimes marshy tundra grasses in brief stretches on the upper parts of Lost Trail and Pole creeks. In the case of Pole Creek, it is important that you carefully maintain your bearings at the head of Cataract Gulch or you may find yourself headed down the trail to Cataract Lake by mistake. As in the previous segments, plan to have a map and compass handy.

Campsites abound along Lost Trail Creek and the broad, grassy meadows of upper Pole Creek, where trout splash in the meandering stream. Mountain bikers may opt to detour around this segment using the Cinnamon Pass Road.

The old Carson mining district began when Christopher J. Carson discovered gold-bearing ores here in the early 1880s. The town of Carson, which still exists as a well-preserved ghost town, developed at the head of Wager Gulch about a mile north of the mining district. Most of the supplies, however, were sent in from the south via the road, built in 1887, up Lost Trail Creek. The most prolific producers here were the Bonanza King and the St. Jacob's Mines, but by the early 1900s even these properties had been abandoned.

Trailhead/Access Points

Carson Saddle, Wager Gulch Trail Access: From Lake City, travel south on Colorado Highway 149 approximately 1.5 miles to a turnoff that leads right to Lake San Cristobal. Continue 9.3 miles on the road up the valley of the Lake Fork to the 4WD road turnoff at left that leads to Wager Gulch and Carson. It is approximately 5 miles up this rough road to the Carson Saddle, so called because it is a low point on the Continental Divide about a mile beyond the old townsite of Carson.

Rio Grande Reservoir – Stony Pass Road: See Segment 24.

Supplies, Services, and Accommodations

Available in Lake City (see Segment 22).

Maps

CT Series: Maps 23 and 24 (see pages 200-201 and 208-209).
USFS: Gunnison National Forest, Rio Grande National Forest.
USGS Quadrangles: Finger Mesa, Pole Creek Mountain.

Trail Description

From the three-cornered jeep road intersection at Carson Saddle, gradually descend southward on the road past the ruins of the old mining district. Be alert for the trail to bear obscurely off the jeep road at mile 0.5 (12,200), just before the road turns east for a steep descent into the valley ahead. The trail angles away from the road, then quickly rounds a ridge and assumes a westerly heading high above Lost Trail Creek. The trail descends slowly to a side stream and a low point at mile 1.5 (12,000), although still well above the wide, marshy valley bottom of the main creek drainage. Dead ahead is a formidable-looking rock outcropping. The CT weaves it way through these rocks for the next 0.3 mile. This area is notorious for remaining heavily snowed in during early summer.

Once through this rock-and-talus obstacle course, the CT opens into the upper portion of a wide, gently inclined, grassy meadow at the head of Lost Trail Creek. Trending a few degrees northwest, the trail, which is obscure at times in the thick alpine grasses, stays in the upper part of the meadow away from the tangled mass of willows near the creek. It then ascends to the right of the rather ominous cliffs visible at the head of the valley.

The CT bears west-northwest as it gains elevation on the hillside. At mile 3.0 (12,560), the trail makes a quick double switchback and continues an ascent past the unusual gnome-like figures so typical of the geology in this part of the San Juans. Your ascent ends at the unnamed pass at mile 3.6 (12,920).

From the pass, the trail makes a gradual descent to the west, high above the headwaters of Pole Creek. Follow the trail southwest as it settles onto a broad, descending ridge of the Continental Divide and approaches a prominent cliff at the head of the cirque that forms Cataract Gulch. Reach a rather obscure but important trail intersection at mile 5.0 (12,360) near the cliff above Cataract Lake. The CT bears to the left (southwest) here as another trail continues ahead to eventually descend northward into Cataract Gulch. Proceed south-southwest, dropping down into the headwaters of Pole Creek on an intermittent trail across a broad, marshy alpine meadow. The trail reappears at mile 5.5 (12,120) on the north side of the creek and continues a sometimes steep descent into the long and spacious upper valley, carpeted with fringed gentian in late summer.

Continue south-southwest on a nearly flat, and sometimes faint, trail that follows the meanderings of Pole Creek. The broad valley narrows into a tighter V-shaped gap beyond mile 6.9 (11,680). At a deep and difficult ford, cross briefly to the east side of Pole Creek at mile 7.8 (11,480), then return to the west side 800 feet beyond.

The trail leaves the narrow gap at mile 8.3 (11,280) and leads into another rolling meadow at timberline. A side trail forks sharply to the right (northwest) here and ascends the North Fork then the Middle Fork of Pole Creek. Continue south-southeast 150 feet beyond the trail junction and make a final ford to the east side of Pole Creek. The trail follows a grassy bench slightly above the creek. Another intersecting side trail at mile 9.0 (11,200) forks sharply to the right (west) and ascends the West Fork of Pole Creek. Continue south 400 feet beyond this trail junction. Be sure to take a short walk off the trail to view scenic Pole Creek Falls.

The CT continues a gradual descent to the south, staying on a grassy, spruced-lined bench while Pole Creek drops off further and further below. Several intersecting side streams provide water for those considering camping here. The trail drops to the level of Pole Creek at mile 10.4 (10,960) and enters another long, grassy meadow ringed with willow and spruce. Pass through a gate at mile 11.1 (10,920) and pause briefly to check out the CT's route up the valley of Bear Creek, visible for several miles to the south-southwest. Begin a short but steep descent from the elevated meadows. Pole Creek roars as it accelerates in the cascade at right. Avoid an intersecting side trail that forks to the right at mile 11.7 (10,600) and continue ahead (south) through a meadow. This segment ends where the trail intersects the Rio Grande Reservoir-Stony Pass Road at mile 12.0 (10,560). A sign indicates that the reservoir is down the road to the left (southeast and east) and Stony Pass to the right (northwest and west).

Notes

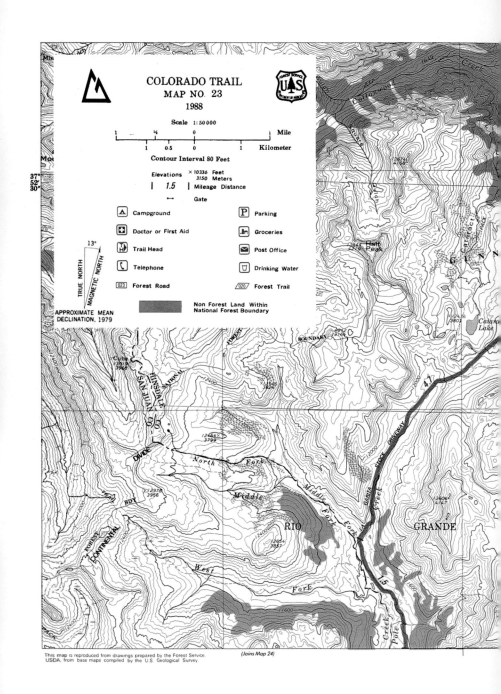

COLORADO TRAIL
MAP NO. 23
1988

Scale 1:50 000

Contour Interval 80 Feet

Elevations × 10336 Feet
3150 Meters

| 1.5 | Mileage Distance

↦ Gate

⬜ Campground   ⓟ Parking

⬜ Doctor or First Aid   ⬜ Groceries

⬜ Trail Head   ⬜ Post Office

⬜ Telephone   ⬜ Drinking Water

⬜ Forest Road   ⬜ Forest Trail

Non Forest Land Within
National Forest Boundary

APPROXIMATE MEAN
DECLINATION, 1979

13°

TRUE NORTH
MAGNETIC NORTH

This map is reproduced from drawings prepared by the Forest Service.
USDA, from base maps compiled by the U.S. Geological Survey.

(Joins Map 24)

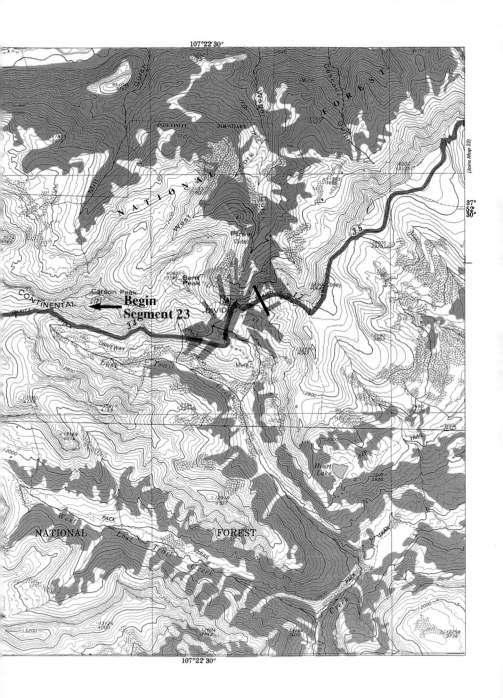

Looking down Elk Creek from the Continental Divide, Weminuche Wilderness

⚠ SEGMENT 24   21.1 Miles

Rio Grande Reservoir Rd. to Molas Pass   **+4,600 Feet Elevation Gain**

Location	Mileage	From Denver	Elevation
Rio Grande Reservoir Road	0.0	378.5	10,560
Continental Divide	7.3		12,680
Animas River	16.1		8,940
Molas Pass	21.1	399.6	10,880

CT Series Maps 24 & 25 (see pages 208-209 & 216-217).

The mystical San Juan Mountains reach a crescendo in the rugged and beautiful Needle Mountains and Grenadier Range. This 21.1-mile segment penetrates much of this spectacular scenery and here the trail crosses the Continental Divide for the last time. Mountain bikers will have to bypass this segment because it passes through the Weminuche Wilderness.

Hikers have plenty of challenges in this segment, starting with the crossing of the Rio Grande. This is the longest ford on the entire CT. It is precarious, deep, and frigid. Another possible difficulty is the extreme, almost dizzying, steepness of the trail at the headwaters of Elk Creek. Snow fields here may linger well into summer and could be a hazardous obstacle, even for experienced mountaineers. Some CT trekkers have reported becoming disoriented on the rolling divide highlands above Beartown where the trail is sometimes obscure and not well marked. In addition, there are other trails and markers here that compound the confusion; so be attentive in this area.

The first 4 miles of this segment follow a 4WD road up Bear Creek. Kite Lake, at the head of the creek, is a popular destination for jeepers and you may even be able to hitch a ride across the Rio Grande or all the way to Beartown. With the exception of a few mine dumps, nothing remains of Beartown today, which was a bustling mining community in the 1890s.

Once backpackers arrive at the Animas River, they are confronted with a unique choice — either to finish the last 70 miles of the CT or to take a nostalgic shortcut to Durango via the narrow-gauge railroad. This curious remnant of the past was constructed in 1882 by the D&RG Railroad and remained part of the line into the early 1980s, when it was sold to a company that now maintains it as one of Colorado's historical highlights. Don't be tempted to hike along the railroad tracks in the narrow Animas River canyon as a shortcut to Silverton; locomotives can appear quickly around blind corners and it is illegal anyway.

The enthusiasm that Captain Charles Baker had for the San Juans was unfortunately never justified by the scant quantity of gold he panned from its rivers. But after his death at the hands of the Utes, on whose land he was trespassing, other prospectors discovered a bonanza in the area's silver lodes. Eventually, enough pressure was exerted on the Utes to force them to cede a large portion of their land in the infamous Brunot Treaty of 1873. Soon after, the valleys around Bakers Park echoed with activity. The little town of Silverton sprang up in the park and thrived for nearly 20 years until the Sherman Silver Purchase Act was repealed in 1893, devastating the economy of the area. By then, however, the region had received its legendary nickname, which it is still known by many today: the Silvery San Juan.

Trailhead/Access Points

Rio Grande Reservoir Road – Stony Pass Road: From Creede, drive west on Colorado Highway 149 for 21 miles and turn left on the side road marked "Rio Grande Reservoir." Continue 19 miles to where the graded road ends and the 4WD road begins. From here on, the road is rough, occasionally steep, often muddy, and sometimes impassible. Continue 7 miles to where the CT crosses the road at a sign reading "Pole Creek Trail." This road continues to Silverton via Stony Pass.

US-550 – Molas Trail Trailhead: See Segment 25.

Supplies, Services, and Accommodations

There are no services available within this segment.

Maps

CT Series: Maps 24 and 25 (see pages 208-209 and 216-217).
USFS: Rio Grande National Forest, San Juan National Forest.
USGS Quadrangles: Pole Creek Mountain, Rio Grande Reservoir, Storm King
  Peak, Snowdon Peak.

Trail Description

Starting from where the CT joins the Rio Grande Reservoir Road near Pole Creek, go right (northwest) on the road about 150 feet, then make a sharp left (south) on the intersecting jeep road. A sign here marks this as the way to Beartown. Gradually descend on the jeep road to the long ford of the Rio Grande at mile 0.4 (10,440). If you are lucky, you might catch a ride with 4WD enthusiasts across the river, which runs deep and cold in early summer.

Once across the Rio Grande, follow the jeep road as it ascends west, then southwest, through a grassy, inclined valley bordered by a thick spruce forest. Pass through a gate at mile 3.1 (10,920) and ascend 0.5 mile further to the lower end of a large meadow. As the jeep road enters several scattered groups of spruce and begins an ascent out of the upper end of the meadow at mile 4.5 (11,320), it passes through the townsite of Beartown. All that is left are a few long-abandoned mine dumps. Fields of columbine now bloom on slopes once trampled by the feet of fortune seekers.

Be on the lookout here for the trail to leave the road at right (north). It rises quickly through a series of switchbacks to timberline. The trail then traverses west at about the 11,880-foot level into a lovely little side drainage covered with wildflowers until early August. After a few more switchbacks, the CT links up with a wider trail at mile 6.1 (12,080) in a larger side drainage. Across the drainage are the remains of several cabins that might provide shelter during one of the frequent San Juan showers. Continue at right (northwest) a few hundred feet to a fork in the trail. This is where the CT route can get confusing. From here, your objective is to get to the top of the Continental Divide (the long, flat, grassy ridge visible about 0.5 mile to the west), where the trail then descends west into Elk Creek. This point on the divide is visible from where you now stand by looking almost due west. If you have sharp eyes, or field glasses, you may even be able to pick out the sign post on the divide marking this spot.

The source of the confusion stems at least in part from the variety of routes in this area and the lack of trail markings. From the fork in the trail above, continue ahead (northwest) and avoid the old jeep track on the left that descends slightly into the drainage. Proceed about 0.3 mile to the head of the drainage. Here, the trail ascends into a short but very pronounced V-shaped gully.

This is where many people have been confused, so pay very close attention. At the top of this gully, where it opens into the rolling divide highland country, you want to leave the trail (which continues ahead to Stony Pass) and bear left, trending to the west-southwest, until you pick up an obscure jeep track that takes a more southwesterly heading toward the crest of the Continental Divide.

Indian paintbrush wildflowers

Follow the jeep track as it bends to the southwest and slowly mounts the divide at mile 6.9 (12,600). Lingering snow fields here might obscure the route in early summer. The jeep track eventually bears due south as it follows the wide, rolling crest of the Continental Divide. The divide here is speckled with marsh marigolds that bloom on tundra saturated by melting snow. On a clear day, it is possible to pick out massive San Luis Peak and the long, horizontal profile of Snow Mesa to the east-northeast.

At mile 7.3 (12,680), the CT takes a sharp right (west), leaving the jeep track that continues south along the divide. As you begin a long descent into Elk Creek, the trail immediately loses 500 feet of elevation as it maneuvers through nearly 30 switchbacks on an extremely steep mountainside, seemingly held in place by the intertwining roots of an exquisite alpine flower garden.

The trail levels out briefly near an old mine cabin near the headwaters of Elk Creek at mile 8.3 (12,080), a convenient place for a campsite. Below the cabin, the valley narrows dramatically into a tight gorge bordered by sheer cliffs with numerous precipitous waterfalls. The decent from the Continental Divide through this gorge could be dangerous if it is blocked by snowfields.

The trail briefly crosses to the south side of upper Elk Creek at mile 8.6 (11,800), then returns to the north bank 0.2 mile beyond. Elk Creek plunges farther down the gorge, leaving the trail perched ledge-like a dizzying distance above. Enter the security of a spruce forest at mile 9.3 (11,400) and continue a steep descent bearing generally west. The trail levels off and takes on a north-westerly heading closer to the creek at mile 9.8 (10,720). Campsites are more numerous in the valley below the gorge.

Ford a large side stream at mile 10.7 (10,320) as the CT swings to the west and gradually pulls away from the creek. Descend a rocky trail in a sunny Douglas fir and aspen forest at mile 12.6 (10,000), where the impressive faces of Vestal and Arrow peaks are reflected in a picturesque pond at trailside. The trail continues its descent, steeply at times, to mile 14.0 (9,360), where it parallels the creek in a narrowing canyon. Listen for the whistle of the narrow-gauge locomotive as the CT ascends slightly and pulls away from Elk Creek.

A sign and register at mile 15.5 (9,040) mark your exit from the Weminuche Wilderness. There are two trails to choose from here. For those who would like a shortcut to Durango, the left fork descends to a whistle stop on the D&SR Railroad at the Elk Park siding. If you are continuing on the CT, take the right fork, which traverses northwest slightly above the Animas River and Elk Park. Descend to and cross the tracks at mile 16.1 (8940), then continue north 700 feet to a footbridge spanning the river.

About 600 feet beyond the bridge, ford Molas Creek and begin a monotonous, 1,300-foot ascent on a zigzagging trail with more than 30 switchbacks. One benefit of this section is watching the spectacular Animas Canyon and Grenadier Range come into view. Notice the dramatic metamorphic folds in the huge rock wall just opposite the trail.

The trail finally tops out at mile 18.6 (10,280) and leaves the trees behind in a gently sloping meadow. Climb steeply through two switchbacks at mile 19.3 (10,360) as Molas Creek rushes down a nearby deep ravine. Take the left fork as the trail levels off just beyond. Ascend to the edge of a spruce forest at mile 19.8 (10,600) where the trail splits. The right (north) fork goes 0.2 mile further to the Molas Trail parking area just off US-550. To stay on the CT, bear to the left (west) and follow the trail as it curves around and assumes a southerly bearing, then ford Molas Creek at mile 20.1 (10,520). The trail makes several wide, meandering switchbacks as it ascends, at times following a posted route through an alpine meadow. This segment ends at mile 21.1 (10,880), as the CT crosses US-550 just 600 feet north of the highway's summit on Molas Pass.

Notes

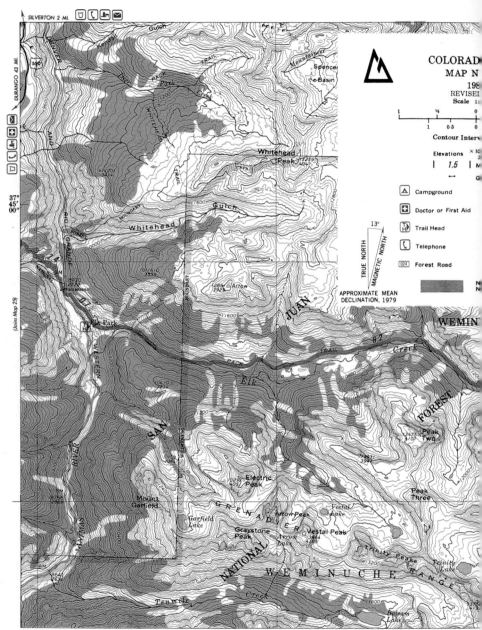

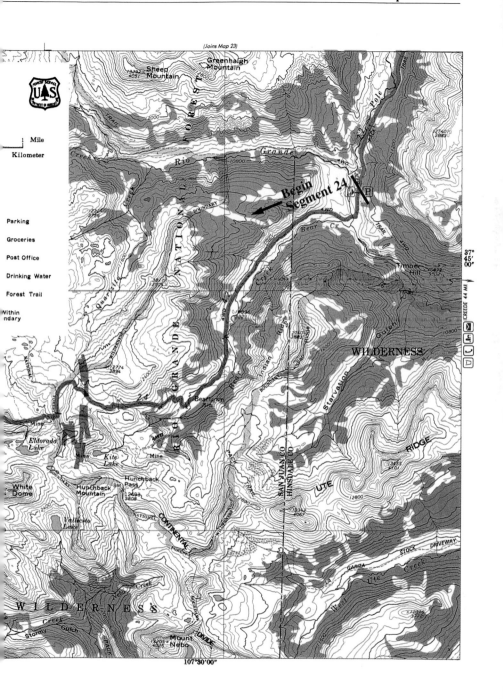

Greenhalgh
Mountain

Sheep
Mountain

FOREST

Rio   Grande

Begin
Segment 24

Bear   Cr.

Parking

Groceries

Post Office

Drinking Water

Forest Trail

Within
ndary

Timber
Hill

WILDERNESS

Starvation   Gulch

Beartown
Smill

RIDGE

Eldorado
Lake

Kite
Lake

Mine

UTE

White
Dome

Hunchback
Pass

Hunchback
Mountain

CONTINENTAL

Vallecito
Lake

STOCK   DRIVEWAY

GARITA

Ute   Creek

West

W I L D E R N E S S

Stormy   Gulch

Nebo   Creek

Mount
Nebo

37°
45'
00"

CREEDE 44 MI.

107°30'00"

Cascade Creek, San Juan National Forest

▲ SEGMENT 25   19.9 Miles

Molas Pass to Bolam Pass Road   **+2,720 Feet Elevation Gain**

Location	Mileage	From Denver	Elevation
Molas Pass	0.0	399.6	10,880
Unnamed Pass	11.3		12,490
Cascade Creek	13.8		10,820
Bolam Pass Road	19.9	419.5	11,120

CT Series Map 25 (see pages 216-217).

The CT traverses a unique, rolling highland in this segment. Once heavily forested, the terrain was devastated by a fire in 1879 and has still not recovered, despite efforts at reforestation. One result of the fire is the unequalled panoramas south to the La Plata Mountains and west to the Needle Mountains and Grenadier Range. Prominent in the initial portion of this segment are 12,968-foot Engineer Mountain, known as Station 31 to the Hayden Survey, and 13,077-foot Snowdon Peak, which was named after the founder of Silverton, Francis Marion Snowdon.

From US-550, the CT gradually climbs and then contours above Lime, North Lime, and West Lime creeks under an impressive pediment of cliffs high above the trail. Large portions of this segment have no forest cover and snow fields may linger well into July. Backpackers will want to tarry in this segment and perhaps set up a high-altitude camp in the shadow of the Twin Sisters or Rolling Mountain. Mountain bikers can rejoin the official route of the CT at Molas Pass after a long detour around the Weminuche Wilderness.

Some trekkers have been confused by the two Molas Lakes in the vicinity of Molas Pass at the beginning of this segment. Molas Lake is east of US-550 near the Molas Trail Trailhead. It is privately owned and encircled with attractive camping sites. Some limited services are available at the general store here. Little Molas Lake is west of US-550 and is located on Forest Service property. There is no official campground here, although many use it for dispersed, primitive car camping. Little Molas Lake is popular with fishermen, campers, and picnickers.

Trailhead/Access Points

US-550 – Molas Trail Trailhead: This segment begins at Molas Pass, but there are no parking facilities here. Long-term parking is available nearby at the Molas Trail Trailhead. From Molas Pass on US-550, drive north about a mile to a dirt road on the right marked as "Molas Trail" (this point is about 5.5 miles south on US-550 from Silverton). From the parking area, an unmaintained road (the beginning of the Molas Trail) leads south 0.2 mile to the CT.

Little Molas Lake Trailhead: From Molas Pass on US-550, go north 0.4 mile and turn left (west) on a dirt road. Continue a mile to the Little Molas Lake fishermen parking area. The CT passes on the west side of the lake.

Bolam Pass Trail Access: See Segment 26.

Supplies, Services, and Accommodations

Silverton has groceries, accommodations and regular bus service. Molas Lake Campground, near Molas Trail Trailhead, carries some limited grocery items, but they do seem to have an accommodating supply of the essentials for backpackers just emerging from the wilderness — cold beer and hot showers.

Maps

CT Series: Map 25 (see pages 216-217).
USFS: San Juan National Forest.
USGS Quadrangles: Snowdon Peak, Silverton, Ophir, Engineer Mountain, Hermosa Peak.

SILVERTON SERVICES — Distance from Trail: 5 miles

Bank	Citizen's State Bank	1218 Greene St.	(303) 387-5502
Bus	Greyhound	Silverton Drive-in	(303) 387-5658
Dining	Chattanooga Cafe	116 E. 12th	(303) 387-5892
	Romero's	1151 Greene St.	(303) 387-0213
Gear	Outdoor World	1234 Greene St.	(303) 387-5628
Groceries	Greene Street Market	717 Greene St.	(303) 387-5652
	M&D Market	959 Greene St.	(303) 387-5341
Information	Chamber of Commerce	414 Greene St.	(303) 387-5654
Laundry	The Silverton Wash Tub	on Greene St.	(303) 387-9981
Lodging	Prospector Motel	1015 Greene St.	(303) 387-5466
	Smedley's B&B	on Greene St.	(303) 387-5423
Medical	Silverton Clinic	1450 Greene St.	(303) 387-5354
Post Office	Silverton Post Office	138 W. 12th	(303) 387-5402
Showers	None		

Trail Description

This segment begins on US-550, about 600 feet north of the sign that reads "Molas Pass Summit, Elevation 10,910." Look for the trail on the west side of the highway. The CT soon crosses a cut in on old snow fence and meanders through gently rolling terrain, at times following a posted route, toward Little Molas Lake less than a mile away.

The trail travels around to the west side of the lake, close to the shoreline at times, then crosses another trail that heads north several hundred feet to the fishermen parking area. Proceed north-northwest on the CT as it drops into a small group of trees and then travels west to intersect a road. Follow the road at left (south-southwest) a few steps, then look for the trail to continue again at right (west). From here, the CT ascends the terraced terrain on a series of gentle switchbacks. Notice the lodgepole pines planted after the 1879 fire.

After 0.7 mile, go right and uphill on the intersecting old road, bearing southwest then west. In 0.5 mile, a short section of trail leaves the old road to the right and ascends to an old jeep track that continues the ascent to the north-northeast. In about 0.6 mile up this jeep track, as you approach the dark grey cliffs of 12,849-foot West Turkshead Peak, look for a well-built trail to exit the jeep track to the left (north to northwest). For the next several miles the CT follows the approximate route of an old pack trail rebuilt by volunteers in 1987.

Approach the saddle between North Lime and Bear creeks at mile 4.0 (11,520). Looking north, there are views of Bear Mountain on the left and Sultan Mountain on the right. About 0.5 mile west of the saddle, a pack trail comes in from the right, although it is difficult to find. This side trail takes you down Bear Creek and US-550 northwest of Silverton. There is a commanding view at mile 5.0 (11,520) as you face the valley below: visible from right to left are Twin Sisters, Jura Knob, Engineer Mountain, Potato Hill, Snowdon Peak, and the Needle Mountains.

Descend several switchbacks and cross upper Lime Creek at mile 6.1 (11,340). The next couple of miles take you generally west to southwest into the upper West Lime Creek drainage. Notice the large conglomerate rocks that appear to have broken off the cliffs above and scattered about the area. There are many cascades and waterfalls here and fields of wildflowers in mid-summer. At mile 9.6 (11,920), just before you reach a small lake on the right, a stream comes out of the side of the mountain. Continue an ascent to the southwest.

At mile 10.3 (12,120), near a scenic alpine lake hidden from view by a willowy rise, the CT intersects the Engineer Mountain Trail and the Engine Creek Trail. Make a sharp right turn here (north then northwest) and continue on the CT. As you rise above the lake, the extensive ridge system of appropriately named Rolling Mountain is visible ahead. Shortly, the CT bears left (west to northwest) and bounces over a rocky hummock that may be drifted with snow into August. At mile 11.0 (12,320), the trail joins up with the historic Rico-Silverton Trail, a former mine trail. From here, you can take a side trip to South Fork Mineral Creek (FS-585) by descending north on the Rico-Silverton Trail. The CT ascends the Rico-Silverton, following it 0.3 mile southwest over a 12,490-foot unnamed pass south of Rolling Mountain. From the pass, the CT descends into the Cascade Creek drainage on several comfortable, newly built switchbacks passing fields of paintbrush and yellow compositae before entering the protection of trees.

At mile 12.3 (11,640), there are two consecutive trail intersections where care must be taken. At the first, avoid the trail coming in from your right; this leads to a nearby lake nestled in the trees and an excellent campsite. To continue on the CT, bear downhill to the left (southwest). About 200 feet beyond at the second trail intersection, go right (west) to stay on the CT. For the rest of this segment, you may see old sign posts marking the way as the Rico-Silverton Trail, which coincides for several miles with the CT. At mile 13.3 (10,920), the trail makes a cumbersome crossing of the cascades on White Creek.

Cross Cascade Creek at mile 13.8 (10,820), where the falls plunge into a seemingly bottomless gorge below. At this point, you may notice that the valley is squeezed together into a narrow cleft by the basement rocks of towering Grizzly Peak to the west and massive Rolling Mountain to the east. This is one of the scenic highlights of the Cascade Creek Valley. Just beyond the creek crossing, the trail descends slightly and precariously approaches the edge of the gorge before assuming a more secure position higher on the canyon walls. Those with steady nerves may want to check out the gorge up close.

On the west side of Cascade Creek, the trail mostly levels out at mile 14.2 (10,800) and then begins an ascent contouring in and out of several side drainages. At mile 16.3 (11,280), a short side trail descends to the end of the Cascade Divide Road (FS-579), which is visible below. This long, rough 4WD road provides a mid-segment trail access to mountain bikers and sturdy vehicles by exiting the Hermosa Park Road above Purgatory Ski Area (see Bolam Pass Trail Access, Segment 26). From the Cascade Divide Road side trail, continue an ascent south, then west on the CT. At mile 18.1 (11,760) the trail crosses a saddle — the divide between Cascade and Hermosa Creeks — and drops into the upper part of Tin Can Basin in the Hermosa Creek drainage. Almost due west and about 2 miles distant is Hermosa Peak, a prominent landmark visible for miles around. Lizard Head and the San Miguel Mountains are visible to the northwest.

Descend to the north, following posts and a faint trail through the meadow. These soon lead to an old road closed to vehicular traffic. Turn left here (west) and follow it downhill to trees and a road open to vehicles. Turn left (south then west) on this road and in 0.6 mile look for a cairn on the left (southwest) that marks the trail as it leaves the road. From the cairn, the trail goes into the forest for less than 0.3 mile and emerges on FS-578, the Bolam Pass Road, at mile 19.9 (11,120) near the south end of Celebration Lake, where this segment ends. If you miss the turn at the cairn, the road will also take you to Celebration Lake.

Sunset, San Juan Mountains

Notes

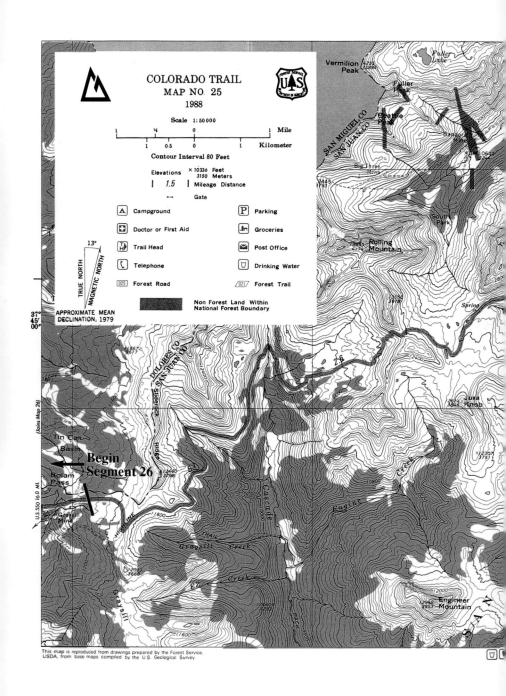

COLORADO TRAIL
MAP NO. 25
1988

Scale 1:50000

Contour Interval 80 Feet

Elevations ×10336 Feet
3150 Meters

| 1.5 | Mileage Distance

↔ Gate

△ Campground
⬡ Doctor or First Aid
Trail Head
☎ Telephone
025 Forest Road

P Parking
Groceries
✉ Post Office
Drinking Water
021 Forest Trail

Non Forest Land Within
National Forest Boundary

TRUE NORTH
MAGNETIC NORTH
13°

37°
45'
00"

APPROXIMATE MEAN
DECLINATION, 1979

Begin
Segment 26

This map is reproduced from drawings prepared by the Forest Service.
USDA, from base maps compiled by the U.S. Geological Survey.

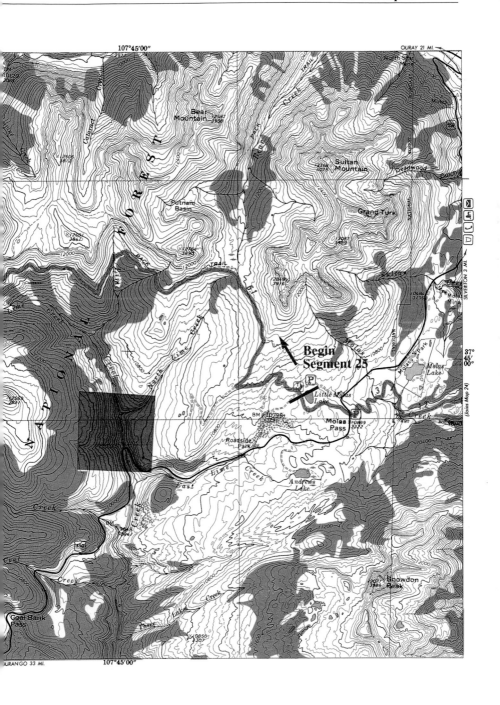

Rico Mountains, San Juan National Forest

◭ SEGMENT 26   11.0 Miles

Bolam Pass Road to Hotel Draw Road   **+1,320 Feet Elevation Gain**

Location	Mileage	From Denver	Elevation
Bolam Pass Road	0.0	419.5	11,120
Blackhawk Pass	6.9		11,970
Straight Creek	8.5		10,980
Hotel Draw Road (FS-550)	11.0	430.5	10,400

CT Series Maps 25, 26, & 27 (see pages 216-217, 222-223 & 230-231).

Hikers along this segment continue to enjoy exceptional views as they make their way through the little-known Rico Mountains. However, there are not as many water stops here as in the previous segment. This is primarily because the CT route follows at or near the crest of the scenic divide between the Animas and Dolores rivers for most of this segment. Snow fields may linger here well into July.

These isolated ramparts were explored by a Hayden Survey team in 1874, one year after the Utes ceded a large part of their mineral-rich reservation. The expedition, led by the well-respected geographer Allen Wilson and topographer Franklin Rhoda, ascended many peaks in the area, including Hermosa Peak, Blackhawk Mountain, Mount Wilson, Engineer Mountain, and Vermillion Peak. This early team of surveyors can at least be partially credited with making sense out of the rugged jumble of mountains and valleys in southwestern Colorado.

Trespassing prospectors were testing the soil at the headwaters of the Dolores River long before the Brunot Treaty actually wrestled the land from the Utes. But the boom did not come until 1879 when lead carbonates rich in silver were discovered. So optimistic were the miners that they named their town and the surrounding mountains Rico, meaning "rich" in Spanish.

Trailhead/Access Points

Bolam Pass Road (FS-578) Trail Access: The trail access point on the Bolam Pass Road is accessible from two directions, US-550 and Colorado Highway 145. Both require a 4WD or at least a strong, high-clearance, vehicle. For the US-550 approach, travel approximately 28 miles north of Durango to the Purgatory Ski Area entrance. At the upper parking area, bear right onto FS-578 and follow the road as it ascends through several switchbacks. At the top of the ridge, the road heads north briefly, then forks left at signs for Sig Creek Campground and Hermosa Park. (FS-579, the Cascade Divide Road, continues ahead here as a long, rough 4WD approach into Segment 25). Follow FS-578 west, then north to a long fork at Hermosa Creek. Just beyond the ford, take the right fork as the road splits. Continue about 7 miles up the rough road to Celebration Lake, about a mile before the road tops out at the pass. The CT skirts the south end of the lake. There is room to park a few cars here. For the approach from Colorado Highway 145, travel 6 miles north from Rico and turn right on FS-578, Barlow Creek Road. The road climbs steadily for 7 rough miles then levels off. Go left where the road forks, continue to Bolam Pass, then descend to Celebration Lake, where the trail crosses the road.

Hotel Draw Trail Access: See Segment 27.

Supplies, Services, and Accommodations

Some supplies, but no groceries, are available at Purgatory Ski Area.

Maps

CT Series: Maps 25, 26, and 27 (see pages 216-217, 222-223 and 230-231).
USFS: San Juan National Forest.
USGS Quadrangles: Hermosa Peak.

Trail Description

This segment begins at Celebration Lake on the west side of FS-578. The trail, which may not be obvious here if the sign has been vandalized, crosses the road on the south end of the lake on something of an east-northeast to west-southwest diagonal. The trail becomes noticeable as you progress southwest of the lake, once you enter the trees. It begins a gradual ascent west-southwest then northwest as it goes around an extended ridge that reaches east from Hermosa Peak. The CT then heads over a flat spot in the ridge. From here, follow blazed posts, cairns, and a faint trail bearing generally west-northwest along the edge of the talus coming off the north slope of Hermosa Peak. In about 0.4 mile, the trail turns abruptly to the right (north), ascending slightly through a skunk cabbage field. The trail bears northwest then west and comes to a jeep track, where you turn right (north-northwest) and proceed for 0.1 mile to a jeep road (FS-149) that is closed to vehicles. Turn left (west-southwest) and follow the road as it continues 1.6 miles around the north side of Hermosa Peak. As the road ascends through a switchback, and just before it tops out at an open saddle west of the peak, look for the faint trail to leave the road to the right (west). The first several hundred feet of the trail may be difficult to find if the markers have been vandalized, but in a few more steps the trail picks up a reliable tread.

The CT continues west from the road at the saddle, staying very near the crest of the Animas-Dolores divide. As you maneuver through the switchback near Section Point, do not be misled by the trail that heads west to northwest down the ridge. The CT goes southwest after leaving the turn.

The trail soon enters a lush basin and begins climbing toward Blackhawk Pass. About 0.3 mile below the pass, a spring bubbles out of a rock cliff. Top out on Blackhawk Pass at mile 6.9 (11,970). The wind can be fierce here as it funnels through this notch in the Rico Mountains. Even so, the views are worth the extra time spent at this summit: to the north is Lizard Head and to the south are the La Plata Mountains and Indian Trail Ridge.

From the pass, the CT begins a descent into the Straight Creek drainage. Once the trail enters the trees, it makes several wide, swinging switchbacks on the west side of the valley to maintain a comfortable grade. At mile 8.5 (10,980), the trail crosses to the east side of Straight Creek. Just before the crossing, a short side trail leads uphill to a six-cascade waterfall. Long-distance trekkers should note that this creek crossing is the last reliable, flowing water on the trail until Taylor Lake at the end of the next segment, about 20 miles away.

The CT follows the valley south for about a mile, while slowly pulling away from the creek. It then bears southeast, away from the drainage and heads back to the broad, forested ridge of the Animas-Dolores divide. As you reach this almost flat crest, the trail seems to end at a cairn. At this point, look for an old road that starts here and follows the crest southward. This road has recently been closed to vehicles and reseeded and is therefore quickly losing its road-like appearance. You may notice an aged Forest Service sign that marks this section of trail as the old "Highline Trail." Stay on the old road as it continues nearly a mile south, on or near the divide. This segment ends at mile 11.0 (10,400), where there is a green closure gate for the old road at an intersection with FS-550. The CT continues south on the Forest Service road into the next trail segment.

Notes

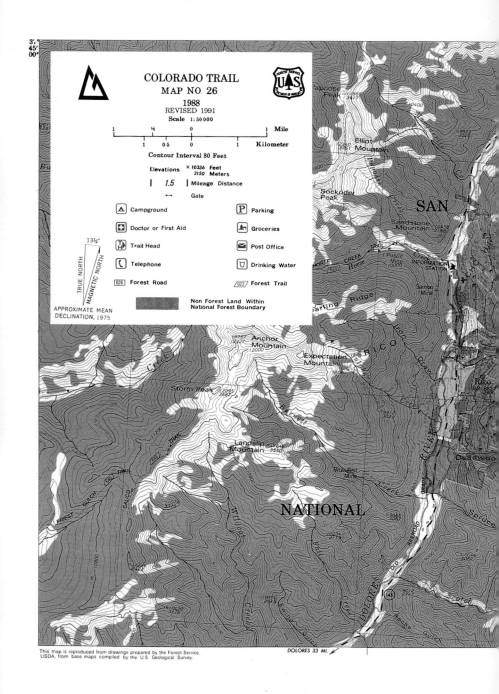

COLORADO TRAIL
MAP NO. 26
1988
REVISED 1991
Scale 1:50 000

Contour Interval 80 Feet

Elevations × 10336 Feet
3150 Meters

| 1.5 | Mileage Distance

←→ Gate

Ⓐ Campground   Ⓟ Parking

Doctor or First Aid   Groceries

Trail Head   Post Office

Telephone   Drinking Water

026 Forest Road   022 Forest Trail

Non Forest Land Within
National Forest Boundary

13½°
TRUE NORTH   MAGNETIC NORTH
APPROXIMATE MEAN
DECLINATION, 1975

This map is reproduced from drawings prepared by the Forest Service,
USDA, from base maps compiled by the U.S. Geological Survey.

DOLORES 33 MI.

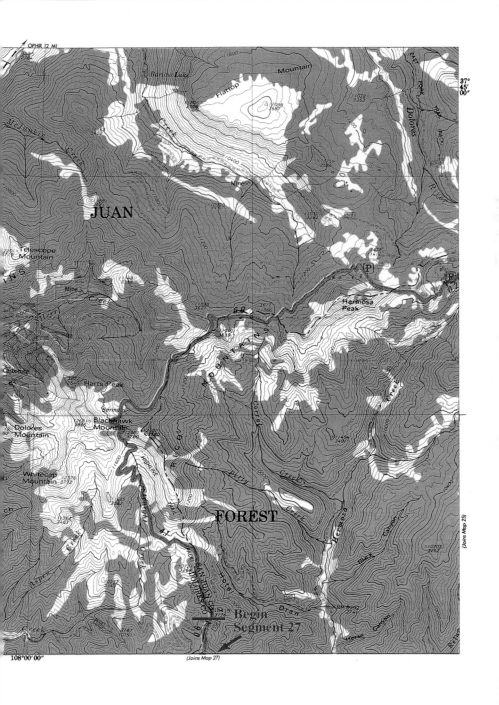

OPHIR 12 MI

Bandao Lake

Flattop Mountain

EAST FORK Dolores River

37° 45' 00"

McJunkin Creek

Mine

JUAN

Telescope Mountain

Mine

Hermosa Peak

Carbonate

Harts Peak

Spring

Dolores Mountain

Blackhawk Mountain

MOUNTAINS

Whitecap Mountain

HIGHLINE

FOREST

RINCON

SAN JUAN NF DOLORES NF

Begin
Segment 27

Black Canyon

(Joins Map 25)

108°00'00"

(Joins Map 27)

Indian paintbrush, La Plata Mountains

⚠ SEGMENT 27   20.1 Miles

Hotel Draw Road to Cumberland Basin   **+3,440 Feet Elevation Gain**

Location	Mileage	From Denver	Elevation
Hotel Draw Road (FS-550)	0.0	430.5	10,400
Big Bend Trail	6.3		10,600
Cape of Good Hope	13.0		11,600
Indian Trail Ridge	18.0		12,258
Cumberland Basin Trailhead	20.1	450.6	11,600

CT Series Maps 27 & 28 (see pages 230-231 & 232-233).

From the start of this segment at FS-550, the CT continues to follow the divide between the Animas and Dolores rivers. Elevation gain is in a series of steps, with some little ups and downs in between. Your reward is the dramatic alpine scenery from Indian Trail Ridge. Much of the trail in this segment is new, rerouted by volunteers around areas of extensive logging. Elsewhere, the trail uses the existing Highline Trail. The CT unavoidably crosses some old clear-cut zones at the beginning of the segment and around Orphan Butte. But those open areas only serve to accentuate the panoramas that are the primary highlight of traversing this little-known San Juan divide.

Water may be difficult to find in this segment. Unless you scamper down from the divide to find the headwater springs of Hermosa Creek (a tributary of the Animas River) or the Dolores River, you will have to be content with a few muddy springs along the way, or wait until you reach Taylor Lake at the end of this segment.

FS-550 follows the approximate route of the historic Rico-Rockwood Toll Road along the Animas-Dolores divide. Completed in 1881, it connected the mining town of Rico to the smelter in Durango. The road was heavily used until Otto Mears built the Rio Grande Southern up the Dolores River to Rico in 1891. At the mouth of Hotel Draw, weary travelers on the Rico-Rockwood Road could rest at an inn. Evidence indicates that these early-day pioneers were not the first to use the Animas-Dolores divide. Indian Trail Ridge further south, as the name suggests, was very likely traversed by the Utes and possibly by people of pre-Columbian cultures.

Trailhead/Access Points

Hotel Draw Trail Access: Travel north from Durango on US-550 approximately 28 miles and turn right into the Purgatory Ski Area entrance. At the upper parking area, turn right onto FS-578, and follow the dirt road as it ascends through several switchbacks. At the top of the ridge, follow the road as it heads north briefly, then take the left fork as marked for Sig Creek Campground and Hermosa Park. Follow FS-578 west and then north to the long ford on Hermosa Creek, which requires a 4WD or high-clearance vehicle. About a mile after the ford, take a sharp left at the fork onto FS-550. A sign, usually shot full of holes, indicates this as the way to Scotch Creek and Hotel Draw. Ascend steadily approximately 3.5 miles on FS-550 to a point where the road levels out near the crest of the Animas-Dolores divide. Look for a side road blocked with a green closure gate on your right (north) that is marked as FS-550A; it indicates the beginning of this segment. The CT northward follows along the ridge beyond the gate to Segment 26; to the south, the trail follows FS-550 a short ways. This spot is also accessible from Colorado Highway 145 about 2 miles south of Rico. Follow FS-550, Scotch Creek Road, about 5 steep and rocky miles to the Animas-Dolores divide, then continue on FS-550 to the start of the segment mentioned above.

FS-435/FS-564 Trail Access: From Colorado Highway 145 about 9 miles south of Rico, turn onto FS-435, Roaring Fork Road. After several miles, avoid the right fork and continue ahead on FS-564, which continues ascending to the Animas-Dolores divide. FS-564 is mostly a gravel road with gradual grades that eventually intersects with FS-550 at the crest of the divide. It is a long drive, but does reach several access points along the CT. Near Orphan Butte, there are numerous logging roads (closed to vehicles) that leave FS-564 and meander over to the CT.

Cumberland Basin Trailhead: See Segment 28.

Supplies, Service, and Accommodations

Limited supplies are available at Purgatory Ski Area.

Maps

CT Series: Maps 27 and 28 (see pages 230-231 and 232-233).
USFS: San Juan National Forest.
USGS Quadrangles: Hermosa Peak, Elk Creek, Orphan Butte, La Plata.

Trail Description

This segment begins where FS-550A meets FS-550, the Hotel Draw and Scotch Creek roads, at the top of the Animas-Dolores divide. FS-550A is a short side road permanently closed to vehicles by a locked, green gate. It has been reseeded and now is suitable only for foot and hoof traffic. At the green gate, go south on FS-550 about 300 feet. Here, another locked gate to the right prevents motorized access to an abandoned logging road. Leave FS-550 here and head southwest on this road. In 500 feet, pass a minor fork at right and continue straight ahead. Shortly, you enter a clear-cut with a panorama of the Straight Creek valley. At mile 0.6 (10,400), ascend the steep side road at left (west). This will take you over a small ridge and reorient you in a few steps to a descent bearing generally south-southeast. In 0.2 mile, the logging road you are follow-ing will begin a mild ascent and then assume a southwesterly heading. At mile 1.2 (10,440), the old road appears to end at a narrow crest on the divide ridge. Notice that FS-550 runs in a deep road cut just below you on your left, and that a rough trail continues ahead (west) from the end of the old log road. This short trail extension will tie into FS-550 in 450 feet. Continue ahead (west) on FS-550 to the intersection of FS-550 and FS-564. Here, FS-550 descends to the right into Scotch Creek and FS-564 goes left, staying near the divide crest and the CT for several more miles. If you are desperate for water at this point, there is a meager seep several hundred feet west-northwest of this intersection. To find it, descend from the intersection to a visible old logging road below and continue on it a few steps to a switchback. The seep, if it is flowing, should be visible.

The CT goes left (south-southwest) on FS-564 from the intersection and follows it only about 350 feet to where a faint tread leaves the Forest Service road at left (west-southwest). This is the beginning of a long pull, as the CT again follows the route of an abandoned log road for nearly 0.5 mile up the east side of the divide. Near the end of this log road, the CT, as a trail now, bears to the right (southwest then west) and continues a steep ascent another 0.2 mile to the top of the divide ridge at mile 2.1 (10,760). From here, the CT mostly fol-lows the route of the old Highline Trail, bearing from west to south as it mean-ders along the divide offering spectacular views from time to time of the Needle and West Needle Mountains to the east and the La Plata Mountains to the south.

Pass the Corral Draw Trail at mile 2.8 (10,840). The CT links up with FS-564 at mile 3.4 (10,760) and follows it south about 700 feet, where the trail resumes at left. The trail crosses FS-564 twice in the next 600 feet, then pulls away from the Forest Service road to an open area just south of the divide —

with more spectacular views. The trail descends to FS-564 at mile 4.7 (10,720) and follows it briefly a few hundred feet southwest, then leaves the road to the left (south). In another 0.6 mile, the trail again ties into FS-564 for 300 feet, then leaves it, again, to the left (southwest). After a short ascent, the trail levels off on the divide, then descends to a saddle where there is an old, but fairly well-maintained, wooden corral. The trail disappears into the grassy meadow just short of the corral and resumes a few steps south of it.

From another shallow saddle on the divide at mile 6.3 (10,600), the Big Bend Trail descends at left into the Hermosa Creek drainage. A short side trail goes right here to FS-564. In 0.5 mile, the CT passes close to FS-564, then joins up with an abandoned log road in another 750 feet. Go left (south-southeast) on this road and continue 300 feet where the trail resumes straight ahead (south-southeast) as the old road bears right. The trail bears generally south as it continues through an old logged-over area, then ascends to an open section of the divide ridge with a view north to the San Miguel Mountains.

Pass the Salt Creek Trail at mile 7.8 (10,840). About 0.2 mile beyond, the trail joins up with an abandoned log road just north of Orphan Butte. For the next mile, the CT follows a potentially confusing combination of roads through the logged area surrounding Orphan Butte. Be aware of the many critical junctions to come in the next mile. Orphan Butte itself is a curious molehill on the divide, noticeable because of its "crew-cut" appearance from logging activity. Follow the log road south, around the east then south side of the butte to a fork in the road at mile 8.7 (10,880). Take the right fork here (south-southwest) and follow it 200 feet to a section of new trail that leaves the old road behind and continues ahead (south). In 800 feet, this section of trail joins an old log road at a faint and somewhat overgrown road fork. Continue at right (south-southwest to southwest) on either fork, for they join back together in a few steps. About 0.2 mile beyond, be on the lookout for a post marking the point on the left (south-southeast) where the trail briefly leaves the old log road. You might have a little trouble initially spotting the trail in the grassy meadow, but several posts mark this junction. From here, the trail continues bearing generally south in and out of old logged over sections, usually on the broad divide crest or slightly below it on the east side.

The trail begins a long ascent to the Cape of Good Hope at mile 11.1 (10,800). In the next 0.5 mile, the CT climbs steadily, then levels out briefly below a sloping rock field to your right. The trail here is usually damp until mid-summer because of the seeps that form Deer Creek. If you need water, there is the likelihood that these seeps will be trickling until then. About 200 feet beyond is the first in a series of three switchbacks that lead to a mid-level bench and sunny meadow at mile 12.1 (11,320). Just as the trail orients from north to west and reenters the trees, there is a side trail to the right that takes you about 200 feet to a magnificent vantage were you can see the route you have just followed. This view point, with many flat areas among the trees, makes a good campsite if the seeps mentioned above are flowing.

The trail continues from the mid-level bench and crosses a few more sporadically flowing seeps that form Roaring Forks Creek. It then switchbacks left (south-southeast) and tops out at mile 13.0 (11,600) on the Cape of Good Hope, which extends east from this point. Here, in an inviting meadow, the trail intersects the Good Hope Stock Trail and the Flag Point Trail. Continue bearing generally south on the CT, and after about a mile of pleasant ridge hiking with periodic views to the east, angle southwest on newly built tread. At mile 14.7 (11,710), you will intersect another trail in an inclined meadow that reaches down from the heights of Indian Trail Ridge. The Highline Loop Trail #608 goes right (west) into Bear Creek. Follow the CT at left (east) here for 0.1 mile, then bear right (south) and continue an ascent to Indian Trail Ridge.

As the trees thin, the display of exquisite alpine flowers multiplies. Once you rise above timberline, the trail dips to cross a saddle then goes back up to a higher part of the ridge. A few places have steep dropoffs to the east side, but the trail is wide enough that it presents no real hazard, at least in good weather. This ridge walk would be very dangerous, however, during afternoon thunderstorms or high winds, and lingering snow fields can hamper travel. From the high point on the ridge, 12,338 feet in elevation, you can survey the La Plata Mountains close-up, as well as the San Miguel Mountains to the north and the Needle Mountains to the northeast.

After passing Point 12,258 on the southern end of Indian Trail Ridge, you come to an old sign reading "Trail 1520." The CT turns east here and descends into Cumberland Basin. Below is Taylor Lake, and visible across the basin are three peaks of the eastern La Platas: Cumberland Mountain, Snowstorm Peak, and Lewis Mountain. At a trail junction near the lake, the CT continues on the left (east) fork.

At mile 20.1 (11,600) you reach the trailhead parking area, where there is a bulletin board. FS-571 descends as a steep, rough road a couple of miles into La Plata Canyon, and then as a better road through the canyon to US-160.

Notes

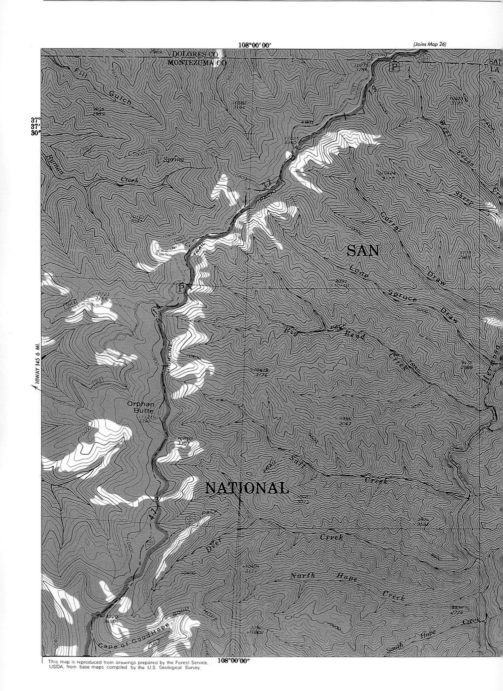

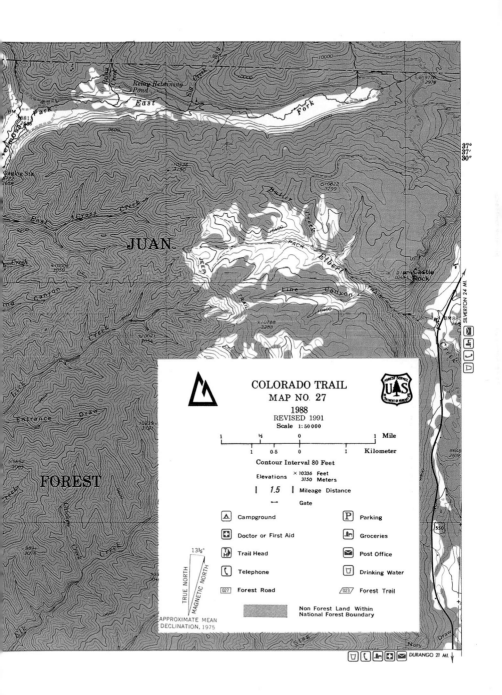

COLORADO TRAIL
MAP NO. 27
1988
REVISED 1991
Scale 1:50 000

Contour Interval 80 Feet

Elevations ×10336 Feet
3150 Meters

| 1.5 | Mileage Distance

Gate

🔺 Campground   🅿 Parking

✚ Doctor or First Aid   Groceries

Trail Head   ✉ Post Office

☎ Telephone   Drinking Water

027 Forest Road   023 Forest Trail

Non Forest Land Within
National Forest Boundary

TRUE NORTH
MAGNETIC NORTH
13½°
APPROXIMATE MEAN
DECLINATION, 1975

JUAN

FOREST

DURANGO 21 MI.

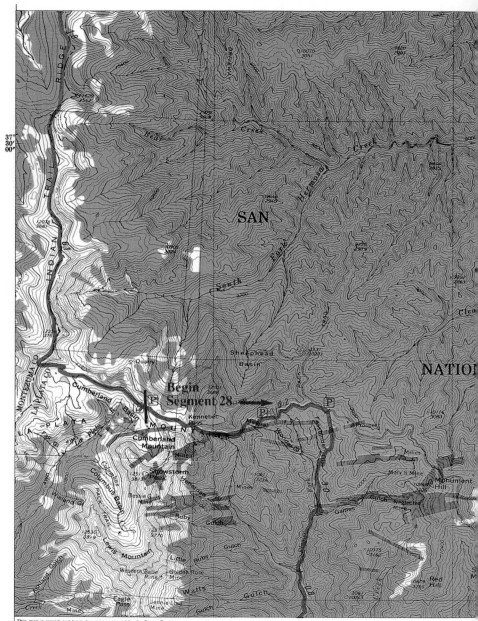

This map is reproduced from drawings prepared by the Forest Service.
USDA, from base maps compiled by the U.S. Geological Survey.

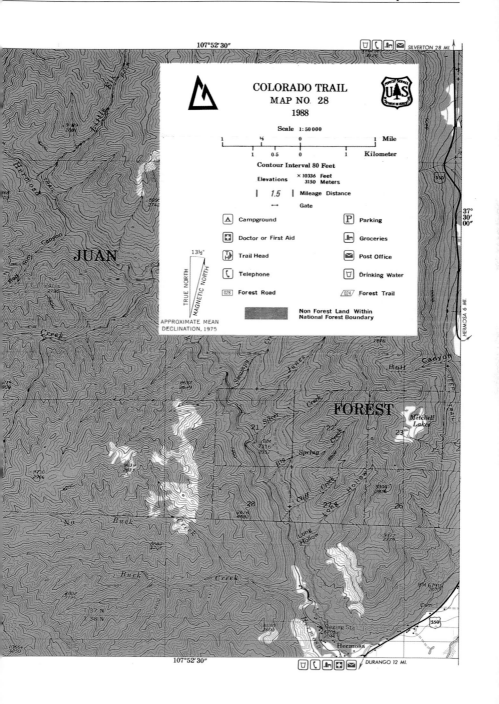

View from Kennebec Pass, above Cumberland Basin

⚠ SEGMENT 28 20.8 Miles

Cumberland Basin to Junction Ck. Trailhead   +1,160 Feet Elevation Gain

Location	Mileage	From Denver	Elevation
Cumberland Basin Trailhead	0.0	450.6	11,600
Kennebec Pass	0.7		11,750
Walls Gulch	6.4		8,520
Sliderock Canyon	8.8		9,140
Junction Creek	18.2		7,390
Junction Creek Trailhead	20.8	471.4	6,960

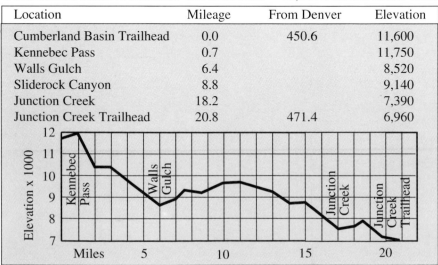

CT Series Maps 28 & 29 (see pages 232-233 & 238-239).

This segment is the final leg of the 471-mile trip from Denver. The trail tops out at scenic 11,760-foot Kennebec Pass and then begins a long descent to Junction Creek Trailhead. The drop from Kennebec Pass to the trailhead is 4,790 feet, the single greatest elevation change on the entire trail. In addition, there is over a thousand feet of ascent to contend with along the way, making the total elevation drop in this segment nearly 6,000 feet.

The trail generally follows the canyon of Junction Creek, winding in and out of numerous steep side drainages, where setting up camp can be challenging. Beyond Walls Gulch, the trail clings to the side of the gorge far above the creek, and water is scarce for 12 miles, until you descend again into the canyon.

Portions of the CT in the upper end of the canyon use the historic Oro Fino Trail, which supplied the mining district of the same name during the early 1900s. This trail had almost totally surrendered itself to the forest when volunteer trail crews began working in the Junction Creek area in 1986. It took two difficult summers for the volunteers to build new trail and to reconstruct the old Oro Fino for the nearly 18 miles between Junction Creek Trailhead and FS-543.

Trailhead/Access Points

Cumberland Basin Trailhead: From Durango, travel west on US-160 approximately 0.5 mile beyond Hesperus and turn right (north) on FS-571. A sign here points out the turn as La Plata Canyon. The trailhead is approximately 14 miles north from US-160. The last 2 miles continue as a 4WD road, which may be snowed in until late June.

Junction Creek Trailhead: Go north on Main Avenue in Durango and turn left (west) on 25th Street. Drive approximately 3 miles and go left where the road splits. Continue approximately 0.4 mile to a cattle guard and a sign announcing your entrance into San Juan National Forest. The CT begins on the left, a hundred feet past the cattle guard. There is room for only a few cars here. The road continues beyond this point as FS-543. There is additional parking about a mile up from the official Junction Creek Trailhead at a switchback on the right. A short side trail from the switchback takes you to the CT. Trail access to the upper part of this segment near Kennebec Pass is possible by continuing on FS-543 for 17.5 miles beyond the cattle guard to a side road on the left (west), identified by two large wooden posts. Continue up the side road 0.7 mile to where the CT crosses the road and ascends at right toward Kennebec Pass.

Supplies, Services, and Accommodations

Durango has all the amenities you would expect from a town of its size, including a variety of hotels and grocery, hardware and sporting good stores. The town also has regular bus and airline service.

Maps

CT Series: Maps 28 and 29 (see pages 232-233 and 238-239).
USFS: San Juan National Forest.
USGS Quadrangles: La Plata, Monument Hill, Durango West.

Trail Description

From the Cumberland Basin Trailhead, ascend southeast on the road for 0.2 mile and turn left onto another road that has been closed to vehicular traffic.

DURANGO SERVICES		Distance from Trail: 3 miles	
Bank	Norwest Bank	1063 Main	(303) 247-3242
Bus	Greyhound	275 E. 8th Ave.	(303) 259-2755
Dining	Aroma's Restaurant	2659 Main	(303) 259-0188
	Griego's Mexican Rest.	2603 Main	(303) 259-3558
Gear	Backcountry Experience	780 Main	(303) 247-5830
	Hassle Free Sports	2615 Main	(303) 259-3874
Groceries	Albertson's	311 W. College Drive	(303) 382-2224
Information	Chamber of Commerce	111 S. Camino del Rio	(303) 247-0312
Laundry	North Main Laundry	2980 Main	(303) 247-9915
Lodging	Brookside Motel	2331 Main	(303) 259-0150
	Day's End	2202 Main	(303) 385-5203
Medical	Mercy Medical	375 E. Park Ave.	(303) 247-4311
Post Office	Durango Post Office	222 W. 8th St.	(303) 247-3434
Showers	Cottonwood Camper Park	21636 Hwy 160	(303) 247-1977
	North Main Laundry	2980 Main	(303) 247-9915

There is a sign here for Kennebec Pass, 0.7 mile farther. From the pass at 11,760 feet, there are views toward Durango and the Junction Creek drainage, with Cumberland Mountain as a grassy cone nearby to the south. At the pass, the CT begins an immediate descent toward the east as the old road continues up to the ruins of the Muldoon Mine a short distance away. The CT descends rapidly, with the redrock cliffs above and the headwaters of Junction Creek below. Use caution when crossing lingering snow fields here, as the drop-offs are steep. The trail continues its steep descent and soon enters a spruce forest. Avoid the trail coming in from the right.

At mile 2.0 (10,340), the trail crosses an unmarked Forest Service road that connects to FS-543 in 0.7 mile on the left. A sign at this crossing reads "Sliderock Trail, Kennebec Pass." The CT continues on the opposite side of the unmarked Forest Service road as a well-built new trail, descending slowly in and out of several side gullies. Not too far beyond the road crossing, the trail ascends slightly to a meadow just below FS-543, then drops steeply into Fassbinder Gulch.

This recently built section of trail continues down the gulch past the confluence of the Flagler Fork. The CT makes a brief easterly swing into Gaines Gulch, passing a 50-foot waterfall. Once back in the main canyon, the trail crosses to the west side of the Flagler Fork. For the next mile, the trail stays close to the creek and crosses it on a long, newly constructed bridge. The CT ascends the west bank in a series of switchbacks and in this way eliminates the need to ford Flagler Fork during high water.

The last ford of upper Junction Creek, at mile 6.4 (8520), is near the mouth of Walls Gulch. Here the trail crosses to the west side of the creek and begins a 4.0-mile ascent, gaining about 1,000 feet as it winds in and out of side drainages. This is rugged terrain with steep slopes down into the Junction Creek gorge. Water flows in the side drainages are meager and most likely found in Sliderock and First Trail canyons. The CT tops out at one last rise and begins the final descent to the Junction Creek Trailhead.

At Road End Canyon, the trail gradually turns into an old 4WD road, which it follows for the next 3 miles. As the road slowly changes its direction from southwest to east, you will pass through a red gate on the road. Continue 0.2 mile past the gate and be alert for the trail to leave the road at left (east). This point might be difficult to spot if the small trail sign has been vandalized.

Once it leaves the road, the CT contours east, almost level, for a mile through a sunny ponderosa pine forest. If you walk quietly here, you might see some grazing elk. Toward the end of this pleasant contour, the trail goes over a ridge, drops into a small drainage, then passes through another gate.

The trail continues 400 feet down through an aspen grove and passes through a third gate. There are remnants of an old brush fence here, which suggests that the area must have been grazed for many years. The CT takes on the appearance of an old road in places as it descends east to southeast in the forest. About a mile beyond the gate, the Hoffhiens Connection Trail intersects the CT at right. From this trail intersection, the CT resumes an easterly bearing. In about 0.3 mile, you will come to an overlook at the edge of a rock cliff that gives a dramatic bird's eye view of the last few miles of the trail as it descends Junction Creek Canyon. This striking overlook has been named Gudy's Rest for Gudy Gaskill, the moving force behind the building of the CT.

Beyond Gudy's Rest, the trail ambles through several switchbacks on its descent into Junction Creek. A wide bridge takes you to the east side of Junction Creek at mile 18.2 (7,390). Bear to the right (south) on the trail just beyond the bridge and continue to the tiny side tributary of Quinn Creek, where you begin a short ascent to 200 feet above Junction Creek. This area is lush with vegetation and hosts many birds. You may see a Western tanager here, or perhaps a dipper diving into the whirling pools along the creek.

Hikers should be aware of several hazards along this section of trail. First, Junction Creek is subject to flash floods, so do not set up camp in the flood plain. Second, this area abounds in poison ivy and poison oak. Be careful where you walk and sit; trail crew volunteers learned about this hazard the hard way. Third, there are two areas where mudslides on the steep canyon walls have caused serious damage to the trail during spring rains. Crossing these sections before trail maintenance crews have cleaned them could be a little precarious and unnerving. Also, keep in mind that this area is popular with mountain bikers and you will most likely see many along this stretch.

About 1.3 miles after the bridge crossing, you again descend to the level of the creek and then come to a fork in the trail; the CT continues straight ahead and down the final mile. There are several side trails along here that ascend to FS-543. Along this narrow stretch of canyon are cascades and pools perfect for dipping on hot summer afternoons. It is a outdoor paradise with sun, shade, grasses, flowers, birds and — poison ivy.

Soon the canyon widens and you cross a small irrigation ditch that takes you through the flood plain for 0.3 mile to the trailhead and the official western terminus of the Colorado Trail at mile 20.8 (6960). Turn right (southeast) onto a road that takes you across the cattle guard and out of the San Juan National Forest. It is a 3.4-mile walk on the blacktop into town. Welcome to Durango!

When you have completed the CT, please contact the Colorado Trail Foundation to have your hame listed on a permanent registry.

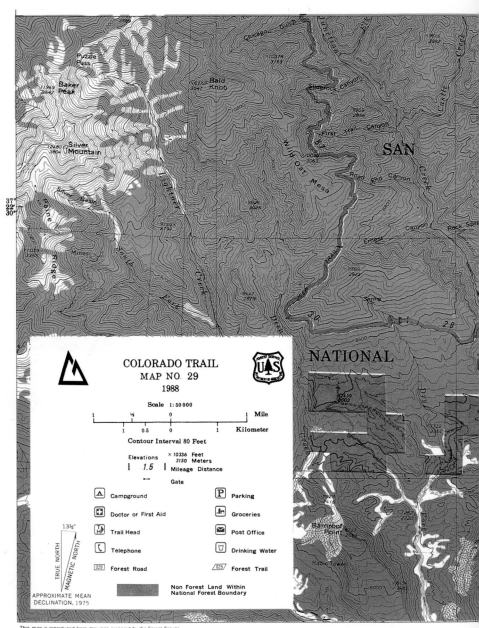

COLORADO TRAIL
MAP NO. 29
1988

Scale 1:50 000

1   ½   0   1 Mile

1   0.5   0   1 Kilometer

Contour Interval 80 Feet

Elevations   × 10336 Feet
                      3150 Meters

| 1.5 | Mileage Distance

Gate

△ Campground   P Parking

✚ Doctor or First Aid   🛒 Groceries

🅗 Trail Head   ✉ Post Office

☎ Telephone   ▽ Drinking Water

029 Forest Road   025 Forest Trail

Non Forest Land Within
National Forest Boundary

13½°

TRUE NORTH

MAGNETIC NORTH

APPROXIMATE MEAN
DECLINATION, 1975

This map is reproduced from drawings prepared by the Forest Service.
USDA, from base maps compiled by the U.S. Geological Survey.

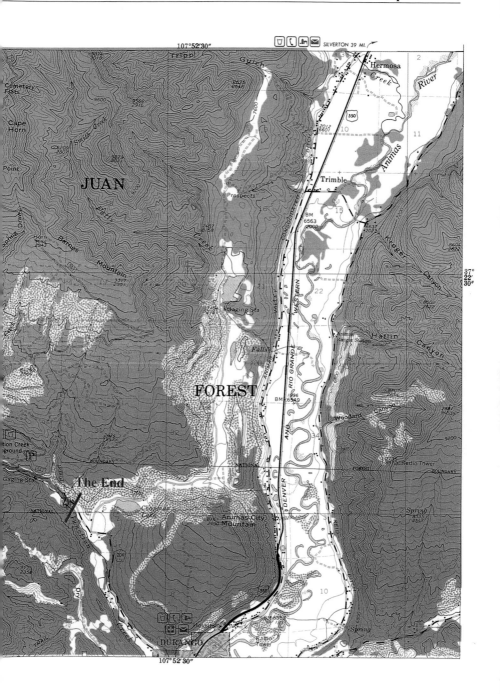

MOUNTAIN BIKE DETOURS

Mountain bikes are allowed on almost all of the CT, the only exceptions being those sections that pass through designated wilderness areas. In addition, there are other areas that mountain bikers may choose to bypass, for they end up pushing their bikes more than riding them, especially if loaded down with gear. These areas are most likely to be above timberline where no built trail exists and where the terrain is particularly rough. This section identifies suitable detours — optional or mandatory — around these areas.

The detours described here use primarily 4WD, Forest Service, and county roads. However, it is sometimes necessary to use paved highways, where appropriate precautions should be taken to make yourself visible to motorists. Safety gear, which is also important on steep, narrow trails, is a must for maneuvering on curving mountain roads with blind corners. Cattle guards, an obvious hazard to bikes, are encountered often on Forest Service and county roads. Be aware that, in most cases, private property is immediately adjacent to county roads and highways but is rarely marked as such.

Many sections of the CT are experiencing heavy mountain bike traffic, such as in the Buffalo Creek Recreation Area (Segment 3). All mountain bikers should follow a simple ethical code to prevent conflicts with other trail users and to preserve the physical integrity of the trail itself. Please remember to: ride safely and equip yourself properly with safety gear; courteously yield the trail to other users; be particularly cautious around pack animals that may panic by your sudden appearance; and ride responsibly with the knowledge that cutting switchbacks and skidding around corners and water bars can destroy a well-designed and laboriously built trail.

The detours identified in this section are not the only options available. Mountain bikers might prefer to plan their own routes using a Colorado state highway map and appropriate Forest Service maps. These maps are also helpful with general navigation, identifying campgrounds, etc. If planning a mountain bike trip on the CT, it's a good idea to contact the appropriate Forest Service districts to inquire about any restrictions or other considerations. Remember, you **must** detour wilderness areas.

Mountain bikers should not be disappointed by the fact that they need to make occasional detours, for the alternate routes hold as much fascination as the main CT corridor.

A summary of the bicycle detours listed here are:

- A mandatory detour around Lost Creek Wilderness, using a series of Forest Service roads over Stoney Pass via Wellington Lake and then up the Tarryall River.
- A highly recommended optional detour of the alpine route over the Tenmile Range, using the Tenmile Bike Path.
- A mandatory bypass around Holy Cross and Mount Massive wilderness areas using Forest Service roads and a section of US-24.

Biking the CT (Photo by G. Gangel-Fayhee)

- An optional detour around steep and difficult Hope Pass using busy highways.
- A mandatory detour around Collegiate Peaks Wilderness using county roads and a section of US-24.
- An optional detour around Raspberry Gulch using county roads.
- A mandatory detour around the La Garita Wilderness using a section of Colorado Highway 149 and Forest Service road over Los Piños Pass.
- A highly recommended detour around Coney Summit using sections of Colorado Highway 149, county roads and Forest Service roads.
- A mandatory bypass around the Weminuche Wilderness using US-550 and Forest Service roads.
- An optional detour around the Junction Creek gorge using a Forest Service road.

LOST CREEK WILDERNESS DETOUR
Segments 3, 4, and 5 (Pike National Forest)

This long detour follows Forest Service and county roads around the southern perimeter of Lost Creek Wilderness. It passes several campgrounds and provides vistas of the Tarryall Mountains and the Rampart Range south to Pikes Peak. You pass through the old mining town of Tarryall, founded in 1896 as Puma City. The story goes that an unsociable miner, known only as Rocky Mountain Jim, grew tired of the non-stop activity in Cripple Creek and moved to this picturesque valley where, he discovered the first lode in the area. Unfortunately for Jim, many others quickly followed until the town grew to a population of a thousand. A more direct but more dangerous detour than the one described below follows FS-550 and FS-543 to Bailey and continues on US-285, a busy, narrow, winding mountain road that goes to the summit of Kenosha Pass.

Detour Description
Begin this detour about midway through Segment 3 where the CT first crosses FS-543 at mile 8.9 (7,400). Continue west and south up FS-543 for 2.7 miles to Wellington Lake. Go left onto FS-560 and top out 2.4 miles later at Stoney Pass (8,560). Then proceed along the Forest Service road another 7 miles, passing a side road that leads to the Flying G Ranch. Go right onto FS-211 at mile 13.6 (7,470), and then go right again in another 5.4 miles, following the signs to Goose Creek Campground. Continue to mile 35.8 (8,220) and go right on paved County Road 77. The hardtop road gives way to gravel in about a mile. Continue through the town of Tarryall and pass the entrance to Spruce Grove Campground a few miles beyond. Pass the Tarryall Reservoir to mile 63.0 (9,220) and go right onto County Road 39 (FS-128), marked also as Rock Creek Hills Road. Continue north and go right (east) onto Lost Park Road (FS-127) at mile 68.6 (9,560). Pedal to mile 70.7 (9,410) and go left onto FS-133 at the sign reading "Colorado Trail, Rock Creek Trailhead." Regain the official CT at mile 72.0 (9,720), where it crosses the road. In the description of Segment 5, this point is mile 7.7 (9,720).

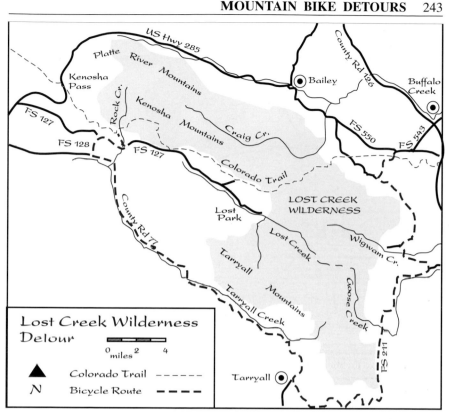

Lost Creek Wilderness Detour

0 miles 2 4

▲ Colorado Trail - - - - - -

N Bicycle Route - - - -

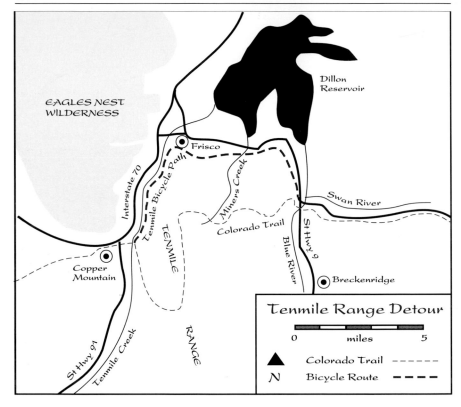

TENMILE RANGE DETOUR
Segment 7 (Arapaho National Forest)

This optional detour bypasses all of Segment 7 and the challenging high-altitude route over the Tenmile Range by using the very convenient Tenmile Bike Path. This detour is highly recommended, partly because it avoids a long, trailless alpine route along the crest of the range and the difficult, steep approaches on either side. Another reason to use this route is that it would be a shame not to take advantage of this well-planned, paved path designed especially for bicycles.

Detour Description
This optional detour begins at the Gold Hill Trailhead at the start of Segment 7. Pedal north and then west on the bike path that parallels Colorado Highway 9 to Frisco. Head south as you enter Tenmile Canyon and pedal up the bike path, following the approximate route of the DSP&P Railroad's Tenmile Canyon line. After approximately 12 miles of pleasant pedaling, you will arrive at Wheeler Flats Trailhead near Copper Mountain. This is the starting point of Segment 8.

HOLY CROSS/MOUNT MASSIVE
WILDERNESS DETOUR

Segments 9 and 10 (San Isabel National Forest)

In order to detour around the Holy Cross and Mount Massive wilderness areas, it is necessary to use a section of US-24. This highway is busy, without adequate shoulders, and care must be taken when riding this portion.

Detour Description

Pedal to mile 2.7 (10,480) in Segment 9, where the detour begins on Wurtz Ditch Road. Leave the CT and descend 0.3 mile on the road, then go left on FS-100. Continue to US-24 at mile 1.3 (10,120) and go right (south) on the highway. Follow US-24 to Leadville and continue south beyond the town to mile 14.0 (9,540), where you will turn right (west) onto Colorado Highway 300. Proceed 0.8 mile and then turn left (south) onto Halfmoon Creek Road. Take a right (west) for 1.2 miles and follow the signs to Halfmoon Creek Campground. Continue past the campground to mile 21.5 (10,080), where you pick up the CT again, heading south from the Halfmoon Creek Trailhead. This is the starting point of Segment 11.

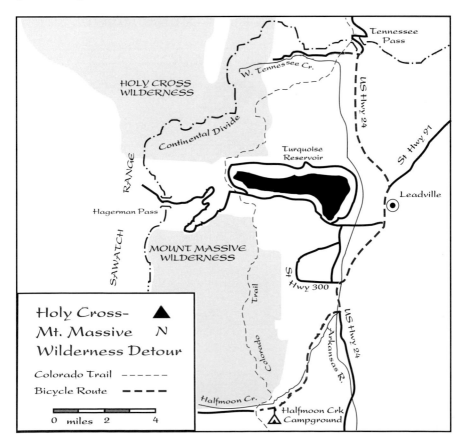

HOPE PASS DETOUR
Segment 11 (San Isabel National Forest)

The approaches to Hope Pass are steep and difficult on either side. It has received many complaints in the past and you may want to bypass this section. The disadvantage is that the bicycle bypass route is on Colorado Highway 82 and US-24, both busy highways. US-24 is particularly dangerous where it follows the narrow, winding Arkansas River gorge.

Detour Description
Start this detour at mile 7.1 (9,320) where there is a pedestrian underpass at Colorado Highway 82. Follow the highway east around the north shore of Twin Lakes Reservoir approximately 5 miles to the intersection with US-24. Take extra care as you go south on US-24 for 4 miles to the intersection with County Road 390. From this point, you continue south on US-24, following the description for the "Collegiate Peaks Wilderness Detour."

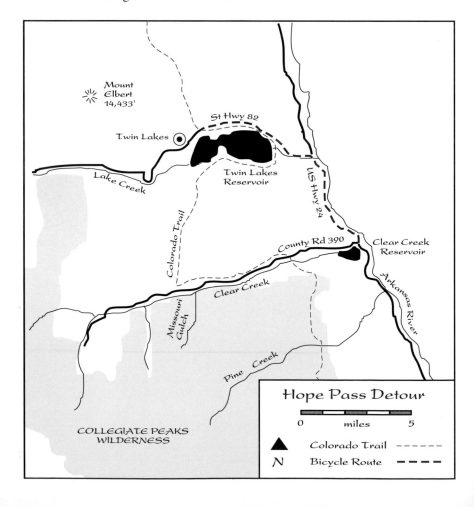

COLLEGIATE PEAKS WILDERNESS DETOUR
Segment 12 and 13 (San Isabel National Forest)

It is necessary to use a section of US-24 for this detour, but the distance spent on the highway can be reduced by using County Road 371 for the last 10 miles. This road follows the abandoned route of the Colorado Midland Railway, built in 1886 along the east bank of the Arkansas River. The formation known as Elephant Rock was so popular with passengers that they often pleaded with the conductor to stop the train so they could take photographs.

Detour Description
Begin this detour at the start of Segment 12 on County Road 390. Pedal east 3 miles and turn right (south) onto US-24. Carefully continue for 5.9 miles, then turn left onto County Road 371. You can continue on US-24 to Buena Vista if you wish, or you can cross the Arkansas River on County Road 371 and then resume a southerly course on the abandoned Colorado Midland grade at mile 18.8 (7,690). Once you reach Buena Vista, turn right (west) onto Main Street and continue a few blocks to the stoplight. Proceed west across Main Street, which becomes County Road 306 (Cottonwood Pass Road) beyond the city limits. Continue to the Avalanche Trailhead parking area at mile 28.4 (9,360), where you will rejoin the CT. This point is mile 6.6 (9,360) of Segment 13.

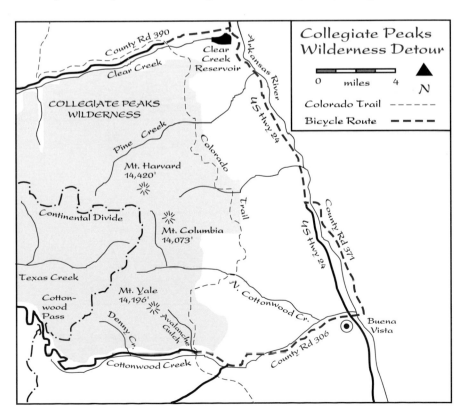

RASPBERRY GULCH DETOUR
Segments 13 and 14 (San Isabel National Forest)

This optional detour was once recommended in order to avoid a steep and poorly maintained section of the trail in the northern part of Segment 14. However, the trail has been rerouted around this problem section and therefore the detour is not as critical as before. We leave it in because some mountain bikers may prefer the smooth, graded county road and also because the steep, gravely switchbacks at the beginning of Segment 14 continue to be a difficulty for cyclists.

Detour Description
Follow the official CT route to mile 19.7 (8,160) in Segment 13. Turn left (east) onto County Road 162 and pedal 0.7 mile to County Road 270. Proceed southeast, then east, on this road, which soon takes on a southerly heading. Continue to mile 4.6 (8,200) and go right (west) on County Road 272. Turn left (south) at an intersection 2 miles beyond and continue to mile 8.2 (8,920), which is the Browns Creek Trailhead. Continue up the Browns Creek Trail to mile 9.6 (9,600), where you will rejoin the CT again. This point is mile 6.4 (9,600) in Segment 14.

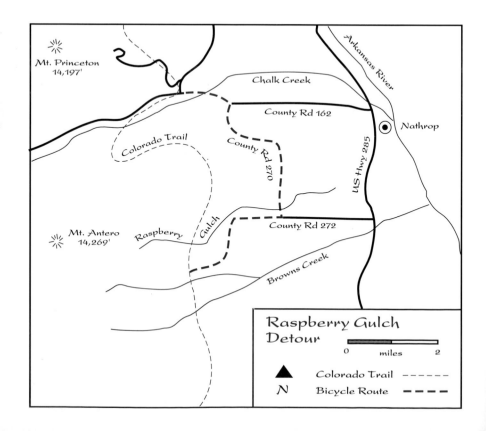

LA GARITA WILDERNESS DETOUR
Segments 18, 19, 20, and 21 (Gunnison National Forest)

This mandatory detour bypasses the La Garita Wilderness and avoids an extended high-altitude, mostly trailless route across Snow Mesa and the Continental Divide. The La Garita Wilderness detour and the following optional detour around Coney Summit (see below) are designed to be used together.

To skirt the wilderness, mountain bikers pedal along backcountry Forest Service roads that follow parts of the historic Saguache-San Juan Toll Road, which was built by Otto Mears in 1874. They also pass by the site of the original Ute Agency on Los Piños Creek. The detour passes several National Forest campgrounds on Cebolla Creek. The final miles are spent ascending Colorado Highway 149 to Spring Creek Pass, where you can join the high-altitude route of Segment 22, or you can descend Colorado Highway 149 to Lake San Cristobal and continue to the Coney Summit detour.

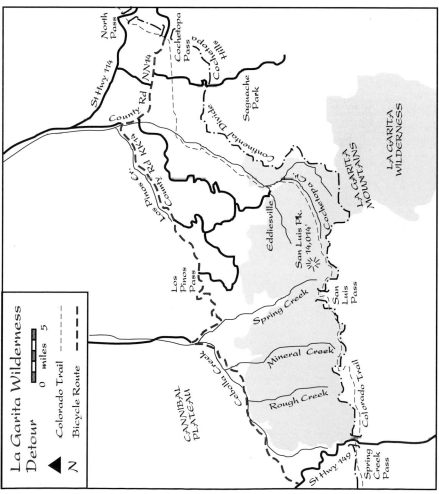

Detour Description

This detour begins on the Cochetopa Pass Road (County Road NN14) at mile 6.4 (9,760) of Segment 18. Descend on the dirt road past two switchbacks and continue pedaling ahead (northwest) on the road as the CT bears to the left up Archuleta Creek. Continue past Dome Reservoir to mile 10.8 (8,979) and turn left onto County Road KK14 (Los Piños-Cebolla Road). Pass beyond the old Ute Agency to mile 19.6 and continue ahead on Los Piños-Cebolla Road, avoiding Big Meadows Road, which forks to the left. Continue 10 miles to Los Piños Pass. Descend from the pass to mile 33.9 and join up with FS-592. Continue ahead (northwest) on the Los Piños-Cebolla Road for 1 mile and go left (west) at the intersection. Gradually ascend along Cebolla Creek to mile 50.0 (11,320), where the Forest Service road joins up with Colorado Highway 149. If you insist on pedaling the high altitude route over Coney Summit (which is not recommended), go left here and ascend 7.6 miles farther to Spring Creek Pass, where you will rejoin the CT at the beginning of Segment 22. If, however, you decide to continue the detour, pick up the Coney Summit detour route by descending to Colorado Highway 149.

CONEY SUMMIT DETOUR
Segment 22, 23, and 24 (Gunnison National Forest, San Juan National Forest)

This optional, lengthy detour from Colorado Highway 149 to Molas Pass avoids Segments 22, 23, and 24, and it is intended to be a continuation of the La Garita Wilderness detour. Mountain bikers are encouraged to continue the detouring around Segment 22 because of the difficulty of the official, trailless route in the vicinity of 13,334-foot Coney Summit and because of the tundra's vulnerability to tire tracks. Starting at Carson Saddle in Segment 23, the CT is still rough but mostly uses trails. Purists who insist on rejoining the official CT here may do so by leaving this detour about half way up the Lake Fork Road at Wager Gulch.

Mountain bikers using this route are not to be deprived of stunning scenery. This detour passes Lake San Cristobal, continues up the valley of the Lake Fork, which is ringed with 14,000-foot peaks, and then ascends 12,640-foot Cinnamon Pass. The pass is a well-known 4WD road that was originally constructed by Otto Mears and Enos Hotchkiss as part of the Saguache-San Juan Toll Road in the 1870s.

Detour Description

Continue the La Garita Wilderness detour by turning right onto Colorado Highway 149 from the Los Piños-Cebolla Road and descending the steep highway toward Lake City. Turn left off the highway at mile 7.1 (8,880) and follow a paved road to Lake San Cristobal. Continue beyond the lake and past the side road up Wager Gulch to Carson Saddle. Pedal up the narrow valley, following the signs to Cinnamon Pass, as the road gets progressively rougher. Top out on Cinnamon Pass at mile 28.9 (12,640). Descend 2.2 miles from the pass and make a sharp left (south) onto an intersecting jeep road just above the ruins of the old mining town of Animas Forks. Continue south, then southwest, down the upper Animas Valley on County Road 2 until you reach Silverton. Pedal through town and join US-550 at mile 43.9 (9,240). Go south on busy US-550 and carefully ascend to mile 50.0 (10,880) just 600 feet north of the highway's summit on Molas Pass, where you will pick up the CT going west. This point is the beginning of Segment 25.

WEMINUCHE WILDERNESS DETOUR
Segment 24 (Rio Grande National Forest, San Juan National Forest)

Mountain bikers who attempt the challenge of Segment 22 and Segment 23 will have to detour Segment 24, which traverses the Weminuche Wilderness. This detour crosses the Continental Divide at 12,600-foot Stony Pass and joins the official CT route at Molas Pass — as does the Coney Summit detour. The Stony Pass route, like Cinnamon Pass, is an historic and scenic bypass, originally built in 1879. Prior to that date, a burro trail over Stony Pass carried most of

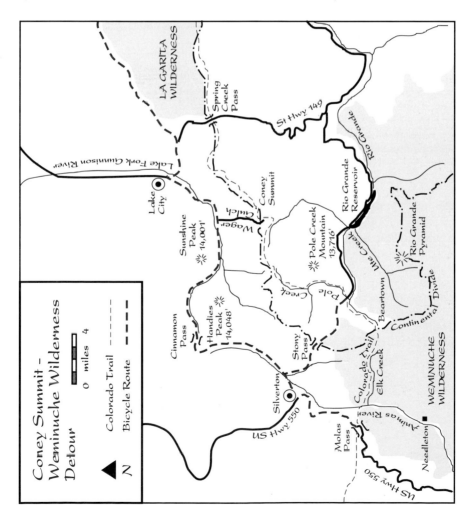

the traffic into Silverton, primarily because it was one of the few routes into the area that did not cross Ute reservation lands.

Detour Description

This detour leaves the official route at the end of Segment 23, where the CT intersects the Rio Grande Reservoir Road. Pedal ahead (northwest) on the road toward Stony Pass. The ford of Pole Creek a short distance beyond can be deep and swift until late summer. Top out on Stony Pass at mile 6.3 (12,600). Descend steeply to Cunningham Gulch Road at mile 10.3 (10,120) and continue 2.5 miles north to an intersection at the old site of Howardsville. Turn left (west) onto County Road 2 which follows the broad Animas River valley. Descend into Silverton and pick up busy US-550 on the opposite end of town at mile 17.7 (9,240). Carefully ascend south on US-550 to mile 23.8 (10,880) just 600 feet north of the highway's summit on Molas Pass, where you will join the official CT going west. This point is the beginning of Segment 25.

JUNCTION CREEK CANYON DETOUR
Segment 28 (San Juan National Forest)

The portion of the official CT in Junction Creek is mostly on good trail, but it does traverse some precipitous spots in rough terrain, and there are several long, deep fords, particularly in the upper end of the canyon. By contrast, there is a very good road that begins just east of Kennebec Pass and descends along the edge of the canyon to the trailhead on Junction Creek. This bypass is intended for mountain bikers anxious for a speedy descent to Durango, or for those interested in making a long loop trip up Junction Creek and then down the road to their starting point.

Detour Description

This detour begins at mile 2.0 (10,340) in Segment 28 just east of Kennebec Pass where the trail crosses a side road. Descend 0.7 mile on the side road and turn right at an intersection onto FS-543. Continue downhill. As you drop quickly in elevation, you will pass through several life zones. Do not become so distracted by the scenery that you fail to notice the many hazardous cattle guards on the road. Pass the entrance to Junction Creek Campground and continue 1.4 miles to the San Juan National Forest boundary and Junction Creek Trailhead, the western terminus of the CT. This is the end of Segment 28. Durango is 3.4 miles down the road.

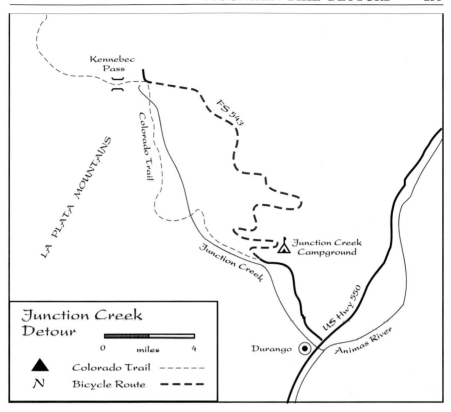

Kennebec
Pass

FS 543

Colorado Trail

LA PLATA MOUNTAINS

Junction Creek

Junction Creek
Campground

US Hwy 550

Durango

Animas River

**Junction Creek
Detour**

0   miles   4

▲   Colorado Trail   ------

N   Bicycle Route   ▪ ▪ ▪ ▪

Notes

Notes

GUDY GASKILL'S CT HIGHLIGHTS

▲ Between Black Canyon and Kenosha Pass, stop to take in the incredible vistas of South Park and the mountainous backdrop.

▲ The hanging glacial valley at 11,000 feet in the Tenmile Range supports a huge colony of pikas.

▲ Be sure to stop for a quick shower under the falls along Cataract Creek near Camp Hale. There's even a resting bench.

▲ In the Holy Cross Wilderness, there is a fascinating tundra walk between Long's Gulch and St. Kevin's Lake Trailhead.

▲ The short but often overlooked five-mile stretch between the Shavano Campground and Colorado Highway 50 wanders through lovely aspen and lodgepole pine forests.

▲ Sargents Mesa teems with its hundreds of grazing elk and numerous trout-filled beaver ponds.

▲ Baldy Lake off Sargents Mesa is worth the quarter-mile detour; it's a watery haven along a dry segment of the trail.

▲ Take in the views from Snow Mesa above Spring Creek. You can see the Rio Grande Pyramid and the Uncompahgre Mountains, where Ute Indians once hunted.

▲ Don't miss the panoramas from Radio Hill on Jarosa Mesa. The view overlooking the Uncompahgre Mountains is worth the climb!

▲ Pole Creek Falls is just a few hundred yards off the trail in a spectacular setting below the double crossing of Pole Creek in the La Garita Mountains.

▲ Between Little Molas Lake and Lime Creek, wildflowers grow knee high in a kaleidoscope of colors.

▲ The north side of Blackhawk Pass is a valley of enchantment with vast herds of elk.

▲ In the Weminuche Wilderness, the Elk Creek drainage and its dramatic geologic walls are topped off with views of Arrow and Vestal peaks.

▲ There is an ice cave below Cataract Falls in the San Juan Mountains where you can chip off ice and make "roller" ice cream.*

▲ From Indian Ridge, a crest of cascading wildflowers, the views of Hermosa Valley and the La Plata Mountains are extraordinary.

*Roller Ice Cream

This is a delightful wilderness treat. When planning a hike, I pack cookies or other foods in a tin can that can later be used as an on-trail ice cream maker. You'll need a tin can, salt, and a wide-mouthed water bottle. Fill the water bottle with powdered milk and powdered eggs, flavor it with fruit, pudding mix, or powdered fruit drinks, and then add water. Put the closed bottle inside the tin can along with salt and ice. Rolling the can back and forth on the ground turns this concoction into "roller" ice cream. You can adjust the recipe to make sherbet by leaving out the milk. Use your imagination to create other flavors.

GUDY GASKILL'S CT PITFALLS

▼ A broken toggle or cotter pin may be difficult to replace along the trail, as sporting goods stores are far apart. Make sure your backpack is in excellent condition before setting off.

▼ The rule of thumb for scheduling your trip is not to leave Kenosha Pass heading west before the middle of June, because Georgia Pass generally has lingering snow banks at lower elevations. From Durango, Cumberland Basin is usually covered by a mile-long snowfield until late June.

▼ When you reach the South Platte historical site, fill up on water as it is a long, dry climb to Top of the World Campground. There is no water at the campground (although there will be in the future), and it's another 6 1/2 miles to Morrison Creek.

▼ You can hike the route from Denver to Lost Creek Wilderness anytime in April or May; after that water sources tend to dry up with hot weather or are fouled by livestock.

▼ The route through Copper Mountain Ski Area is confusing without direction or a guidebook, so take a map — or this book!

▼ Take note of all the shell holes made during World War II training at Camp Hale in the Tennessee Pass-Leadville area. They become "pitfalls" with night walking or with engrossing daytime conversation.

▼ Hope Pass is a temporary route while negotiations continue for a permanent, more direct one. Those climbing Hope Pass know why it is so named: "Hope I never have to go over that pass again with a full pack!"

▼ Watch out for the missing signs at the Chalk Cliffs. The route along the road is a temporary solution to skirt private property.

▼ The La Garita Wilderness is so remote that few travel here and you are unlikely to meet other hikers. The loneliness is offset by the complete solitude that you find.

▼ It is a temptation to climb 14,014-foot San Luis Peak, but the high incidence of lightening storms in that area can make it a dicey proposition. Be sure to check the cloud patterns and weather before ascending.

▼ From Coney Summit to Carson Saddle there is an incredibly steep descent on a rutted four-wheel-drive road. If your boot tread is worn, you'll probably slip and slide here.

▼ Carson Saddle has a surprising number of people in four-wheel-drive vehicles, which can be a shock after the previous isolation of the trail.

▼ All major water crossings have bridges spanning them except for Pole Creek and the Rio Grande. Both can be extremely fast during high water, so use caution.

▼ Along the southern reaches of the trail, towns and local services are few and far between. There is a little store at Molas Pass (by Big Molas Lake) that offers showers and a good variety of staples. Don't miss it!

Colorado Trail Miles Between Segments

SEGMENT→	1	2	3	4	5	6	7	8	9	10	11	12	13
↓		16	26	39	54	68	94	107	131	146	157	186	204	226
1	16		9	23	38	52	77	91	115	130	141	170	188	210
2	26	9		13	29	43	68	81	105	120	132	160	179	201
3	39	23	13		15	29	55	68	92	107	118	147	165	187
4	54	38	29	15		14	39	53	77	92	103	132	150	172
5	68	52	43	29	14		25	39	63	78	89	118	136	158
6	94	77	68	55	39	25		13	37	52	64	92	111	133
7	107	91	81	68	53	39	13		24	39	50	79	98	120
8	131	115	105	92	77	63	37	24		15	26	55	73	96
9	146	130	120	107	92	78	52	39	15		11	40	59	81
10	157	141	132	118	103	89	64	50	26	11		29	47	69
11	186	170	160	147	132	118	92	79	55	40	29		18	40
12	204	188	179	165	150	136	111	98	73	59	47	18		22
13	226	210	201	187	172	158	133	120	96	81	69	40	22	
14	246	230	221	207	192	178	153	140	116	101	89	60	42	20
15	260	244	235	221	206	192	167	154	130	115	103	74	56	34
16	275	259	249	236	221	207	181	168	144	129	118	89	71	49
17	295	279	270	256	241	227	202	189	164	150	138	109	91	69
18	308	292	282	269	254	240	215	201	177	162	151	122	104	82
19	321	305	296	283	267	253	228	215	191	176	165	136	117	95
20	334	318	308	295	280	266	240	227	203	188	177	148	130	107
21	348	332	323	309	294	280	255	242	217	203	191	162	144	122
22	366	350	341	328	312	298	273	260	236	221	210	181	162	140
23	378	362	353	340	324	310	285	272	248	233	222	193	174	152
24	400	383	374	361	346	332	306	293	269	254	243	214	196	173
25	419	403	394	381	365	351	326	313	289	274	263	234	215	193
26	430	414	405	392	376	362	337	324	300	285	274	245	226	204
27	451	434	425	412	397	383	357	344	320	305	294	265	247	224
28	471	455	446	432	417	403	378	365	341	326	314	286	267	245

Mileages are given to the end of each segment.

14	15	16	17	18	19	20	21	22	23	24	25	26	27	28
246	260	275	295	308	321	334	348	366	378	400	419	430	451	471
230	244	259	279	292	305	318	332	350	362	383	403	414	434	455
221	235	249	270	282	296	308	323	341	353	374	394	405	425	446
207	221	236	256	269	283	295	309	328	340	361	381	392	412	432
192	206	221	241	254	267	280	294	312	324	346	365	376	397	417
178	192	207	227	240	253	266	280	298	310	332	351	362	383	403
153	167	181	202	215	228	240	255	273	285	306	326	337	357	378
140	154	168	189	201	215	227	242	260	272	293	313	324	344	365
116	130	144	164	177	191	203	217	236	248	269	289	300	320	341
101	115	129	150	162	176	188	203	221	233	254	274	285	305	326
89	103	118	138	151	165	177	191	210	222	243	263	274	294	314
60	74	89	109	122	136	148	162	181	193	214	234	245	265	286
42	56	71	91	104	117	130	144	162	174	196	215	226	247	267
20	34	49	69	82	95	107	122	140	152	173	193	204	224	245
	14	29	49	62	75	87	102	120	132	153	173	184	204	225
14		15	35	48	61	73	88	106	118	139	159	170	190	211
29	15		20	33	47	59	73	92	104	125	145	156	176	197
49	35	20		13	26	39	53	71	83	104	124	135	156	176
62	48	33	13		14	26	40	59	71	92	112	123	143	163
75	61	47	26	14		12	27	45	57	78	98	109	129	150
87	73	59	39	26	12		15	33	45	66	86	97	117	138
102	88	73	53	40	27	15		18	30	51	71	82	102	123
120	106	92	71	59	45	33	18		12	33	53	64	84	105
132	118	104	83	71	57	45	30	12		21	41	52	72	93
153	139	125	104	92	78	66	51	33	21		20	31	51	72
173	159	145	124	112	98	86	71	53	41	20		11	31	52
184	170	156	135	123	109	97	82	64	52	31	11		20	41
204	190	176	156	143	129	117	102	84	72	51	31	20		21
225	211	197	176	163	150	138	123	105	93	72	52	41	21	

APPENDIX A

Forest Service Addresses
The Colorado Trail crosses ten Forest Service districts, each of which maintains information concerning the portion of the trail within its jurisdiction. Addresses for the districts are:

South Platte District: Pike National Forest, P. O. Box 25127, 11177 West Eighth Avenue, Lakewood, CO 80225.

South Park District: Pike National Forest, P. O. Box 219, Fairplay, CO 80440.

Dillon District: Arapaho National Forest, P. O. Box 620, 135 Colorado Highway 9, Silverthorne, CO 80498.

Holy Cross District: White River National Forest, P. O. Box 190, 401 Main, Minturn, CO 81645.

Leadville District: San Isabel National Forest, 2015 North Poplar, Leadville, CO 80461.

Salida District: San Isabel National Forest, 230 West 16th Street, Salida, CO 81201.

Saguache District: Rio Grande National Forest, P. O. Box 67, Saguache, CO 81149.

Creede District: Rio Grande National Forest, P. O. Box 270, 220 Creede Avenue, Creede, CO 81130.

Cebolla District: Gunnison National Forest, 216 North Colorado, Gunnison, CO 81230.

Animas District: San Juan National Forest, 110 West Eleventh, Durango, CO 81301.

APPENDIX B

Recommended Equipment Checklist

Day Hikes

Lightweight daypack
Snacks or lunch
Raingear
Sweater
Hat or sun visor
Wool hat
Gloves
Binoculars
Water or purification system
Trail guide and maps
Headlamp

First aid kit
Flower, bird, or other field guides
Compass
Suncreen and sunglasses
Lighter or firestarter
Toilet paper
Insect repellent
Camera and film
Knife
Extra food for emergencies

Additional Gear for Overnight Hikes

Sturdy backpack
Sleeping bag
Groundcloth
Change of clothing
Stove and fuel
Cup and spoon
Toothbrush
Biodegradable soap
Trowel for digging "catholes"
Garbage bags
Thin rope or cord
Tent or bivouac sack

Sleeping pad
Camp chair
Booties or slippers
Cooking gear
Food
Pack cover
Comb
Towel
Playing cards
Reading material
Journal

APPENDIX C

Colorado Conservation Groups

Colorado Environmental Coalition
777 Grant Street, Suite 606
Denver, CO 80203
(303) 837-8701

Colorado Mountain Club
2530 West Alameda Avenue
Denver, CO 80219
(303) 922-8315

Colorado Wildlife Federation
7475 Dakin Street
Westminster, CO 80210
(303) 429-4500

Sierra Club
Rocky Mountain Chapter
777 Grant Street, Suite 606
Denver, CO 80203
(303) 861-8819

Sierra Club
Southwest Regional Office
2037 10th Street
Boulder, CO 80302
(303) 449-5595

Trout Unlimited
655 Broadway Street #475
Denver, CO 80203
(303) 595-0620

Western Colorado Congress
P.O. Box 472
Montrose, CO 81402
(303) 249-1978

The Wilderness Society
7475 Dakin Street
Westminster, CO 80210
(303) 650-5818

APPENDIX D

Map Sources

Colorado Atlas & Gazetter
DeLorme Mapping
P.O. Box 298
Freeport, ME 04032
(207) 865-4171

Maps Unlimited
899 Broadway
Denver, CO 80203
(303) 623-4299

Trails Illustrated
P.O. Box 3610
Evergreen, CO 80439
(303) 670-3457
(800) 962-1643

United States Geological Survey
Denver Federal Center
P.O. Box 25286
Lakewood, CO 80225
(303) 236-7477

USGS Topographic Maps
National Cartographic Center
507 National Center
Reston, VA 22092
(703) 648-6045

Colorado Geological Survey
1313 Sherman Street, Room 715
Denver, CO 80203
(303) 866-2611

APPENDIX E
Recommended Reading

Bartlett, Richard A. *Great Surveys of the American West*. Norman, Okla.: University of Oklahoma Press, 1962.

Brown, Robert L. *An Empire of Silver*. Sundance Pubs., 1984.

Bueler, William. *Roof of the Rockies*. Boulder: Pruett Publishing Company, 1974.

Chronic, John and Halka Chronic. "Prairie, Peak and Plateau." *Colorado Geological Survey Bulletin 32*, 1972.

Colorado Trail Management Direction Route Selection Environmental Assessment Report. Washington, D.C.: United States Forest Service, 1984.

Digerness, David S. *The Mineral Belt*. Sundance Publications, 1977.

Fielder, John and Fayhee, M. John. *Along the Colorado Trail*. Englewood: Westcliffe Publishers, Inc., 1992.

Gantt, Paul H. *The Case of Alferd Packer*. Denver: University of Denver Press, 1952.

Gilliland, Mary Ellen. *Summit: A Gold Rush History of Summit County, Colorado*. Silverthorne: Alpenrose Press, 1980.

Hall, Frank. *History of the State of Colorado*. Chicago: Blakely Printing, 1895.

Harbour, Midge. *Tarryall Mountains and the Puma Hills*. Colorado Springs: Century One Press, 1982.

Hart, John L. Jerome. *Fourteen Thousand Feet*. Denver: Colorado Mountain Club, 1925.

Lavender, David. *The Big Divide*. New York: Doubleday, 1948.

Mutel, Cornella Fleischer and John C. Emerick. *From Grassland to Glacier*. Boulder: Johnson Books, 1984.

Ormes, Robert. *Guide to the Colorado Mountains, Sixth Edition*. Sage Books, 1970.

Tracking Ghost Railroads in Colorado. Colorado Springs: Century One Press, 1980.

Pearson, Mark. *The Complete Guide to Colorado's Wilderness Areas*. Englewood: Westcliffe Publishers, Inc., 1994.

Pettit, Jan. *Utes, the Mountain People*. Colorado Springs: Century One Press, 1982.

Quillen, Ed. "Trail to Nowhere." *Denver Empire*, December 9, 1984.

Sprague, Marshall. *Great Gates*. New York: Little, Brown, 1964.

Sumner, David. "The Colorado Trail Takes Shape." *Colorado Magazine*, July-August 1974.

Wolle, Muriel Sibell. *Stampede to Timberline*. Sage Books, 1949.

INDEX

A

Agate Creek Trail, 147
Alpine tundra, 44p
Altitude sickness, 32
Angel of Shavano Trailhead, 137, 140
Avalanches, preparing for, 33
Avalanche Trailhead, 129, 130

B

Bailey, services in, 65, 66
Baker, Charles, 19, 203
Baldy Lake, 158p
Beartown, 203, 204
Benton, Thomas Hart, 16
Big Bend Trail, 227
Bolam Pass Road, 214
Bolam Pass Road (FS-578) Trail
 Access, 219
**Bolam Pass Road to Hotel Draw
 Road**, 218-21
Breckenridge, services in, 83, 84
Brookside-McCurdy Trail, 66
Browns Creek Trail, 139
Browns Creek Trailhead, 137
Brunot Treaty, 15, 19, 203, 219
Buena Vista, services in, 123, 124,
 129
Buffalo Creek, services in, 53, 54, 59
Buffalo Creek Gun Club Road, 60
Buffalo Creek Recreation Area, 59, 241

C

Camp Hale, 21, 89, 92, 94
Camp Hale (Eagle Park) Trailhead, 90,
 92
Carson, Christopher J., 197
**Carson Saddle to Rio Grande
 Reservoir Road**, 196-98
Carson Saddle, Wager Gulch Trail
 Access, 197
Cascade Creek, 30p, 210p
Cascade Divide Road, 213

Chalk Cliffs, 128p
Chalk Creek, 131p
Chalk Creek to US Highway 50,
 136-41
Chalk Creek Trailhead, 137
Cinnamon Pass Road, 197
Clear Creek Road Trailhead, 123
**Clear Creek to North Cottonwood
 Creek Road**, 122-25
Clothing, 25
Cochetopa Hills, 164p
Cochetopa Pass Road, 165, 166
Cochetopa Pass Road (County Road
 NN14) Trail Access, 166
Collegiate Peaks, 116, 123
Collegiate Peaks Wilderness, 123,
 124, 129, 130
 detour of, 242, 247, 247m
**Colorado Highway 114 to Saguache
 Park Road**, 164-67
Colorado Highway 114 Trail Access,
 165-66
Colorado Magazine, 12
Colorado Mountain Club (CMC),
 12, 14, 23
Colorado Mountain Trails Foundation
 (CMTF), 12, 14
Colorado Trail
 ecosystems of, 39-43, 45
 geology of, 34-37, 36m
 heritage of, 15-16, 18-21
 history of, 12, 14
 map of, 2-3
 markers on, 26-27
Colorado Trail Foundation (CTF), 11,
 14, 23
Coney Summit, detour of, 242, 249,
 250-51
Continental Divide Trail (CDT), 27,
 145

Copper Mountain Resort, 85, 89
  pack animal bypass from, 94
  services at, 90, 91
Copper Mountain to Tennessee Pass,
  88-92, 94
Corps of Topographical Engineers, 16
Corral Draw Trail, 226
**County Road 126 to Forest Service
  Road 543**, 58-60
Craig Creek Trail, 65
Creede
  poem about, 181
  services in, 177, 178, 182
Creede, Nicholas, 181
**Cumberland Basin to Junction Creek
  Trailhead**, 234-37
Cumberland Basin Trailhead, 235

D

Deane, C. A., 48
De Anza, Juan Bautista, 16, 165
Dexter, James, 113
Dominguez, Father, 16
Drinking water, 26, 31
Durango, services in, 235, 236
Dutchman Creek Trail, 160

E

East Mineral Creek Trail, 183
Eddiesville Trailhead, 171, 172, 177,
  178
**Eddiesville Trailhead to San Luis
  Pass**, 176-79
Elbert, Samuel, 114
Elk Creek, 202p
Engine Creek Trail, 213
Engineer Mountain Trail, 213
Escalante, Father, 16
Essentials, list of, 25-26
Ethics, 27-29
Evans, John, 19, 47, 75

F

Ferchau, Hugo, 12
Fires, building, 28
Flag Point Trail, 227
Food, packing, 26
Fooses Creek Road, 145
Ford, Bob, 181
Forest Service Road 435/Forest
  Service Road 564 Trail Access,
  225-26
**Forest Service Road 543 to Long
  Gulch**, 64-66
Forest Service Road 543 Trailhead, 65
Forest Service Road 550 Trailhead, 59
Fremont, John Charles, 16, 18, 75,
  89, 99, 165, 181
Friend of the Colorado Trail, 11-12
Frostbite, 33
Fryingpan-Arkansas Project (Pan-Ark
  Project), 20, 99, 113

G

Gannett, Henry, 129
Garfield, services in, 145, 146
Gaskill, Gudy, 12, 14, 237, 256-57
Georgia Pass, 74p
Georgia Pass Trail Access, 76
Giardiasis, 31
Glacier Ridge Road, 75, 78
Gold Hill Trailhead, 75, 83
**Gold Hill Trailhead to Copper
  Mountain**, 82-85
Good Hope Stock Trail, 227
Granite outcrops, 52p
Greenhorn, Chief, 16, 165
Green Mountain bike path, 60
Grey, Asa, 75
Group size, limits on, 28
Gudy's Rest, 237
Gunnison, John W., 16, 18
Gunnison, services in, 159, 160
Guyot, Arnold, 75

H

Hagerman, John J., 19, 99, 107
Hagerman Pass Road, 102, 108
Hagerman Pass Road (FS-105) Trail
  Access, 107
**Hagerman Pass Road to Halfmoon
  Creek,** 106-8
Hagerman Tunnel, 20, 99, 107
Hale, Irving, 89
Halfmoon Creek Road, 108
**Halfmoon Creek to Clear Creek
  Road,** 112-16
Halfmoon Creek Trailhead, 113
Harvard Trail, 125
Hastings, Merrill, 12
Hayden, Ferdinand, 18
Herbert, Clark, 75
Hermosa Park Road, 213
Highline Trail, 108, 221, 225, 226,
  228
Hikes, planning, 24-26
Hoffhiens Connection Trail, 237
Holy Cross Wilderness, 99, 101
  detour of, 241, 245, 245m
Homestake Peak, 98p
Hooper, W. H., 65
Hooper Road, 65, 66
Hooper Trail, 66
Hope Pass, detour of, 242, 246, 246m
Hotchkiss, Enos, 19, 165, 250
Hotel Draw Road, 226
**Hotel Draw Road to Cumberland
  Basin,** 224-28
Hotel Draw Trail Access, 225
Human waste, disposal of, 28
Hypothermia, 31-32

J

Jacque, J. W., 89
James, Edwin, 16
Jarosa Mesa, 188p

Jay Creek Road, 155
Jefferson, services in, 69
Jefferson County Road 126 Trailhead,
  59
Jefferson Creek Road, 77
Jefferson Lake Road, 75, 77
Jefferson Lake Road Trail Access, 76
Junction Creek Canyon, detour of,
  242, 252, 253m
Junction Creek Trailhead, 235, 236

K

Kassler to South Platte Townsite,
  46-49
Kassler-Waterton Canyon Trailhead,
  47
Kennebec Pass, 234p
Kenosha Mountains, 64p
Kenosha Pass, 68p
Kenosha Pass to Gold Hill Trailhead,
  74-78
Kenosha Pass Trailhead, 76

L

La Garita Wilderness, 165, 171, 172,
  177, 178, 181, 182
  detour of, 242, 249-50, 249m
Lake City, services in, 190
Lake Fork Road, 250
Lakeview Campground Trailhead/Twin
  Lakes Reservoir Trail Access, 114
Lamm, Richard, 14, 115
Leadville, services in, 100, 107
Lee, Abe, 107
Lightning, 32
Lily Lake Road, 100
Little Molas Lake Trailhead, 211
Long, Steven, 16, 47
Long Gulch to Kenosha Pass, 68-69
Long Gulch Trail Access, 69

Lost Creek Wilderness, 59, 65, 69
    detour of, 241, 242, 243m
Lost Park Road, 66
Low impact camping, 27
Lucas, Bill, 12
Lujan Creek Road, 159, 161
Lujan Creek Road Trail Access, 159

M

McIntyre, John, 75
Main Range Trail, 99
Marshall, William, 153
Marshall Pass Road, 147
Marshall Pass to Sargents Mesa,
    152-55
Marshall Pass Trail Access, 153
Mears, Otto, 15, 19, 153, 165, 225,
    249, 250
Meeker, Nathanial, 15
Miller, Jim, 94
Mineral Creek, 180p
Miners Creek Trail, 84
Molas Pass to Bolam Pass Road,
    210-14
Molas Trail, 206
Mountain bikes
    detours for, 241-53
    regulations for, 33, 241
Mount Etna, 136p
Mount Evans, 58p
Mount Massive, 106p
Mount Massive Trail, 108
Mount Massive Wilderness, 107, 108
    detour of, 241, 245, 245m
Mount Ouray, 34p, 144p, 152p
Mount Shavano, 136p
Mount Shavano Trail, 139-40
Mount Tabegauche, 136p
Mount Taylor, 136p

N

Nelson, Craig, 115
Noise pollution, 29
North Cottonwood Creek Road, 125
**North Cottonwood Creek to Chalk
    Creek Road**, 128-30, 132
North Cottonwood Creek Trail Access,
    129
Notch Lake, 22p

O

Oro Fino Trail, 235
Ouray, Chief, 15-16

P

Pack animals, 28, 29
Packer, Alferd, 165
Palmer, William Jackson, 19
Peak bagging, ethics of, 29
Peaks Trail, 84
Pine Creek Trail, 124
Plant communities, 42
Pole Creek, 196p
Poncha Springs, services in, 145
Prout, H. G., 189
Purgatory Ski Area, services at,
    219, 226

Q

Quillen, Ed, 14

R

Rainbow Trail, 153, 154
Raspberry Gulch, detour of, 242, 248,
    248m
Raspberry Gulch Road, 139
Reilly, William, 21

Revett, Ben Stanley, 75
Rhoda, Franklin, 219
Rico Mountains, 218p
Rico-Silverton Trail, 213
Rio Grande Reservoir Road, 198, 204
Rio Grande Reservoir Road-Stony Pass
    Road Trail Access, 203
**Rio Grande Reservoir Road to Molas
    Pass**, 202-4, 206-7
Roads, types of, 24
Roberts Tunnel, 20-21
Robidoux, Antoine, 165
Robinson, George B., 89
Rolling Creek Trail, 65
Routes, types of, 24

S
Saguache, services in, 153, 154
Saguache Park Road, 167, 171, 172
**Saguache Park Road to Eddiesville
    Trailhead**, 170-72
Saguache Park Road Trail Access, 171
St. Kevins Gulch Trailhead (FS-107),
    99-100
Salida, services in, 137, 138, 145
Salt Creek Trail, 227
San Luis Pass, 176p
San Luis Pass to Spring Creek Pass,
    180-85
San Luis Pass Trail Access, 182
Sargents Mesa (FS-855) Trail Access,
    159
**Sargents Mesa to Colorado
    Highway 114**, 158-61
Scotch Creek Road, 226
Searle Pass, 93p
Silver Creek Trail, 154
Silverton, services in, 211, 212
Skyline Trail, 177, 181, 183, 184
Smith, Soapy, 181
Snowdon, Francis Marion, 211
Snow Mesa, 8p, 17p

South Cottonwood Creek Road, 132
South Platte River, 46p
**South Platte Townsite to County
    Road 126**, 52-55
South Platte Townsite Trailhead, 53
Spring Creek Pass to Carson Saddle,
    188-92
Spring Creek Pass Trailhead, 189
Spring Creek Trail, 178-79
Stewart, William M., 177
Stewart Creek, 170p
Stoves, using, 28
Sun exposure, 33

T
Tabor, Horace Austin Warner, 19, 20
Tenmile Bike Path, 83, 85, 90, 241,
    244
Tenmile Range, 82p, 88p
    detour of, 244, 244m
**Tennessee Pass to Hagerman Pass
    Road**, 98-102
Tennessee Pass Trailhead, 99
Toll, Roger, 123
Torrey, John, 75
Trailhead/trail access, 23-24
Trail markers, 26-27
Twin Lakes (village), services in, 114
Twin Lakes, 112p

U
Uncle Bud's Hut, 102p
US-50 South Fooses Creek Trailhead,
    145
US-550-Molas Trail Trailhead, 211
U.S. Forest Service (USFS), 11, 12, 14
    maps by, 23
U.S. Geological Survey (USGS), 18
    maps by, 23, 37
US Highway 50 to Marshall Pass,
    144-47
Ute Indians, exile of, 15-16

V
Vegetation, 40, 41, 42
Volunteers, 11, 13p, 14

W
Wannemaker, Nathaniel, 137
Wapaca Trail, 125
Warman, Cy, 181
Waterton Canyon, 46p
Waterton Canyon Trailhead, 47, 48
Weminuche Wilderness, 203, 206, 211
  detour of, 242, 251-52, 251m
West Jefferson Trail, 77
West Mineral Creek Trail, 184
Wheeler, George, 18
Wheeler, John S., 89
Wheeler Flats Trailhead, 85, 90, 91
Wheeler Trail, 85
Whitney, Josiah Dwight, 123
Wildflowers, 10p, 38p, 122p, 180p,
  205p, 224p
Wildlife, observing, 39-41
Williams, Bill, 165
Wilson, Allen, 219
Womack, Bob, 20
Wurtz Ditch Road (FS-100) Trail
  Access, 99
Wurtz Ditch Road, 100

"m" indicates map
"p" indicates photo

John Fielder has been photographing the natural world since 1973. The photographer of nineteen books, including fifteen on his adopted state of Colorado, he has most recently undertaken a two-year project to photograph Rocky Mountain National Park. In 1993 Fielder was awarded the Sierra Club's Ansel Adams Award for Conservation Photography, and he was also appointed to the board of Great Outdoors Colorado by Governor Roy Romer. Fielder is active in conservation issues, civic affairs, photography instruction, and publishing. In addition to this book, his latest titles include *A Colorado Autumn* and *To Walk in Wilderness: A Colorado Rocky Mountain Journal* with environmental writer T. A. Barron. Fielder and his family live in Greenwood Village, Colorado.

Other books by John Fielder:
A Colorado Autumn
To Walk in Wilderness: A Colorado Rocky Mountain Journal
Colorado, Rivers of the Rockies
Along the Colorado Trail
Colorado, Lost Places and Forgotten Words
The Complete Guide to Colorado Wilderness Areas
Colorado BLM Wildlands: A Guide to Hiking & Floating Colorado's
    Canyon Country
Colorado Reflections Littlebook
Colorado Aspen Trees Littlebook
Colorado Lakes & Creeks Littlebook
Colorado Wildflowers Littlebook
Colorado Waterfalls Littlebook

Also look for John Fielder's Colorado wall and engagement calendars.

The Colorado Trail Foundation
P.O. Box 260876, Lakewood, CO 80226

The Colorado Trail: The Official Guidebook *by Randy Jacobs**
40 color photographs, 29 maps, 272 pages, 5½ x 8½ format
       Softcover **$19.95** _____

Along the Colorado Trail *by John Fielder & M. John Fayhee*
100 color photographs, 128 pages, 9x12 format *Hardcover* **$33.00** _____
         Softcover **$22.00** _____
Day Hikes on the Colorado Trail *by Jan Robertson*
35 color photographs, 48 pages, 4x9 format **$ 6.25** _____

Topographic waterproof CT maps (11x17)
  Full set: 29 maps, Denver to Durango **$20.00** _____
  Northeast set: 16 maps, Denver to Marshall Pass **$12.00** _____
  Southwest set: 13 maps, Marshall Pass to Durango **$12.00** _____

Note Cards, assorted designs *by Jerry Albright* **$ 4.00** _____
Sweatshirts __M __ L __ XL **$22.00** _____

Colorado Trail T-Shirts, short-sleeved with CT map design **$10.00** _____
50% cotton/50% polyester *100% cotton*
White: __S __M __L __X Aqua: __M __L __XL
Cool green: __M __L __XL Raspberry: __S __M __L __XL
Light Blue: __L __XL White: __S __L __XL

Official Colorado Trail Souvenirs with CT logo
Baseball caps (cotton) **$ 5.75** _____
Patch (cotton) **$ 2.75** _____
Pin **$ 2.25** _____
Trail Sign **$ 1.25** _____

All prices are listed postpaid Subtotal _____
Colorado residents add 4.3% sales tax Colo. tax _____
       Total _____

For a FREE certificate for completing the entire Colorado Trail, write to the Colorado Trail Foundation. Completion plaques are available for $27.00.

Friends of the Colorado Trail

$500 Supporter	$100 Patron	$75 Contributor
$50 Family	$25 Individual	$15 Senior/Student

Benefits for Friends Include:
Quarterly newsletter, 10% discounts on CT materials, information on CTF functions, and an invitation on a CT hike.
  ____I would like to work on a trail crew
  ____I would like to "adopt" a section of the trail to maintain.

            ( )____-____
_____
Name   Phone No.

_____
Street Address or P.O. Box

_____
Town or City   State   Zip

* Colorado Trail books are also available at all Colorado book retailers.